History Lessons

*What business and management can
learn from the great leaders of history*

Jonathan Gifford

Marshall Cavendish
Business

Copyright © 2010 Jonathan Gifford

First published in 2010 by Marshall Cavendish Business
An imprint of Marshall Cavendish International

PO Box 65829
London EC1P 1NY
United Kingdom

and

1 New Industrial Road
Singapore 536196
genrefsales@sg.marshallcavendish.com
www.marshallcavendish.com/genref

Marshall Cavendish is a trademark of Times Publishing Limited

Other Marshall Cavendish offices: Marshall Cavendish International (Asia) Private Limited, 1 New Industrial Road, Singapore 536196 • Marshall Cavendish Corporation. 99 White Plains Road, Tarrytown NY 10591–9001, USA • Marshall Cavendish International (Thailand) Co Ltd. 253 Asoke, 12th Floor, Sukhumvit 21 Road, Klongtoey Nua, Wattana, Bangkok 10110, Thailand • Marshall Cavendish (Malaysia) Sdn Bhd, Times Subang, Lot 46, Subang Hi-Tech Industrial Park, Batu Tiga, 40000 Shah Alam, Selangor Darul Ehsan, Malaysia

The right of Jonathan Gifford to be identified as the author of this work has been asserted by him in accordance with the Copyright, Designs and Patents Act 1988.

A CIP record for this book is available from the British Library

ISBN 978-0-462-09936-1

Project managed by Cambridge Publishing Management Ltd

Printed and bound in Singapore by Times Printers Pte Ltd

CONTENTS

INTRODUCTION

*H*istory Lessons starts from the assumption that management, at any level, has a lot to do with leadership. An effective manager needs a whole array of talents, and now that we have begun to take on board the concept that people should not be managed at all, rather that managers should ideally lead their teams to the successful fulfilment of their tasks, so leadership skills for managers have come to the fore.

This book is based on the premise that there is no one kind of perfect manager or leader and that a search for the set of characteristics and skills that represent the ideal leader is doomed (happily) to failure. Leaders, like the rest of us, come in all different shapes and sizes: meticulous and visionary; outgoing and retiring; impulsive and cautious; subtle and direct. This book sets out to look at what the great leaders from history have actually done—to see how they behaved; to learn what we can from their actions. *History Lessons* attempts to give readers enough history to provide some sort of insight into the real issues faced by each of the leaders, and the context in which they made their decisions. There is also, I hope, enough detail about these leaders' lives to give some idea of the kind of people that they were; of the personal background and historical context that helped to shape their personalities and influence the decisions that they took and the plans of action that they devised. Leadership and management are intensely human activities—the leaders of the past were essentially no different from the leaders and managers of today. It is from their entirely recognisable human qualities that we can learn the most useful lessons.

The book does not attempt to set out any particular historical theory about individual leaders: the historical facts presented here are those that are generally accepted to be true (historical truth being, inevitably, an elusive thing). Equally, the book does not follow any particular management theory. In fact, *History Lessons* sets out to be a theory-free zone—readers are invited to draw their own conclusions and to find their own parallels between the decisions and actions of these leaders from history and the issues that they face in their own working lives. The one thing that every manager may take from these accounts of the great leaders from the past and the more recent present is, I hope, inspiration.

There are various things that leaders throughout the ages have all done; various skills, abilities, and characteristics that they have all demonstrated. The complete list of 'things that great leaders do' is no doubt a long one. In *History Lessons* I have selected eight skills and abilities that, in my opinion, represent many of the essential things that any leader should be able to do and—ideally—should be very good at. If you can glance down this list and say to yourself, "On reflection, I do all of those things and, come to think of it, I do them rather well," then your future as a leader in your own field is secure. Many great leaders in history have demonstrated only a few of these particular skills and abilities, but this was still enough to secure their place in history.

The chosen list of things that leaders do and the characteristics that they display is this:

- Changing the Mood
- Boldness of Vision
- Doing the Planning
- Leading from the Front
- Bringing People with You
- Making things Happen
- Taking the Offensive
- Creating Opportunities.

Changing the Mood is chosen to open the book, since this is one of the hardest things that a new manager has to do, and also one of the most subtle. There are no hard and fast rules for achieving this; no easy method even for measuring the current mood and noting its improvement. But when the mood is bad no organization can thrive, and is unlikely even to survive. When the mood is good, then things really start to happen. The leader who manages the switch from the former to the latter will have made a flying start. In some extreme cases, managing such a change would represent a lifetime's work well spent.

Boldness of Vision probably gets enough press already: "*It's the vision thing.*" We tend to assume that only leaders of nation states and Chief Executive Officers need to worry about vision, but, in fact, every manager, at every level, needs to have a vision. Another word for vision is just 'strategy': it informs everything that you do. If you start to do things that do not cohere with your overall strategy—your vision—then you will begin to fail, or at least to waste a great deal of time.

Doing the Planning is often underrated. There is an inevitable sense in which a great deal of planning is an entirely obvious and routine part of any manager's work—you plan to deliver result A by time B. But it is the hidden planning that often reveals the leaders of true genius: they have their vision of what they want to achieve and they labor quietly but diligently to plan how they will bring it about. These are the leaders who suddenly astonish with the dramatic results of their actions. Their results are not, actually, astonishing—they have been carefully planned.

Leading from the Front is another of those apparently dramatic management skills that, in fact, everyone should aspire to. There are many examples of leaders whose selfless and conspicuous bravery has propelled them to fame and glory: men and women who have inspired huge devotion amongst their followers and who have led people to achievements of which they would not have imagined themselves capable. Leading from the front is not necessarily as glamorous as this; in fact there are many deeply unglamorous and unpleasant tasks that have to be done in any organization. The manager who steps in occasionally and does one of these arduous things is leading from the front and demonstrating a core aspect of great leadership—that you do not expect your team to do things that you are not prepared to do yourself. There is another sense to the notion of leading from the front: people lead from the front when they simply stick to their principles; when they insist on doing what seems right to them in the face of all opposition. This is just as brave (and sometimes just as foolhardy) as leading troops into enemy fire.

Bringing People with You is another potentially elusive 'must have' for managers. You can tell people what to do; indeed, you can scream at them until you are blue in the face (I have seen this done on many occasions, in many different and sometimes imaginative ways) and they will not budge. And, indeed, why should they? What, as they rightly say (or mutter), is in it for them? Great leaders are able both to inspire and to create a substantial common interest: we are all in this together; your success is my success. Great leaders also recognize the rights and expectations of others; they are the great diplomats of the world and the antitheses of the great dictators.

Making Things Happen is a less elusive skill. For many people, this is the very essence of leadership—a leader can almost be defined by his or her ability to make things happen: to get people to do things that they would not have done without the leader's inspiration and guidance; to change the world around them. But making things happen can be a bit one-dimensional. Some of the outstanding movers and shakers of history have not been, in the broadest sense, the truly greatest leaders. Their psychological make-up sometimes makes them constitutionally unable not to make things happen—they see the world as a series of errors crying out to be corrected; a collection of other people's messes begging to be tidied up. They tend to be a bit too certain that everything would go to hell in a hand cart without their personal intervention. Sometimes they are right, but the greatest leaders combine this characteristic with several of the other, more subtle leadership skills.

Taking the Offensive is one of those actions that can sort the men from the boys and the women from the girls. It is arduous and potentially dangerous and very often it would be much less painful simply to put up with things as they are; to hunker down in our foxholes and try to cope with what the opposition is throwing at us. But no really great leader will allow the opposition to keep him or her permanently on the defensive, nor will they accept that things are simply as they are and can never be changed. Taking the offensive is one of the many leadership abilities that are most clearly demonstrated in the military world—in the world of physical confrontation—but that is in fact needed in every field of human endeavor. The manager who takes the offensive against any apparently intractable problem in their organization is demonstrating the same leadership skills as the battle commander who takes the fight to an apparently invincible enemy and wins an audacious victory against all odds. Some people also take the offensive not in organizational but in personal terms. The individual who stands up for change in the face of ingrained and established custom and practice is as daring as the most glamorous cavalry commander.

Finally, **Creating Opportunities** is perhaps one of the most subtle of the arts of management and leadership; a kind of making your own luck. Funnily enough, the end result—the apparently surprising run of good results; the optimism that begins to flow through the organization; the dawning of a golden era in which everything seems to go right for your team—stems precisely from your having successfully demonstrated all (or most) of the key leadership attributes set out in this particular list. If you have created the right mood in your organization, set out your vision and done your planning; if you are leading from the front and bringing your people with you in other ways; if you are making things happen and are taking the offensive, then, strange as it may seem, your luck will improve. You will find that you have set up opportunities that your team can now happily seize upon. You are now, thanks to all of your diligent preparation, magically in the right place at the right time. The end result will (by definition) be a team effort—your leadership skills will have created the conditions and the environment in which success can be achieved by everyone in the organization. Your team begin to bring successes to your door; unexpected and unplanned-for opportunities present themselves.

Choosing great leaders from history is an inevitably contentious matter. Many of the leaders in *History Lessons* are included because they would be expected to feature on anybody's list of 'great leaders': Hannibal and Napoleon; Abraham Lincoln and Winston Churchill; Pericles of Athens and Nelson Mandela. Several leaders are chosen from the great events of recent history; from World War II and from the great ideological and political struggles in the Far East that preceded and followed that conflict. The twentieth century is over-represented as a result, but for the (I hope) justifiable reason that this time of global change and violent upheaval is still very recent history, and that the scale of the struggle demanded that people who might otherwise have led quite mundane lives, and to whom we can very easily relate, were suddenly called upon to make the most difficult leadership decisions in the most desperate of circumstances.

There is an inevitable bias towards empire-builders and generals. Most of recorded history, sadly, pays little or no attention to the great educators, the great merchants, or the great business leaders of the day. There are not enough female leaders included in this book. There has been an attempt to include people who have had great influence on people's lives without being *leaders* in quite the normal sense: people who have inspired others, changed their point of view, or set them off in new directions, rather than having *led* or *directed* them: Marco Polo; Talleyrand; Martin Luther King; Elizabeth Garret Anderson; Muhammad Ali.

Finally, there has been an attempt—doomed, sadly, to failure—to break out of the straightjacket of a Western perspective. Great leaders of the East have been included to remind us in the west that there have always been great civilizations—and great leaders—south and east of the Mediterranean. There are huge omissions that it is beyond the scope of this book to address: many great nations and cultures have no leaders included here to represent them.

1
CHANGING
THE MOOD

One of the most significant, and difficult, tasks that can face a new manager is to change the mood of their team or organization. It could be argued that this is always a job that needs to be done, since the mood before your arrival is not *your* mood, just as the overall culture of the organization is not yet your culture. But in many cases the situation is more urgent, or significant, than that.

This can take many forms; in a results-driven organization it is likely to mean that people have stopped believing that they can succeed. There is some insurmountable obstacle in the way: the product is not right; there is not enough marketing support; the competition are too clever; the machines are too slow; the buyers have bought the wrong merchandise; suppliers keep letting you down; senior management don't know what they are doing; the current economic climate makes success impossible; the targets are too high; the bonuses are too low; the team can't cope with the workload; nobody has any back-up. It's just not working.

In a service organization the bad mood can take many forms, but it amounts to a similar thing: the team don't feel that they have to put themselves out; they're not paid to be nice to people; customers are ridiculously demanding; there are too many customers; it's not possible to keep everybody happy all of the time; this is somebody else's job not theirs; it can wait; it doesn't matter.

In extreme cases, genuinely bad conventions take hold. Print workers on Fleet Street newspapers in the bad old days became accustomed to 'Spanish practices'. Management, desperate to get newspapers out on time, would do anything to avoid a stoppage. A complete culture of abuse became the norm: phantom casual workers signed on as M. Mouse and receiving a shift payment; money changed hands in brown envelopes to fix a mysterious problem with the presses; people did a brisk trade in counterfeit goods from lockers that 'custom and practice' dictated should never be inspected. The worst cases have a parallel with accusations of institutional racism: the organizations concerned have become so infected with a particular attitude that they no longer even recognize that they have a problem.

Changing the mood in cases like this is a very tough job, but it can be done. The one certainty is that the mood will not be changed by confrontation, by telling people that this will all change—or else. The three leaders from history in this section demonstrate three different approaches to the problem.

☙

The most direct example is probably that of Lieutenant-General Bernard Montgomery, who took over the British Eighth Army in North Africa following a series of defeats by the brilliant German tank commander, Erwin Rommell. Eighth Army command had lost faith in their ability to defeat Rommel. There were elaborate plans for defending against Rommel's next attack, and a whole drawer-full of fall-back positions; there were no plans for driving Rommel out of North Africa. Montgomery was not Churchill's first choice for the command; Churchill was persuaded to offer the job to Montgomery when his predecessor was shot down on an internal flight across the Libyan desert.

Montgomery sized up the situation with astonishing speed and took immediate control. In a classic speech he electrified his staff with his clear vision of what they would do next and how they would ultimately win. An army that was convinced of its own worth but baffled by its failures against Rommel could suddenly believe in itself again. There was a clear plan of action and infectious self-confidence. "This Rommel chap is definitely a nuisance, so we will hit him a crack and be done with him," said Montgomery. The previous command had become so spooked by Rommel that the army was forbidden to mention his name; the Commander in Chief had issued an order insisting that Rommel be referred to as "the enemy" or "the Germans," signing off (and rather undermining his position) by saying, "PS. I am *not* jealous of Rommel."[1]

The transformation in mood achieved by Montgomery in a matter of days was startling. Winston Churchill, visiting the army a week or so after Montgomery's arrival, could hardly believe the change. Eighth Army stopped Rommel in his tracks for the first time with a well-prepared defensive line and then built up its forces, with American aid, until the final complete defeat of Rommel's *Afrikakorps* at the Second Battle of El Alamein. The Axis forces were driven out of North Africa.

A rather different kind of mood-change in a very different era was achieved by Queen Elizabeth I of England in the sixteenth century. She began her reign with the nation embroiled in uncertainty and fear. Elizabeth's father, Henry VIII, had broken with the Church of Rome and created the Church of England; the new Protestant religion had taken firm hold in England, but a substantial minority of subjects held to their Catholic faith. Elizabeth's sister, Queen Mary, had attempted to turn back the clock to Roman Catholicism and to terrify her Protestant subjects out of their new faith by burning them as heretics. After her death, England faced the real prospect of invasion from Spain: Queen Mary had married King Philip of Spain, who could now argue that he had a claim to the English throne. Fear of Catholicism and fear of the Catholic enemy went hand in hand to create a dangerous atmosphere of suspicion and paranoia. Elizabeth, herself a Protestant, introduced reforms that would establish the Protestant faith in England, but also relaxed punishments for non-conformity and showed, by personal example, that her Catholic subjects were not to be demonized or excluded. In these relatively un-dramatic ways—forcing clear but moderate legislation through in the face of opposition from the Bishops—Elizabeth re-introduced an atmosphere of tolerance that enabled England to avoid the religious wars that plagued the continent for years to come. After the apparently miraculous defeat of the Spanish Armada, she was also able to engender a more general mood of success within the country; a feeling that to be English now amounted to something; that the country was secure and even flourishing. There was great exuberance in the arts, especially in literature, with playwrights such as Shakespeare, Marlow, and Johnson writing some of the finest works of the English theatre.

Nelson Mandela is another kind of mood-changer altogether. To understand Mandela's achievement it is necessary to remember that during the apartheid period and the civil unrest that it created, Nelson Mandela was clearly perceived to be a terrorist and a communist, apparently in league with foreign powers, determined to bring down the South African state and install a black communist regime that would be implacably hostile to whites. Even when a move towards a democratic settlement seemed possible, many white South Africans believed that a black majority government would lead to persecution of the white minority. Mandela's Truth and Reconciliation Commission took much of the poison out of the bitter recriminations that both sides had stored up against the other, but in a real sense it was simply the personality of Mandela himself that provided the cure; calm, smiling, dignified, inclusive. White South Africans realized slowly that they were no longer the reviled outsiders that they had feared they would become. They were all still South African. There was a new mood in the country.

BERNARD MONTGOMERY
(1887–1986)

The war in North Africa had begun well for Britain. Italy had entered the war in June 1940 as an ally of Germany and had invaded Egypt from Italian Libya, in the hope of capturing the Suez Canal. In November 1941, Commonwealth forces successfully pushed Italian forces out of Egypt, overrunning most of Libya and capturing 113,000 Italian prisoners. Before the Commonwealth troops could drive the Italian army out of North Africa, they were diverted to defend Greece. This allowed time for Hitler to support his ally, Mussolini, by despatching the German *Afrikakorps* to North Africa, commanded by Erwin Rommel.

Rommel quickly drove the British out of Libya, striking too quickly to allow the build-up of defensive positions, despite his inferior strength. When one of his commanders protested that he could not continue the drive forward because his vehicles were in poor condition, Rommel made the marvellous, Napoleonic remark that, "One cannot permit unique opportunities to slip by for the sake of such trifles."

Rommel successfully outflanked all of the Allied forces in North Africa. He swept past the strategic port of Tobruk, but failed to trap the bulk of the British Commonwealth Western Desert Force as he had hoped. Rommel then laid siege to Tobruk. He was beginning to run rings around the British and Commonwealth forces in North Africa. Churchill planned to replace the Commander in Chief of the Western Desert Force, Auchinleck, with General Alexander. His own choice to head up Eighth Army itself was Lieutenant-General William Gott; a large and ebullient fighter, loved by his soldiers and an inspiring leader at battalion or divisional level. Gott's plane was shot down on take-off as he was making an internal flight across the desert and he was killed along with 14 other passengers. With Gott's death, and against Churchill's instincts, the Chief of Staff, Alan Brooke, recommended Lieutenant-General Bernard Montgomery for the job. Churchill reluctantly agreed: Montgomery was self-righteous, high-handed, conceited, and boastful. As it turned out, Montgomery was precisely the right man for the job. In many ways, Montgomery was a great general. In his later career as Field Marshall, "Monty" failed to rise to the statesmanlike levels of diplomacy needed for truly successful high command. But in North Africa, he was to turn a dispirited army, expecting to fail, into a successful unit that would turn the tide of the war in the Allies' favour.

The British made two attempts to relieve Tobruk, both of which were costly failures. Rommel was hugely outnumbered, but he neatly avoided an attempt to encircle him, concentrated his forces, and launched a counter-attack. He was stopped only just short of Egypt. Had the Axis forces reached Egypt, the effects on the Allied war effort would have been devastating: supplies that could no longer be shipped through the Suez Canal would have to make the slow journey around South Africa's Cape of Good Hope. German access to the oilfields of the Middle East could have had an even more drastic effect on the balance of power.

Rommel was temporarily forced to retreat to his defensive lines but soon received vital supplies and new tanks; he won a dramatic victory in the Battle of Gazala, west of Tobruk. The British began a headlong retreat to the east to avoid being cut off—known to British Tommies as the 'Gazala Gallop'. Only Tobruk stood between Rommel and Egypt; after a fierce onslaught, the city surrendered. Its 33,000 defenders were all captured: only after the devastating fall of Singapore to the Japanese earlier in the same year had more British Commonwealth troops been captured in a single defeat. It was a disaster. Rommel, with his inferior forces, had completely out-maneuvered the British.

Rommel's new drive to the East was held up at El Alamein, a key defensive position on the North African coast. El Alamein controlled a bottle-neck through which the Axis forces would have to pass in order to reach Egypt. In the first battle of El Alamein—a bitterly fought stalemate—the Eighth Army lost 13,000 men to Rommel's 7,000, though Rommel could afford the losses less than the British. Both sides dug in. The Eighth Army was frustrated and dispirited. Morale was at an all-time low.

Churchill replaced Auchinleck with General Alexander, and, reluctantly, he appointed Lieutenant-General Bernard Montgomery to the key task of commanding the Eighth Army, a role that Auchinleck had taken on in addition to his role of Commander-in-Chief. Montgomery took over command immediately on his arrival and earlier than Auchinleck had planned, much to the latter's annoyance. But Montgomery had no time to lose. There was much to be done. He called his senior staff to a meeting in their desert headquarters:

> "I want first of all to introduce myself to you. You do not know me. I do not know you. But we have got to work together; therefore we must understand each other and we must have confidence in one another. I have only been here a few hours. But from what I have seen and heard since I arrived I am prepared to say, here and now, that I have confidence in you. We will then work together as a team; and together we will gain the confidence of this great army and go forward to final victory in South Africa.
>
> "I believe that one of the first duties of a Commander is to create what I call 'atmosphere'; and in that atmosphere, his staff, subordinate commanders and troops will live and work and fight. I do not like the general atmosphere I find here. It is an atmosphere of doubt, of looking back to select the next place to which to withdraw, of loss of confidence in our ability to defeat Rommel, of desperate defence measures by reserves in preparing positions in Cairo and the Delta. All that must cease. Let us have a new atmosphere.
>
> "The defence of Egypt lies here at Alamein [...] What is the point of digging trenches in the Delta. It is quite useless; if we lose this

position we lose Egypt; all the fighting troops in the Delta must come here at once, and will. Here we will stand and fight; there will be no further withdrawal. I have ordered that all plans and instructions dealing with further withdrawal are to be burned, and at once. We will stand and fight here. If we can't stay here alive, then let us stay here dead.

"I want to impress on everyone that the bad times are over. Fresh divisions from the UK are now arriving in Egypt, together with ample reinforcements for our present divisions. We have 300 to 400 new Sherman tanks coming and these are actually being unloaded at Suez now. Our mandate from the Prime Minister is to destroy the Axis forces in North Africa; I have seen it written on half a sheet of notepaper. And it will be done. If anyone here thinks it can't be done, let him go at once; I don't want any doubters in this party. It can be done, and it will be done; beyond any possibility of doubt.

"Now I understand that Rommel is expected to attack at any moment. Excellent. Let him attack. I would sooner it didn't come for a week, just to give me time to sort things out. If we have two weeks to prepare we will be sitting pretty; Rommel can attack as soon as he likes, after that, and I hope he does.

"Meanwhile, we ourselves will start to plan a great offensive; it will be the beginning of a campaign which will hit Rommel and his Army for six right out of Africa […] What I have done is to get over to you the atmosphere in which we will now work and fight; you must see that that atmosphere permeates right down through the Eighth Army to the most junior private soldier. All the soldiers must know what is wanted; when they see it coming to pass there will be a surge of confidence throughout the army. I ask you to give me your confidence and to have faith that what I have said will come to pass.

"There is much work to be done. The orders I have given about no further withdrawal will mean a complete change in the layout of our dispositions; also that we must begin to prepare for our great offensive [...] The great point to remember is that we are going to finish with this chap Rommel once and for all. It will be quite easy. There is no doubt about it. He is definitely a nuisance. Therefore we will hit him a crack and finish with him."[2]

Montgomery's speech is quoted here nearly in full, partly because it is not widely available and partly because it is a classic of its kind. If the tone of voice is a little contrived—even for the 1940s—this was not missed by his audience. One of Montgomery's Intelligence Officers described the speech as "straight out of school speech day"—but he went on to add that the effect was one of "exhilaration." Other officers talked of the "electrifying" effect of Montgomery's speech; about his "professionalism." One officer said, "Monty absolutely deserved all the credit he could get for the way he changed us. I mean, we were different people. We suddenly had a spring in our step."[3]

Montgomery's great assets were his meticulous planning and his immense (and potentially infuriating) self-confidence. His analysis of the situation at Alamein was perfect: the British armored Corps had been, "[...] too brave. They always attack." German tanks would take shelter behind their anti-tank guns, which had a longer range than the guns of the British tanks; once the anti-tank guns had done their damage, the superior German tanks would join the battle and Rommel could use his cavalryman's genius to the full. As a result, the British had fought a series of losing cavalry engagements and Army headquarters had developed a system of ever-more complicated defensive arrangements. The whole system prevented any concentration of force, either in attack or defence. Behind these defensive/offensive screens was the ultimate defensive line, back near the Nile Delta. This was all about to change, with troops being pulled up from the Delta to reinforce the position at El Alamein.

Montgomery pulled all of the troops up forward, to the strong defensive position offered by the ridge of Alam El Halfa, southeast of El Alamein. Here he dug in not only his anti-tank guns but the tanks themselves, using them as stationary gun emplacements.

Montgomery's plan was to let Rommel attack Alam El Halfa—indeed to encourage him to do so—while building up his forces for a strong counter-attack, using the American-supplied, powerful Sherman tanks that were on their way to North Africa (though not quite so soon as Montgomery had implied in his speech). It was a good plan, well-conceived and well-thought-through. The effect on the Eighth Army of having such a plan laid out clearly before them was, indeed, electrifying.

Montgomery had taken command on August 13th. Six days later, Winston Churchill paid the army a visit. He was astounded. He talked of, "[…] a complete change of atmosphere […] The highest alacrity and activity prevailed. Positions are everywhere being strengthened and extended, forces are being sorted out and regrouped in solid units."[4] He was impressed by the speed with which Montgomery had grasped the essentials of the situation, with the clarity of his plan, and by the way his self-confidence had infected the whole army. Churchill sensed what he and Britain so desperately needed: a victory.

Rommel did launch his expected attack. Nothing illustrates Montgomery's confidence in his planning more graphically than the fact that, when woken by his Chief of Staff to be told that Rommel was attacking, Montgomery lifted his head from the pillow, muttered, "Excellent, excellent,"—and went back to sleep.[5]

Rommel's forces, attacking at night under a full moon, were spotted by the RAF and bombed; they were also harassed by British armored units with instructions to inflict maximum damage and then retreat. These flanking attacks also forced the German forces to turn north towards the prepared defences of Alam el Halfa. The panzers broke through to the lines in the evening.

The combined artillery of the dug-in anti-tank guns and tanks held off the German attack. There was a real danger that individual commanders would launch counter-attacks—which is what Rommel wanted most of all—but Montgomery had drummed the plan into his troops. Rommel was horrified when the British did not move out to meet him. "The swine isn't attacking," he complained. Rommel was being forced to fight on ground chosen by the British, instead of facing brave but badly organized attacks by armored units that he could outmaneuver and outgun. Rommel attacked again next day but could make no headway; he withdrew. The German high-command berated Rommel for not pursuing the offensive. The official reasons given for this were shortage of petrol, Allied air superiority, and the lack of an element of surprise. In fact, Rommel knew that he had been outmaneuvered—in a strategic sense. Rommel, the master of maneuver, had been presented with a powerful defensive line that he could not break through, outflank, or ignore.

Montgomery, in his turn, was criticized for not delivering a killer blow against Rommel's retreating forces. He bided his time while he was reinforced with British Commonwealth forces and American Sherman tanks. Germany, embattled on the Eastern Front with Russia, was unable to resupply the *Afrikakorps*. Montgomery launched a huge air and artillery bombardment and then drove wedges of armor through Rommel's lines, forcing a retreat to the west as far as Tunisia.

Victory in North Africa denied Axis forces access to the oil of the Middle East and was the first major victory of World War II. Churchill, with his usual ear for a telling phrase (but borrowing heavily, in this case, from the French Napoleonic diplomat Charles Maurice de Talleyrand), said, "This is not the end. It is not even the beginning of the end. But it is, perhaps, the end of the beginning." And he also said (not quite accurately, but in homage to the turning point that victory in North Africa represented), "Before Alamein, we never had a victory. After Alamein, we never had a defeat."

ELIZABETH I OF ENGLAND
(1533–1603)

Elizabeth grew up in a time of great religious and political turmoil, in an atmosphere of fear and in the constant shadow of violent death. She proved to be one of life's great survivors: her fierce intelligence, strong will, and quick wits kept her alive when advisors to her sister, Queen Mary, were recommending that Elizabeth's execution was essential for the stability of the kingdom. When she became the Queen of England, she vowed to take "good advice and counsel" and was determined to rule with the support of a broad consensus of the English people. A religious settlement was the most pressing priority, not least because of the impossibility of separating religion from both national and international politics, and Elizabeth's very first Parliament was called upon to enact radical and far-reaching legislation on religious matters. This made the Protestant faith the established Church of England, with the monarch as its head, but reduced the penalties for heresy, so that dissent or non-cooperation were no longer such deadly matters.

Elizabeth successfully trod a middle line between her Catholic and her more radical Protestant subjects. The sheer length of her reign ensured that her essentially moderate approach prevailed, and resulted in a great stabilization of the nation. The country's successful, if partly fortuitous, defeat of the mighty Spanish Armada created a sense of national confidence. The English began to feel at ease with themselves and to be proud of their achievements. There was a great flourishing of the arts, especially in literature (Shakespeare, Marlow, Johnson, Spencer) and a growing sense of having lived in a golden age. Elizabeth saved England from the vicious religious divisions that continued to plague neighbors such as France, and laid the foundations for future prosperity and expansion.

Despite famously marrying six wives, Elizabeth's father, Henry VIII, had only three children by these marriages: Mary, Elizabeth, and Edward. Mary was the daughter of Henry's first wife, Catherine of Aragon, daughter of the King of Spain. Mary was raised (like Henry himself) as a Catholic. Catherine gave birth to four other children, who were either stillborn, or died soon after birth. When the Pope declined to annul Henry's marriage to Catherine, Henry decided to form his own church and to allow his own divorce. A number of Acts of Parliament were passed, recognizing Royal Supremacy over the church. England had broken with Rome. Henry married Anne Boleyn, who gave birth to Elizabeth, but failed to produce the desired-for son and was executed. Henry's third child, Edward, was born to his third wife, Jane Seymour, who died less than two weeks later from infection. On Henry's death, Edward became England's first Protestant King at the age of nine, but was to die, aged only 15, of tuberculosis. Catherine of Aragon's daughter, Mary, became Queen and rode into London with her younger sister, Elizabeth, amidst cheering crowds.

Mary reinstated the Catholic Church and married Philip, heir to the Spanish throne. She restored the heresy laws and set about burning Protestants. A serious rebellion, led by Thomas Wyatt, hoped to put Elizabeth on the throne in her place. The rebellion failed and Wyatt was executed. The young Elizabeth was sent to the Tower of London, protesting her innocence: under close questioning she failed to provide her interrogators with any evidence of her direct involvement in the plot. Mary's advisers nevertheless argued that Elizabeth would have to be executed to prevent future plots centered on her. In the absence of hard evidence against her, and with the reluctance of the Privy Council to see a Tudor Princess executed, Elizabeth was moved from the Tower to house-arrest in Woodstock, Oxfordshire.

It was in this atmosphere of fear and revolt that young Elizabeth learned her lessons in power politics. She was only 20 years old when she had been taken by barge to the forbidding Traitor's Gate at the Tower of London; she was 25 when she became Queen on her sister's death. Her illegitimacy in the eyes of the Catholic Church gave her little option but to pursue her father's break with Rome, and her Protestant faith gave her every incentive.

Since the birth of Protestantism could be ascribed to the letter of Martin Luther protesting about certain practices of the Catholic Church in 1517—a mere 32 years before Elizabeth's coronation—the great majority of Elizabeth's bishops were still, in effect, Catholic. Even Henry VIII himself had been a practicing Catholic; he had simply declared that he, and not the Pope, was the head of the Church in England. Elizabeth set the tone for her administration by arresting two of Queen Mary's more aggressively Catholic bishops—both of whom had taken an active part in the prosecution of Protestants. Both worthies suffered nothing greater, however, than arrest.

In her first Parliament Elizabeth put forward the Act of Supremacy. Her sister Mary had repealed their father's legislation establishing the monarch as head of the Church. Elizabeth's Act established the monarch as Supreme Governor of the Church. This proved a less contentious title than "Supreme Head", which had caused consternation (and some amusement) among senior clerics, since it was obvious from biblical authority that a mere woman could no more be Head of the Church than she could, for example, be a doctor—or indeed a priest. The bill was passed easily by the commons but with difficulty in the Lords, where every bishop voted against the bill. Once passed, however, the Act required anybody taking up an official position in government or church to swear the Oath Of Supremacy recognizing the Queen as head of all matters spiritual as well as temporal, and renouncing all "foreign jurisdictions […] and authorities." Penalties for not swearing the oath were, however, reduced. Under Henry, failure to swear had carried the death penalty. Under Elizabeth, a first refusal could result in a fine and a second in imprisonment. Only the third refusal would be treated as treason, punishable by execution.

Elizabeth then proposed her Act of Uniformity, which compelled the use of the Book of Common Prayer in church services, and made attendance of church on Sundays compulsory, on pain of a fine of one shilling—more than £10 in modern terms, a considerable sum for the poor (money raised by these fines, ironically, was to be used to help the poor). The Book of Common Prayer was toned down to remove some of its more flagrantly anti-Catholic sentiments. References to "The Bishop of Rome and his detestable enormities" were removed and churchgoers were no longer required to pray for the conversion of Roman Catholics, as well as for that of Jews and "infidels." The Act of Uniformity scraped through the House of Lords by three votes. Again, every bishop voted against the Act.

For the rest of her reign, Elizabeth fought to ensure that her Catholic subjects were not unnecessarily persecuted, though their influence in public affairs inevitably declined. She continued publically to associate with prominent Catholic families who had opposed the Acts. She saw Catholic subjects who were supportive of the monarchy as considerably less dangerous than more radical Protestants, whose articles of faith tended against any form of superior authority. Elizabeth's approach to the fundamental and critical issue of religion in English politics was firm, thorough, pragmatic, and essentially fair.

After the passing of the Acts there was a virtual cull of bishops: three were imprisoned for their flagrant support of Catholicism and every bishop other than the Bishop of Llandaff (who had signed the Oath of Supremacy) was removed from their bishopric and replaced with men who accepted Elizabeth's central position—even if, as was often the case, their Protestantism was significantly more extreme than her own.

The two other great crises of Elizabeth's realm were the threats posed by Mary, Queen of Scots and her allies, the French, and the threat of a Spanish invasion.

Mary, Queen of Scots' grandmother was Henry VIII's sister; her father was James V of Scotland; her mother was from the powerful French dynasty of the Dukes of Guise. The French constantly threatened to use their alliance with Scotland as a platform for the invasion of England. This threat was neutralized by a treaty with well-disposed Scottish lairds that effectively ended the 'Auld Alliance' between Scotland and France. Mary, Queen of Scots, was imprisoned.

Spain now began to threaten. England had begun increasingly to side with the Dutch in their rebellion against Spanish rule (of the Spanish Netherlands). Elizabeth's favourite pirate, Sir Francis Drake, had been pillaging Spanish colonial interests with the clear support of his Queen. A Spanish plot to assassinate Elizabeth was uncovered (or partly fabricated) by the spymaster Walsingham. Mary, Queen of Scots was implicated and executed. Philip (who had not been a great supporter of Mary, Queen of Scots, because of her links to his enemy, France) decided for entirely unrelated reasons to invade England, the throne of which had, after all, been left to him in the will of his late wife, the other Mary, Elizabeth's sister. The intrepid Drake burned part of the Spanish fleet at Cadiz, delaying the invasion, but in July 1588, the great Armada—130 ships carrying 8,000 sailors and 18,000 soldiers—sailed for England. The Armada planned to rendezvous with a land army of 30,000 men in Flanders prior to an invasion of England. At Tilbury, in the face of this terrifying invasion, Elizabeth made her greatest speech to her troops and to the nation:

> "My loving people, We have been persuaded by some that are careful of our safety, to take heed how we commit ourselves to armed multitudes, for fear of treachery; but I assure you I do not desire to live to distrust my faithful and loving people. Let tyrants fear. I have always so behaved myself that, under God, I have placed my chiefest strength and safeguard in the loyal hearts and good-will of my subjects; and therefore I am come amongst you, as you see, at this time, not for my recreation and disport, but being resolved, in the midst and heat of

the battle, to live and die amongst you all; to lay down for my God, and for my kingdom, and my people, my honour and my blood, even in the dust.

"I know I have the body but of a weak and feeble woman; but I have the heart and stomach of a king, and of a king of England too, and think foul scorn that Parma or Spain, or any prince of Europe, should dare to invade the borders of my realm; to which rather than any dishonour shall grow by me, I myself will take up arms, I myself will be your general, judge, and rewarder of every one of your virtues in the field."

Drake's fire-ships scattered the Armada from its anchorage off Calais and a well-fought attack by the English drove the Armada off up the east coast of England. The Spanish were forced to sail around the north of the British Isles to reach the Atlantic and return to Spain: fierce westerly storms wrecked some 24 Spanish ships on the coasts of Ireland. More than a third of the great Armada failed to return to Spain.

Elizabeth's later reign was marked by increasing concern about foreign Jesuit Catholic priests entering England from the Continent and spreading sedition; repression of Catholics within English society increased. Elizabeth was equally harsh on the Puritan wing of her Protestant church. Many of her more extreme Protestant subjects had seen the Acts of Supremacy and Uniformity as a compromise—and so, brilliantly, they were. Elizabeth's great success was in establishing some kind of structure—in this case, the Church of England—that could find a middle ground of national support in the face of the potentially hugely damaging forces of differing religious beliefs. Despite her own firm Protestant faith she managed, unlike her sister, Queen Mary, to avoid fanaticism. She viewed religious faith as essentially a personal matter: if that faith strayed into the realm of politics, then it had to be dealt with; if not, it could be left alone. Her contemporary, Francis Bacon, the philosopher and statesman, summed this up brilliantly:

"Her Majesty, not liking to make windows into men's hearts and secret thoughts, except the abundance of them did overflow into overt express acts and affirmations, tempered her law so as it restraineth only manifest disobedience."

Though she outstayed her welcome to the point that there was a sense of national relief at her eventual death (her later reign was marred by unsuccessful minor wars, rising prices, and rising taxation, not helped by poor harvests), Elizabeth's long reign had given the country stability and, most importantly, a sense of identity. Before Elizabeth there was uncertainty as to whether the nation was Catholic or Protestant; it had seemed entirely possible that the nation would acquire a Spanish King (Philip) or a French/Scottish Queen (Mary, Queen of Scots; next in line to the throne after the childless Elizabeth). By the end of Elizabeth's reign, the nation knew that it was Protestant, but that the Church of England had proved to be a broad church where many found continuity of religious observance. Dissenting Catholics were, in general, not persecuted or pursued. More especially, the nation knew that it was English: Shakespeare's 'History Plays' can be seen as a dramatic exploration of 'Englishness', stretching back to medieval times and culminating with the Tudors. Elizabeth's reign had created a new national mood.

NELSON MANDELA
(b. 1918)

Nelson Mandela changed the mood of South Africa to an extent that seems unbelievable, even with hindsight. For decades, black and white South Africans had been embattled in an increasingly bitter conflict. Civil war seemed increasingly likely—at times, South Africa seemed already to be in a state of civil war. Nelson Mandela himself was regarded as a violent terrorist leader, in league with foreign powers, determined to overthrow the government of South Africa and to install a black communist regime that was expected to be implacably hostile to the white minority and their way of life. Even when a democratic solution seemed possible, it was believed by most South African whites that a black majority government would both ruin the country and oppress the white minority. In reality, soon after Nelson Mandela's ANC party won a majority in South Africa's first ever multi-racial elections in 1994, making Nelson Mandela the President of the Republic of South Africa, people began to come together.

Mandela, the son of a chieftain from Transkei, took a first degree by correspondence course while working as an articled clerk at a law firm and went on to study law. He joined the African National Congress (ANC) in 1942. In 1948, the Afrikaner-dominated National Party won the election and imposed a system of segregation—apartheid—of people by race: white, black, colored, and Asian. The 'race' of all citizens was shown on their passes. It was illegal to marry, or to have sex with a person of another race. Committees sat to decide on the appropriate classification of people whose race was difficult to determine, sometimes splitting up families whose members were assigned to different racial groups. Black people were declared to be no longer citizens of South Africa, but of ten 'homelands' based on tribal territories. They were allowed to vote only for the government of their "homeland," which was, in any case, only nominally independent of the South African government: black people had been effectively disenfranchised. Their dispersal to the ten supposedly autonomous homelands ensured that the black majority in South Africa was neutralized electorally.

Movement of black people was strictly controlled to prevent migration to the mainly white cities, where the bulk of employment was to be found. Black workers who wanted a job in 'South Africa' (outside of the homelands) required a work permit. They were not allowed to bring their families to work in the cities, but lived in male-only hostels, separated from their families for long periods. The work permit covered only one area, typically a township. To be found in a different area was to be arrested as an 'illegal immigrant' and deported to one's homeland.

Added to all of this was the indignity of the many measures of 'petty-apartheid'—the racial segregation of trains, hospitals, swimming pools, cinemas, parks, and beaches—and the realities of second-class wages, education, and opportunities. The reality of educational policy for blacks could not be more brutally spelled out than it was by H.F. Verwoerd, Prime Minister of South Africa from 1958–1966, speaking in the debate on Bantu education in 1953:

> "When I have control of Native education, I will reform it so that Natives will be taught from childhood that equality with Europeans is not for them [...] (the Ministry) will know for what class of higher education a Native is fitted, and whether he will have a chance in life to use his knowledge."[6]

In 1944 Mandela and others formed a Youth League of the ANC, calling for non-violent protest to establish black self-determination. In 1950, 18 black workers were killed after a labor walk-out. In 1952, the ANC set out to ask the government to repeal "six unjust laws," promising a campaign of civil disobedience led by volunteers, with Mandela as

Volunteer-in-Chief. The volunteers marched into townships without permits; appeared on the streets after curfew; used whites-only train carriages. Eventually Mandela and 21 other leaders were arrested under the new Suppression of Communism Act: they were sentenced to nine months hard labor, but suspended for two years—a relatively lenient sentence. The judge determined that they were guilty of 'statutory communism' (based on the notion that all protest must be communist-inspired) which he admitted, however, had "nothing to do with communism as it is commonly known."[7] Nevertheless, his judgment required Mandela to resign from his leadership position within the ANC and he was banned from appearing at public meetings.

In 1956 Mandela was arrested, along with the president of the ANC and 150 others, and charged with treason. The Treason Trial dragged on for five years, ending in 1961 with the acquittal of all the accused. In 1960, a crowd of many thousands converged on a police station in Sharpeville, provoking arrest for not carrying their pass books—a deliberate act of civil disobedience. The crowd was buzzed by Sabre jet fighters to try to panic them into dispersing; then Saracen armored vehicles were lined up; then the police opened fire. The official death toll was 69 dead, including eight women and ten children, with 180 injured. In the aftermath of the shootings, the ANC was banned.

It was clear that non-violent protest had run its course and failed. The ANC, now an illegal organization, went underground. Mandela formed the military arm of the ANC—*Umkhonto we Sizwe* or "Spear of the Nation," often abbreviated as MK—which began a campaign of sabotage. Nelson traveled around Africa, seeking support, military advice, and training. On his return he was arrested for leaving the country illegally (black Africans were not allowed passports) and for initiating a strike against the newly declared Republic of South Africa, which had left the British Commonwealth following a referendum from which blacks—some 70 percent of the population—had been excluded. Mandela was sentenced to five years in jail. While serving that sentence, he was linked to acts of sabotage and charged with high treason, which carried the death sentence.

In his statement from the dock at the opening of the defence statement, Mandela admitted from the outset that he had helped to form the MK military wing; that he had played a prominent role in its affairs and that he had planned acts of sabotage. Mandela then eloquently spelled out the background to his actions and his political philosophy.

The ANC had been banned, removing any lawful means of protest. Violence had become inevitable because non-violent protest had been met with new and increasingly harsh laws and, finally, with a massive show of force.

Mandela's actions had not been influenced by outside foreign powers:

> "I have done whatever I did, both as an individual and as a leader of my people, because of my experience in South Africa and my own proudly felt African background, and not because of what any outsider might have said."

Nor was he influenced by communism: the ANC had cooperated with communists because they shared the common goal of bringing an end to white supremacy, but the ANC had never advocated a revolutionary change in the economic structure of the country, nor had it condemned capitalist society. Mandela commented that, from his reading, Marxists seemed to regard the parliamentary system as undemocratic and reactionary: "On the contrary, I am an admirer of such a system."

> "Our complaint is not that we are poor by comparison with people in other countries, but that we are poor by comparison with white people in our own country, and that we are prevented by legislation from altering this imbalance.
>
> "Above all, we want equal political rights, because without them our disabilities will be permanent. I know this sounds revolutionary to the whites in this country, because the majority of voters will be Africans. This makes the white man fear democracy.

"But this fear cannot be allowed to stand in the way of the only solution which will guarantee racial harmony and freedom for all. It is not true that the enfranchisement of all will result in racial domination. Political division, based on color, is entirely artificial and, when it disappears, so will the domination of one color group by another. The ANC has spent half a century fighting against racialism. When it triumphs it will not change that policy [...]

"During my lifetime I have dedicated myself to this struggle of the African people. I have fought against white domination, and I have fought against black domination. I have cherished the ideal of a democratic and free society in which all persons live together in harmony and with equal opportunities. It is an ideal which I hope to live for and to achieve. But if needs be, it is an ideal for which I am prepared to die."[8]

Mandela was found guilty and sentenced to life imprisonment with hard labor. He was to spend the next 27 years in prison, 18 of them on Robben Island. In this time he became an international figure and a symbol of the struggle of black South Africans against apartheid. As the sixties and seventies progressed, opinion moved against the South African government. Anti-apartheid boycotts of South African goods, banks, and sports spread across Europe and America.

In 1982 Mandela had been moved from Robben Island prison to a maximum security prison outside Cape Town, where he spent most of the next six years in solitary confinement. Secret talks between Mandela and representatives offered Mandela his freedom if he would renounce violent action, break with the Communist Party and abandon the principle of majority rule. Mandela refused to renounce violence while the government refused to share power with black people, reiterated that the ANC had never been controlled by communists but that he was not prepared to denounce them, and insisted that the government must accept majority rule. But he proposed preliminary talks to open the way for negotiations, saying that it was time for all leaders to set aside preconditions and start the debate "for a new South Africa."

The extent to which Mandela maintained his leadership position within the ANC while in prison is remarkable. One of the reasons for his move from Robben Island prison may well have been the position of respect that he held with other imprisoned ANC members, and his continued influence over them and the movement. Foreign diplomats visiting Mandela in prison in the search for a settlement had been impressed by his ability to speak for the movement without consulting with colleagues. Despite his apparently isolated position, he obviously knew precisely what the ANC would or would not accept, and was able to speak for them.

By the late 1980s, South Africa was becoming ungovernable. Sanctions were beginning to hurt the economy. Street violence was increasing. President Botha imposed a crackdown: a nationwide state of emergency increased police powers; townships were surrounded, roads blocked. Thousands were detained and sometimes tortured. Opposition bases in neighbouring countries were attacked by the army and air-force in cross-border raids. Militants in the ANC and the Pan African Congress turned to terror tactics, planting bombs in restaurants, shopping centers, and government buildings. The ANC started a campaign to make townships ungovernable through rent boycotts. This ran out of control as 'people's courts' turned on local authorities and accused them of helping the government, handing out brutal punishments including the fatal 'necklacing': murdering victims by placing a burning tire around their neck.

International pressure for the release of Mandela increased. In 1989, President Pieter Willem Botha suffered a mild stroke and was replaced by F.W. de Klerk. A year later, de Klerk announced Mandela's freedom. A gray-haired but upright Mandela emerged into a glare of publicity that took him by surprise; the world was impressed by his dignity, fortitude, and resolution.

De Klerk took the historic step of legalising the ANC and 60 other banned organizations. Oliver Tambo, President in Exile of the ANC, stood down and Mandela was unanimously elected President of the ANC. Within six months of his release, Mandela suspended the ANC's armed struggle, alienating his more hard-line members. De Klerk and Mandela signed the historic Record of Understanding, setting up a freely elected constitutional assembly that would draw up a new draft constitution.

In April 1994 South Africa's first ever multi-racial elections were held, with all citizens eligible to vote. Violence on both sides continued up until Election Day, but 20 million South Africans turned out to cast their vote. The ANC won 63 percent of the vote; Nelson Mandela was the new President of South Africa.

Mandela now began the most impressive phase of his leadership. He had spent a quarter of a century in prison and had every right to feel bitterness toward the party who had put him there. Given their intransigence in government, he would also have been forgiven for denying them ministerial roles. At the same time, he was only now discovering the extent to which the previous government—and even his old negotiating partner de Klerk, with whom he was to shared the Nobel Peace prize—had been complicit with the infamous Third Force: the shadowy group of security and ex-security officers who had fomented and encouraged violence between different black organizations in an attempt to 'divide and conquer' the black majority.

But Mandela set out to create a government of national unity. His first task was to help his own organization, the ANC, to make the immense transition from being a slightly disorganized group of revolutionaries, who had spend most of the last 34 years 'underground' as a banned organization, into a party of government of a complex modern state. His next task was to assemble his cabinet.

Old enemies sat down together, and proved surprisingly cooperative. The cabinet reflected all of the country's racial groups. The Afrikaners of the National Party seemed committed to making the coalition work; they in turn were pleasantly surprised to hear ANC members arguing amongst themselves—they had expected them to have a party line thrashed out in advance. Mandela handled the cabinet with a light touch, listening impassively; making the occasional contribution. In committee meetings he was decisive, coming quickly to a judgment after a short brief.[9]

Mandela set out on a symbolic campaign of personal forgiveness. He had learned to control his emotions during the long years of refinement; he channelled what anger and bitterness he must have felt into positive action. He visited ex-President Botha (whom the Truth and Reconciliation Commission judged to have "facilitated a climate in which [...] gross violations of human rights could and did occur"); he invited the former commander of Robben Island prison to dinner; he had lunch with the Prosecutor from his trial. When the South African rugby team, the Springboks, celebrated their return to international rugby after the lifting of sporting boycotts, Mandela walked onto the field after the Springbok's victory over New Zealand, wearing a green Springbok shirt, and handed the trophy to an astonished captain Francois Pienaar. For many, the Springboks were a symbol of white Afrikaner racial superiority. Afrikaners at the game and watching on television felt that they had been offered understanding and had been welcomed into the new fold.

Mandela's Truth and Reconciliation Commission was a compromise, but a brilliant one. During the hard bargaining of the negotiations, the National Party had insisted on a general amnesty for the security forces for any actions carried out during the struggles. A deal had been thrashed out: there would be no 'general' amnesty, but amnesties would be granted to individuals who told the truth about their action, provided that they could prove that these actions had been politically motivated. Many grisly details emerged of torture and murder by government agencies. Some dark secrets of the ANC and other black groups also emerged. The nation would learn the truth, and could decide if it could forgive or not, but there would be no acts of vengeance.

2

BOLDNESS OF
VISION

Leaders are often judged by the vision that they bring to their organization. It is probably a mistake to imagine that every organization is susceptible to a new grand vision. The great leaders from history tend, by definition, to have been leaders of a nation, an empire, a movement. Winston Churchill set out a vision for the British people that said that they could, and should, resist the spread of Nazi Germany. It seemed impossible for a small nation—still reeling from the effects of the World War I and the Depression—to stop such a mighty war machine, but Churchill persuaded the nation that it could, just somehow, achieve exactly that. There was no doubt about the vision:

> "Victory—victory—at all costs, victory, in spite of all terror, victory, however long and hard the road may be; for without victory, there is no survival. Let that be realized; no survival for the British Empire; no survival for all that the British Empire has stood for, no survival for the urge and impulse of the ages, that mankind will move forward toward its goal."[10]

Most organizations are faced with something less dramatic than imminent invasion by a hostile force bent on world domination (although, in a business sense, that scenario may sound eerily familiar to you). A great vision for any organization is both simple and, well, bold, but it need not be grand. What, after all, are you leading your team or organization *for*? There will be targets to be achieved and directions to be set, but these are the essential running, the unavoidable management of your business. A vision is something else: an overriding sense of purpose, a *raison d'être*, a corporate identity (in the real sense of the phrase, as opposed to the more usual "what-color-should-our-logo-be?" sense).

At this more understandable, more mundane level, it becomes clear that every leader does indeed need a vision. Boldness is, after all, a matter of degree, but a vision, by definition, is something that everybody in the organization can grasp; a simple answer that can instantly be given to the question, "What are we trying to achieve?"

The leaders from history in this section were able to offer their nations a truly momentous vision, a vision that changed the course of history. What is interesting is that they had not been born, as it were, with this vision. They had not been carrying it around, waiting to proclaim it to the right audience. They found themselves in a particular set of circumstances; with a particular set of issues—and suddenly it all became clear. In order to lead their country forward, they were able to articulate what everybody needed to hear.

Abraham Lincoln is perhaps most remarkable for the fact that he started his presidency of the United States of America with, understandably, a conservative position: he was simply desperate to hold the United States—still a very young nation—together. The new nation's radical experiment in republican government was in danger of fragmenting into a collection of loosely associated states; of ceasing to be a nation. Lincoln set out at first only to prevent the secession of the Southern States, and preferred not to address the question of slavery in states where it was long-established, deeply as he loathed the institution of slavery. He sought, at first, only to prevent the spread of slave ownership into new territories as America expanded to the west. As the American Civil War progressed, he realized that the moral issue was in fact the core issue; that the pragmatic solution of merely holding the states together was no solution. The vision that he offered was suddenly crystal clear in his own mind, as it would soon be in the nation as a whole: "A nation conceived in liberty and dedicated to the proposition that all men are created equal."

Pericles of Athens, the great Athenian statesman, gave his fellow citizens a sense, firstly of what it meant to be citizens of the world's first democracy, and then of the greatness that could accompany that.

Athenians, he said, were different from other people; they served no master but themselves; they followed no laws other than those that they had set themselves. This set them apart from other nations and gave them the opportunity for greatness—which, in ancient Greece, meant the opportunity to rule over many of the other city-states, to accumulate great wealth, to encourage the arts and philosophy, and to build great buildings, like the Parthenon, so that all might see the true worth—the glory—of Athens. What was most impressive about Pericles' vision for Athens is that he offered Athenians not what they wanted but what he believed to be in the best interests of Athens. The Periclean Age is one of the golden ages of history; its culture still inspires us today.

Winston Churchill, Prime Minister of Great Britain during World War II, demonstrated that, at times, boldness of vision can take precedence over every other leadership quality. Churchill was in many ways an admirable man and a strong leader: brave, intelligent, eloquent, perceptive, and at times brilliant. At other times he was a one-man disaster area. But his knowledge of the history of the British people—and his conviction that the nation was up to the momentous challenge that faced it—allowed him to articulate what perhaps no other politician would have dared even to conceive. Faced by the overwhelming might of the German army and with insufficient resources to undertake a war of such magnitude, Britain might sensibly have sought an accommodation; might, perhaps, have traded a degree of independence for security from outright invasion. Churchill, through his remarkable speeches, inspired the incredible dedication and self-sacrifice shown by the people of Britain during the war years. He made the nation, still suffering from the effects of the Depression, feel that it was still capable of great resolve and mighty endeavors.

> "Let us therefore brace ourselves to our duties, and so bear ourselves that, if the British Empire and its Commonwealth last for a thousand years, men will still say, 'This was their finest hour.'"[11]

ABRAHAM LINCOLN
(1809–1865)

Abraham Lincoln had most, and possibly all, of the qualities that are needed in a great leader. He had a sharp and enquiring mind, able to absorb large quantities of information. Helped by his study and practice of the law, he could consider every facet of an argument, and then present a closely-argued narrative that spelled out the most compelling interpretation of the salient facts. He was a great orator, speaking sometimes at length and in great detail, and at other times with a breathtaking concision and eloquence. He was prepared and willing to compromize, but held strong bedrock convictions from which he would not budge: he would compromize on the solution, but not on the principle. He had great mental toughness and physical stamina: he worked hard. He was a good judge of people; he assembled good teams and helped to bring people of differing opinions together so that they would work towards the common goal. When he found a colleague whom he could trust, he gave them considerable freedom of action. As President of the nation, he had a clear and detailed vision of the way in which he wanted that nation to develop, and was able to pursue that vision single-mindedly through the most difficult of imaginable political circumstances: a civil war.

"Fourscore and seven years ago our fathers brought forth on this continent a new nation, conceived in liberty and dedicated to the proposition that all men are created equal."

When Abraham Lincoln made one of the world's most famous speeches, at the dedication of the Soldiers' National Cemetery in Gettysburg, Pennsylvania, in November 1863, he made this proposition sound unquestionable. America's Declaration of

Independence, written by Thomas Jefferson in 1776—fourscore and seven years before Lincoln's Gettysburg address—had clearly said, "We hold these truths to be self-evident, that all men are created equal, that they are endowed by their Creator with certain unalienable Rights, that among these are Life, Liberty, and the pursuit of Happiness." Every American knew that.

The problem was that the definition of liberty at the time was contentious and far from self-evident. As Lincoln himself said later, "The world has never had a good definition of the word liberty and the American people, just now, are much in want of one. We all declare for liberty; but in using the same word we do not all mean the same thing. With some the word liberty may mean for each man to do as he pleases with himself, and the product of his labor; while with others the same may mean for some men to do as they please with other men, and the product of other men's labor."[12] What Lincoln was referring to was, of course, slavery. But to the farm-owning citizens of the slave states, slaves were a part of their property—as essential to their capacity to work the soil and raise crops as were their tools, wagons, and other items. To take away their *property* was to deny them the ability to create their own livelihood, and thus to deny them their *liberty*. In this the Southern States were harking back to an early American definition of what it meant to be a citizen and a 'free man'—a citizen was able to support himself; he had property, or at least his skills and the tools of his trade. The idea of a wage laborer being a full citizen was novel, while slaves were not considered to be citizens in any meaningful sense. A Supreme Court decision in 1857 concerning slave-owners' rights to take their property (including slaves) into the new territories simplified matters with a fearsome clarity: slaves were not persons under the Constitution, and therefore had no right to liberty themselves.

At the time of the War of Independence, it was already clear to many Americans that slavery would become a dangerously contentious issue amongst the thirteen states that made up the new United States. George Washington himself was a Virginian plantation owner who, like all of his peers, owned slaves. The big, labor-intensive plantations of the South were entirely dependent on slaves; slave-labor underpinned the whole economy of the Southern States and slaves represented a significant proportion of the property of land-owners. The Constitution (adopted in 1787) addressed the issue of slavery, but entirely inconclusively: the importation of slaves was permitted; escaped slaves should not be assisted and should be returned to their owners; slaves were to be recognized in terms of the population of any state as 'other persons' who should be counted as three-fifths of a citizen. Slavery was implicitly rather than explicitly recognized, and a specific article forbade any amendments or new legislation at a national, Congressional level regarding slavery for 20 more years, until 1808. The Constitution was, in effect, ducking the issue and hoping that some kind of consensus might emerge in 20 years time. It did not.

Many individual states did abolish or phase out slavery, establishing themselves as 'free states' as opposed to 'slave states'. As early as 1787, Congress had passed the Northwest Ordinance, which set up the principle that the original 13 states on America's east coast would expand westwards by the creation of new states rather than by the expansion of the existing states. Slavery was banned in these new western territories; the Ohio River became the border between the free states to the north and the slave states to the south.

In 1803, Napoleonic France sold their last remaining American territories to help fund the new revolutionary republic's wars against the monarchies of old Europe. The French territory of Louisiana was big: it encompassed modern-day Arkansas, Iowa, Missouri, Oklahoma, Kansas, Nebraska, parts of Minnesota, most of North and South Dakota, parts of New Mexico, Texas, Montana, Wyoming, Colorado, and Louisiana west of the Mississippi. The territory represents about 828,000 square miles or 23 percent of the modern United States. The Americans paid France 15 million dollars (including cancellation of debt).

The opening up of the new territories began a political wrangle as to whether they would be 'free' or 'slave' states—a serious political issue since two Senators per state were elected to the Senate and there was great concern that neither faction should predominate. In 1820 a compromize was reached that would allow the new state of Missouri to be a slave state, but which banned slavery in the rest of the 'Missouri Territory'—the territory bought from France. The inclusion of Missouri into the Union tipped the balance of slave to free states in the former's favor by 12 states to 11. Maine was admitted to the Union as a free state to keep the political balance.

In 1854, an Act to open the new northwestern territories of Kansas in the mid-west and Nebraska to its north, confirmed that settlers would be allowed to vote as to whether territories should be free or slave states. This appeal to "popular sovereignty" attempted to establish the principle that slavery was an issue on which Congress should not impose its will on the people. It drew a 45-year-old lawyer from Illinois, Abraham Lincoln, to return to politics and to help in the formation of the new Republican Party. In a famous speech, Lincoln's deep-seated hatred of slavery was made clear:

> "This [...] covert *real* zeal for the spread of slavery, I can not but hate. I hate it because of the monstrous injustice of slavery itself. I hate it because it deprives our republican example of its just influence in the world—enables the enemies of free institutions, with plausibility, to taunt us as hypocrites—causes the real friends of freedom to doubt our sincerity, and especially because it forces so many really good men amongst ourselves into an open war with the very fundamental principles of civil liberty—criticizing the Declaration of Independence, and insisting that there is no right principle of action but *self-interest*."[13]

The new Republican Party was opposed to slavery and espoused a modernizing agenda, with emphasis on building railroads, industry, and cities, improving education, and establishing a national banking system. They promised free homesteads to new farmers and propounded the benefits of the free labor market. The new Republican

Party represented a real and direct threat to the southern slave states' entire way of life. In many ways, it was not simply the issue of slavery that divided the nation, but a way of living: the patrician, affluent, landed, agrarian society of the south opposed to the new, modern, increasingly industrialized states of the north, built on the free labor market and the rights of the individual.

In 1858, Lincoln accepted the Republican nomination to the Senate. Lincoln's eloquent and forceful speeches against slavery made him something of a national figure. In 1860, Lincoln won the nomination as Presidential candidate for the Republican Party. He was far from the strongest candidate at the outset but his origins as a poor homesteader's son from the new western territories (born in a log cabin in Kentucky; moved to Illinois) gave him a strong appeal to settlers in the new western states. Ironically, his 'moderate' stance on slavery was in his favor—several abolitionists in the Republican Party presented the anti-slavery case in the light of a new and more perfect 'second American revolution' that would free black Americans from slavery, just as the first revolution had freed Americans from British rule. Lincoln's main advantage was a split in the opposing Democratic Party. He was elected with only 40 percent of the popular vote.

Lincoln's moderate stance over slavery may have helped to get him elected as the first ever Republican President, but it didn't do any good. Seven Southern States, led by South Carolina, declared that they would secede from the Union to form a new nation—the Confederate States of America. They argued that the new Republican government was no longer working in their best interests and they exercised their Constitutional right to a new form of government: a confederacy.

From the outset, Lincoln's primary aim was to maintain the Union. He supported an Amendment that would have prohibited the banning of slavery in the border states where it was currently permitted. This was hoped to encourage states such as Missouri and Kentucky to remain in the Union—though their support was less whole-hearted than Lincoln at first imagined. Lincoln was against the spread of slavery into new states, but he did not set out to abolish slavery in states where it was established. He saw the war at first as a kind of police operation—a question of putting down a rebellion within the nation.

Lincoln had hoped to persuade the border states to begin a policy of gradual emancipation of slaves, with slave-owners compensated by the government. He believed that if the border states moved away from slavery, this would persuade the Southern States that they could never hope for the border states' support in the war, and would demonstrate that the tide of opinion was turning against them. When the border states rejected the plan, Lincoln changed his mind. He began work on an emancipation plan with the fervor of a man who has resisted his best instincts in order to pursue a policy of possible compromize, and can now follow his heart. Lincoln announced that, as of January 1st 1863, he would proclaim freedom for all slaves in states then in rebellion against the North: "I never, in my life, felt more certain that I was doing right, than I do in signing this paper." He then began to work on the Thirteenth Amendment to the Constitution, banning slavery throughout the United States.

In July 1863, Union forces won the bloody three-day battle of Gettysburg and halted the Confederate General Lee's second attempt to invade the north. Lee retreated to the south. There had been around 50,000 American casualties at Gettysburg; at the dedication of the Soldiers' National Cemetery, Lincoln made the famous address which, in effect, redefined the aims of the war. The war was no longer an attempt to bring rebellious states back into the union, it was a moral struggle to achieve the "rebirth of freedom" and of the distinctive, and still precarious form of government that the American Revolution had created, a "government of the people, by the people, for the people:"

"Fourscore and seven years ago our fathers brought forth on this continent a new nation, conceived in liberty and dedicated to the proposition that all men are created equal.

"Now we are engaged in a great civil war, testing whether that nation or any nation so conceived and so dedicated can long endure. We are met on a great battlefield of that war. We have come to dedicate a portion of that field as a final resting-place for those who here gave their lives that that nation might live. It is altogether fitting and proper that we should do this.

"But, in a larger sense, we cannot dedicate, we cannot consecrate, we cannot hallow this ground. The brave men, living and dead who struggled here have consecrated it far above our poor power to add or detract. The world will little note nor long remember what we say here, but it can never forget what they did here. It is for us, the living, rather to be dedicated here to the unfinished work which they who fought here have thus far so nobly advanced. It is rather for us to be here dedicated to the great task remaining before us—that from these honored dead we take increased devotion to that cause for which they gave the last full measure of devotion—that we here highly resolve that these dead shall not have died in vain, that this nation under God shall have a new birth of freedom, and that government of the people, by the people, for the people shall not perish from the earth."

One day after Lee's defeat at the Battle of Gettysburg, there had been another Unionist victory at Vicksburg on the Mississippi, when General Ulysses S. Grant had driven Confederate forces back into the city of Vicksburg and successfully besieged the city. From now on, Lincoln put his trust in Grant, who showed a dogged tenacity and a will to push forward. Grant, with William T. Sherman, launched a coordinated attack against the Confederacy on all fronts. Where there had previously been an attempt to avoid destruction of property in the Southern States, there was now the merciless intent to remove their capacity to wage war. Crops and livestock were destroyed, rail tracks were ripped up and bent around trees; any useful infrastructure was destroyed. Civilian deaths, however, remained low.

Despite Grant's advances, the war still looked like a bloody stalemate and in 1864 Lincoln's re-election as President seemed unlikely. A war-weary North began to contemplate the possibility of an independent South. There were informal peace negotiations, but both sides were intransigent: the South wanted independence; Lincoln would offer nothing but unconditional surrender. The days of possible compromize were over.

Lincoln was saved by a stunning victory in the south: Sherman captured Atlanta, Georgia. Lincoln was re-elected. Sherman began to fight and burn his way further south towards Savannah while Grant drove Confederacy forces back down the Shenandoah Valley. The war was being won. Early in 1865, Robert E. Lee was forced to retreat from Richmond and after a retreat of nine days, surrendered to Grant at Appomattox Court House. Grant offered generous terms of surrender and worked hard to allow the Confederate Army to stand down with their pride intact.

Grant accepted Lee's surrender on April 9th 1865; on April 14th Lincoln was shot at Ford's Theatre by John Wilkes Both, a Confederate spy who had previously planned to kidnap Lincoln and exchange him for Confederate prisoners, but had finally been driven to murder by Lincoln's recent speech promoting voting rights for black Americans. Lincoln died the next day.

Lincoln had set the tone for a spirit of reconciliation in his Second Inaugural Speech:

> "Fondly do we hope—fervently do we pray—that this mighty scourge of war may speedily pass away [...] With malice toward none; with charity for all; with firmness in the right, as God gives us to see the right, let us strive on to finish the work we are in; to bind up the nation's wounds; to care for him who shall have borne the battle, and for his widow, and his orphan—to do all which may achieve and cherish a just and lasting peace, among ourselves, and with all nations."[14]

Lincoln's political light-footedness was remarkable in someone so relatively inexperienced. He was a master at keeping conflicting groups working together towards the common goal, even when there were great ideological differences between them and when his own leadership was not particularly highly-rated. He dealt masterfully with the slave-owning border states who stayed in the union, seeing them as an essential ideological buffer zone between the free state members of the union and the slave state secessionists ("I hope to have God on my side, but I must have Kentucky"); when it seemed that a war-weary north would give up the fight and allow the Southern States to become independent, he maneuvered them into a position of total non-compromize that clarified the only possible successful outcome of the war for the north: unconditional surrender and the reinstatement of the union. His timing with regards to the emancipation of slaves was impeccable. Had he entered the war on a strong abolitionist platform, he would not have brought the border states, or even general northern opinion, with him. If he had delayed pursuing the emancipation issue much longer, the war, and an exhausted nation, might have swung in favor of an independent Confederacy. He gave the nation the vision that it needed at exactly the moment when most people were ready to receive it.

PERICLES OF ATHENS
(c.495–429 BCE)

Pericles, the great Athenian statesman, was born around 490 BCE. Greece at the time was a collection of city states engaged in a more-or-less permanent state of rivalry and warfare, occasionally managing to form a united front against the common enemy, Persia. Though Pericles was only one of several elected generals, he came to be the effective leader of Athens. In Athens, every free (that is, not enslaved) male Athenian was a member of the Assembly. This was a relatively small number—perhaps 43,000 people, of which a quorum of 6,000 was sometimes required to pass business. These manageable numbers allowed a remarkable experiment in total democracy. This was not representational democracy; *everybody* got to vote, by show of hands, on the key issues of the day (apart from women and slaves, obviously). Pericles' 'leadership' of Athens was based entirely on his powers of persuasion. Though accused of populism for introducing, for example, payment for members to attend the Assembly (before this measure, only citizens wealthy enough to spend time away from their home and their land could afford to attend the Assembly), Pericles was not a populist. A calm and famously incorruptible man, he inspired Athenians to believe in the potential greatness of their city state. The Golden Age of Athens attracted the greatest poets, playwrights, philosophers, architects, and artists to the city. This Golden Age of Athens is synonymous with Periclean Athens.

In Greece around the sixth century BCE, some city states were ruled by kings and others by the aristocratic heads of great families in an essentially tribal structure. Occasionally a political opportunist or "tyrant" would seize power, often with popular support: the word acquired its negative connotations a little later. Rule by aristocrats favoured the rich; the growing class of merchants and the poorer members of society might fare better under the leadership of a tyrant. It was the power struggle between aristocracies and tyrants—between oligarchy and tyranny—that was to create the conditions for the birth of democracy. When the last tyrant of Athens was overthrown by a leading clan, one family seized power with the aid of Sparta, and began to expel other families hostile to them. The people of Athens rose up and besieged the upstarts and their Spartan allies on the Acropolis for two days before expelling them from the country. One of the triumphant great families—the Alcmaeonids —had little option but to reward the citizens who had seen off their rivals with some form of power-sharing. Their leader, Cleisthenes, created ten new tribes drawn from different parts of Attica—the country surrounding Athens. Old tribal loyalties were broken. Each of the ten new tribes was now represented in a Council, the central administrative body; on key issues Council needed the endorsement of the Assembly, to which every free adult male belonged.

This radical form of democracy was to last for another 180 years, evolving over time but never straying from the basic principle that the citizen body—the *demos*—made all of the decisions about the government and administration of the state. In Athens the *demos* consisted of every free Athenian male over the age of 18. Citizens over the age of 30 could put themselves forward for membership of the Council. Members were finally appointed by lot. They served for one year, and could serve not more than twice. They met daily, prepared business for the assembly and ensured that decisions were implemented and kept within budget. The key administrative positions—financial controllers, inspectors, architects—were also elected by lot for one year and only for one period of service. At the top of the pyramid were the military generals—the *strategoi* (from which the word strategy is derived)—which was the only role that was elected and not chosen by vote. Generals could serve indefinitely, but were elected annually.

Although the election to government post by lot rather than merit looks alarming to modern eyes, there was a strict system of supervision, audit, and control. Council members were scrutinized before they were able to put their name forward for selection by lot.

Incompetence was punished by fines, exile, or—ultimately— execution. Many military commanders were prosecuted for failure and could be executed. Even the great Pericles was prosecuted, stripped of his rank of general, and fined, though he was re-elected a year later. Despite Pericles' role as General, he had no executive power to impose decisions and, like any other citizen, had just one vote in the Assembly. If Pericles was to lead Athens to follow a particular course of action, he had to rely on his powers of persuasion.

Pericles was born some years after the creation of a democratic Athens. The democratic reformer, Cleisthenes, was his mother's uncle. He grew up in a time of radical change brought on by invasions from Persia, as Darius the Great attempted to extend his empire. Some Greek city states were already under Persian rule; others were allies. The remaining states were forced to cooperate to defend themselves. At the great battle of Marathon, in 490 BCE, the Athenians, supported only by neighboring Plataea, defeated a much larger Persian army. After Marathon, an Athenian statesman, Themistocles, persuaded the national Assembly to use money from a newly-discovered silver mine to build a fleet of warships.

Ten years after their defeat at Marathon, the Persian returned under Xerxes, son of Darius. Their route through central Greece was famously blocked by Leonidas and the 300 Spartans at the narrow pass of Thermopylae; their sacrifice bought the Athenians time. The Persians advanced from Thermopylae, burning towns in their path, including Athens. Sparta argued for sealing off the Peloponnese (the southernmost tip of mainland Greece, where Sparta was located) with a defensive wall across the narrow Isthmus of Corinth. Themistocles argued, correctly, that the Persian fleet could still land armies behind the wall at will. He lured the Persians to attack the Athenian fleet in the narrow straits at Salamis. The onshore morning breeze hemmed the Persian ships into the narrow straits, leaving little room for maneuver.

Ships rammed each other and locked together; what was essentially a land battle on board a mass of ships ensued. The Greeks triumphed: some 200 Persian ships were sunk; many Persians (who could not swim) were drowned; those who reached the shore were slaughtered.

Without a navy, the Persians were unable to supply their army. They retreated over the bridge of ships that they had built across the Hellespont—the narrow strait separating Europe from Asia Minor, where the city of Constantinople would later be founded. Xerxes left a large army behind to defend captured Greek territories, but this was defeated by combined Greek armies.

At this time, Pericles was a teenager. His family was rich and aristocratic, and the young Pericles was given the best education that money could buy. Since Athens in the fifth century BCE was the birthplace of one of the most significant intellectual revolutions in the history of mankind, that education was very good indeed. Pericles mixed with the great philosophers of the day: he heard Zeno lecture; Protogoras and Anaxagoras were his friends. Anaxagoras had a particular influence on Pericles, instilling in his student something of his own spirit of rational, scientific inquiry into the natural world.

Pericles took himself and high office very seriously indeed. In the vibrant atmosphere of Athens, this of course led to a degree of criticism, and even abuse. The poet Ion accused Pericles of being "over-assuming and pompous." He felt that beneath Pericles' aristocratic poise was an element of superiority and scorn for lesser mortals. Pericles also suffered some less high-minded criticism. He seems to have been born with an odd-shaped, elongated skull. His contemporaries called him "squill head" (*Schinocephalos*), after the bulbous sea onion plant, or squill. There was no place to hide in democratic Athens, even for the aloof young Pericles. Plutarch records an anecdote about Pericles being "reviled [...] all day long" in the market place by somebody who was obviously not a fan. Pericles maintained a dignified silence and went about his business. The man then followed him home, still shouting abuse. Pericles—ever the aristocrat—sent a servant out with a torch to light the man's way home.

Pericles was famosly calm and measured. Nothing, it seems, could disturb his composure. He was also famously incorruptible—his family wealth being a guarantee that Pericles had no reason to be so tempted. He kept himself aloof, avoiding dinner parties, putting in an appearance at family weddings but quickly excusing himself.

Perhaps the most distinctive characteristic of Pericles was his skill as an orator. The closest that we have to a record of Pericles' real speeches are those written down by his contemporary, the historian Thucydides. We cannot be certain whether it is the voice of Pericles or that of Thucydides that we read today; what is certain is that Thucydides felt that these speeches were impressive enough to be recorded—presumably as accurately as possible—while the effect of Periclean oratory on the Athenian Assembly is a matter of record. Like any great speaker, Pericles used his powers to inspire and to persuade, but contemporaries agree that he never took a populist approach; he never tried to sway people's emotions. His great strength seems to have been in conveying something of his own lofty concerns: he set out a vision of the greatness of Athens, and the Athenians rose to the challenge. They knew that they were different: unlike that of other Greek city-states, the future of Athens lay in its own hands. Pericles was elected as a general (the only official post that he ever held) every year from 443 to 429 BCE, but the Athenian people could choose not to elect him; even the great Pericles could be removed from office.

The goals that Pericles put in place for this new democracy were unashamedly imperialistic. Athens was the leader of the Delian League, a league of Greek states allied against Persian attacks. Tributes were collected from the Allies to fund the League's defence. Athens removed the treasury of the League from the island of Delos, with the excuse—perhaps genuine—that it was exposed to being raided by the Persians. Athens did indeed provide the necessary weapons, ships, and armor for the League's defence but soon found, in peaceful times, that the fund was in surplus. The excess was used to fund a lavish building program in Athens, the most notable aspect of which was the Parthenon, temple of Athene—protector of the Athenians—which also became the new treasury. Pericles and Athens were unashamed. The glory of Athens reflected the glory of all Greece. Their protecting goddess Athene was, appropriately, the goddess of war. She was also the patroness of craftsmen—the perfect symbol for the industrious and ingenious Athenians. The Athenians saw something god-like in their striving for glory as they rose above the envy and resentment of the allies.

Periclean Athens attracted the great poets and playwrights of the day: Aeschylus was an established tragedian; Euripides and Sophocles were contemporaries. The comic playwright Aristophanes was a relative youngster (born around 456 BCE). The great philosophers Socrates, Anaxagoras, Parmenides, and Protagoras, and the historian Herodotus, were all Periclean Athenians.

Athens had always been ruthless in her control of the empire: rebellions by disaffected oligarchies within the league were vigorously put down. Some smaller rebel states became colonies of Athens, populated by Athenians. Colonials retained their citizenship of Athens and were given land from which to earn their livelihood. They were also obliged to maintain arms in order to defend the colony.

Athens faced other, more serious revolts, and was not always successful in containing them. Sparta, Athens' old rival for pre-eminence in Greece, formed its own league of states from the Peloponnese archipelago. Around 432, Pericles imposed a trade embargo on Megara, one of Sparta's allied states, on the grounds that they had trespassed on sacred grounds. Sparta threatened war and demanded the expulsion of the Alcmaeonid family, including Pericles, from Athens, in a clear attempt to create a rift between Pericles and the Athenians. Pericles persuaded the Assembly to make no concessions to the Spartans on the grounds that if they made concessions now, the Spartans would be sure to return with further demands later. Sparta invaded Attica. Pericles persuaded the rural population of

Attica to retreat to within the walls of Athens. With access to the sea, Athens was able to raid allied Spartan territories—though not Sparta itself, safe in the interior of the Peloponnese.

After a raid on Megara, Pericles made a funeral oration for the fallen, part of which has become famous for its description and praise of Athenian democracy:

> "Our constitution does not copy the laws of neighbouring states; we are rather a pattern to others than imitators ourselves. Its administration favours the many instead of the few; this is why it is called a democracy. If we look to the laws, they afford equal justice to all in their private differences; if to social standing, advancement in public life falls to reputation for capacity, class considerations not being allowed to interfere with merit; nor again does poverty bar the way, if a man is able to serve the state, he is not hindered by the obscurity of his condition. The freedom which we enjoy in our government extends also to our ordinary life. There, far from exercising a jealous surveillance over each other, we do not feel called upon to be angry with our neighbour for doing what he likes [...] But all this ease in our private relations does not make us lawless as citizens. Against this fear is our chief safeguard, teaching us to obey the magistrates and the laws, particularly such as regard the protection of the injured, whether they are actually on the statute book, or belong to that code which, although unwritten, yet cannot be broken without acknowledged disgrace."[15]

The Spartans looted the Athenian countryside. Plague broke out in overcrowded Athens. Pericles was finally brought to trial for his policies, stripped of his title as *strategos*, and fined. Pericles lost many friends, his sister, and his two legitimate sons to the plague. At the death of his last legitimate son, Pericles' famous reserve and self-control collapsed. This was the end of his dynasty; he broke down in tears. Later, Pericles pleaded with the Athenians to change his own law demanding that citizens have Athenian parents on both sides. In tribute to Pericles they did so, legitimizing his 'half-Athenian' son by his long-standing mistress, Aspasia.

Pericles himself died of the plague in 429 BCE but not before he had been reinstated as *strategos*. On his deathbed, he said that his proudest boast was that, "No Athenian ever put on mourning because of me"—a reference to the fact that Pericles was unable to command, only to persuade, so that any Athenians who had died in battle had not died because of him; what the Athenians did, they did not because Pericles imposed it on them, but as a result of their own decisions.

After Pericles, the power of Athens declined. The damage done by the war with Sparta was perhaps irreparable, and subsequent statesmen failed to inspire and lead as Pericles had done.

Pericles' greatest error was his failure of diplomacy in allowing the Thirty Year Peace with Sparta to come to an end. The ultimate failure of Athenian democracy was caused, sadly, by what critics had always foretold: total democracy is easily subverted and led astray by leaders who seek merely popular approval. Relying on chance to produce a constant supply of statesmen like Pericles is not a good plan.

Perhaps the last word should go to Pericles, as quoted by Thucydides:

> "All who have taken it upon themselves to rule over others have incurred hatred and unpopularity for a time: but if one has a great aim to pursue, this burden of envy must be accepted, and it is wise to accept it. Hatred does not last for long; but the brilliance of the present is the glory of the future stored up forever in the memory of man."

WINSTON CHURCHILL
(1874–1965)

Winston Leonard Spencer-Churchill was born into the English aristocracy in the family's ancestral home of Blenheim Palace, built for John Churchill, Duke of Marlborough, on behalf of a grateful nation, after his victories in the wars of the early eighteenth century. As a young man, Winston was brave and audacious, fighting in the many little wars of a British Empire on which the sun had not yet begun to set. He entered Parliament and rose to the rank of minister—not before, however, he had 'crossed the floor' of the House of Parliament, moving from the Conservative party to the Liberal party and making long-standing political enemies in the process. As President of the Board of Trade for the Liberal government Churchill became the perhaps unlikely proponent of a number of social measures, revolutionary for their time. Later, as First Lord of the Admiralty, Churchill built up the navy in response to Germany's dramatic program of naval expansion: a dangerous challenge to Britain's naval supremacy. At the outbreak of the World War I, Churchill had done more than most to put his country onto a war footing. He entered the war with resolution and determination, using the navy to land brigades in Northern Europe in an attempt to slow down the advancing German army. And then Churchill made a very big mistake: far from the last mistake of his long career.

At the outbreak of World War I, the Ottoman Empire had sided with Germany. The Ottoman Empire, with its capital at Constantinople, controlled the Dardanelles, the narrow straits (less than one mile wide at the narrowest point) leading from the Mediterranean to the Black Sea via the inland sea of Marmara. At their northern limit lies the Bosporus, the entrance to the Black Sea. Straddled across the Bosporus lies the great city of Constantinople. The Dardanelles are the ancient Hellespont—the divide between Europe and Asia.

Churchill wanted control of the Dardenelles, allowing the Allies to support Russia via the Mediterranean and the Black Sea. Russian success on the Eastern Front would take pressure off the Western Front, in France. Churchill, as First Lord of the Admiralty, seemed to believe that this was a job that the Navy could handle by itself. A fleet of obsolete battleships—obsolete in the sense that they could not be put up against the newly-built German battleships in the North Sea, unlike Churchill's recently commissioned fleet of new dreadnoughts—could be put to good use in the Mediterranean theatre. There was to be no troop support on the ground: the flotilla carried enough troops to control an area that was confidently expected to be subdued by British sea power.

Churchill had underestimated the number of Turkish troops in the area, partly as the result of a faulty report by T.E. Lawrence—an intelligence officer who was to become famous as Lawrence of Arabia. Nevertheless, the Dardanelles forts shelling the attacking fleet soon began to run out of ammunition. Their communications were cut; guns were being knocked out by the naval bombardment; an easy passage into the Sea of Marmara and on to Istanbul was forecast by the Allies. Then Allied ships began to blow up.

A French battleship exploded and sank. The minesweepers—manned by civilian crews and under fire from the forts on shore—retreated, leaving the straits largely un-cleared of the charted minefields. What was worse was that an entirely new line of mines had been laid, in secret, ten days before the attack. It should have been expected and planned for. Three British battleships were hit by mines; two sank. Two further French battleships were badly damaged. The naval commander called for a retreat. Churchill maintained that had they persisted, the attack would have been successful—but a more likely scenario is that the ships would have been stranded in the Sea of Marmara with a minefield between them and the Mediterranean and insufficient troops to force an attack on Constantinople. The naval failure was bad; worse was to follow.

Australian and New Zealand troops stationed in Egypt were sent to the Dardanelles, along with British and French contingents. It took them six weeks to assemble the invasion force; the Turks (amply forewarned by the failed naval attack) prepared their defences. Mustafa Kemal, a 34-year-old lieutenant colonel in the Turkish army (and the future President of the Independent Republic of Turkey) played a key role in the defence. The Allied troops disembarked on defended beachheads as if nothing had been learned from the Western Front about the devastating effect of modern weapons in defensive positions: several landing forces lost between 60 and 90 percent of their force in casualties.

A beachhead was achieved, but the battle continued for nearly nine months, through the fierce heat of summer, with its plagues of flies and epidemics of disease, and into the freezing, wet winter. At one point storms flooded the battlefield, washing unburied bodies into the trenches. At other times troops died of exposure in fierce blizzards. Allied troops were evacuated in January 1916; the political fall-out in London had already begun. The Liberal Prime Minister, Henry Asquith, was forced to form a coalition government with the Conservatives; a condition of this coalition was the dismissal of Churchill from his post as First Lord of the Admiralty. Churchill retained a post in cabinet in the meaningless role of Chancellor of the Duchy of Lancaster.

In a typically Churchillian move, Winston resigned from the cabinet to fight on the Western Front in command of an infantry battalion. He is reputed to have asked to be posted to the front line, possibly because front line troops were allowed alcohol, whereas his battalion headquarters were teetotal. He endured real hardship alongside his troops, but after six months on the frontline, Churchill asked to be allowed to return to his pressing Parliamentary duties. His timing was fortunate though his bravery, as ever, is unquestioned; had he delayed by six weeks his battalion would have been caught up in the Somme offensive, with its appalling casualty rates. Churchill was back in Parliament, but his career seemed to be over.

As a young man, Churchill had scraped into the Royal Military Academy at Sandhurst, thanks to the private tuition that his father had paid for in order to coach Winston through the examinations at which he had never excelled. Military life suited Churchill; he set off on his chosen career, aided at every step by his family connections. His mother's influence secured a place in the glamorous 4th Hussars, who were posted to India for routine service. His mother was also to prove extremely useful in helping Winston to fulfil his ambitions as a writer: she persuaded the *Daily Telegraph* to accept his despatches, for the handy sum of five pounds per column. Churchill also managed to get himself commissioned by the Allahabad *Pioneer*, which could count Rudyard Kipling amongst its previous correspondents.

Churchill saw action in northwest India (modern-day Pakistan). His account of the siege of Malakand, in *The Story of the Malakand Field Force*, sold very well. He later fought in the Sudan under Lord Kitchener with the 21st Lancers and took part in one of the last cavalry charges made by the British army. Churchill wrote of his experiences in *The River War*. By the time Churchill sailed to South Africa to take part in the war between Britain and the Boers, as a correspondent for the *Morning Post*, he was on his way to becoming famous and commanded high fees for his lectures. When his troop train was ambushed by the Boers, Churchill was captured along with the rest of the British. He escaped and was smuggled, on a rail truck, helped by sympathetic strangers, to British South Africa. His exploits made him a household name throughout the British Empire. His book, *London to Ladysmith via Pretoria*, sold well enough to make him financially independent. Churchill returned home in 1900 to become a Member of Parliament.

Elected as a member of the Conservative party, Churchill crossed the floor of the British Parliament in 1904 to join the Liberals, largely over the issue of his support for free international trade and against the tariffs that the Conservatives sought to impose in order to protect Britain's economic pre-eminence.

Under Liberal Prime Minister Herbert Asquith, Churchill joined the cabinet as President of the Board of Trade. There, this son of the aristocracy helped to introduce Britain's first minimum wage, set up the first Labor Exchange to help the unemployed find work, and helped to introduce a National Insurance Act to provide a limited form of unemployment, health, and pension insurance for working families. Later he supported the People's Budget—a reforming budget aiming to increase tax on the rich in order to support welfare reforms. Subsequent governments and other ministers (especially the Liberal firebrand Lloyd George) were to receive more credit than Churchill himself for the revolutionary social policies that he helped to set in motion.

In 1910 Churchill became Home Secretary, and later First Lord of the Admiralty. Germany was expanding its navy in an attempt to challenge Britain's command of the oceans, a supremacy unchallenged since the battle of Trafalgar. Britain's merchant navy, which carried over 50 percent of the world's goods, would have to be protected. Churchill fought in cabinet to match the German Navy's force. He even attempted to negotiate with the German Kaiser to stop this particular arms race. By the time of the outbreak of World War I in 1914, Britain had a fleet of modern oil-powered dreadnoughts and a fledgling naval air arm. Churchill had also been instrumental in the development of the tank: naval research funding was used to develop "Landships." The first tanks used naval guns, as the army had no canon designed to be fired in a confined space. The tank program was seen by most people at the time as a waste of money.

Churchill started the war well but came to grief after the Dardanelles disaster. He was brought back as Minister of Munitions by his old ally in the earlier Liberal Reforms, David Lloyd George, now Prime Minister. After the end of the war, Churchill became Secretary of State for War and for Air, where he became determined to stop the growth of Bolshevism in Russia and supported Allied intervention in the Russian Civil War. In 1922, Churchill lost his seat in the general election. He failed to be re-elected in another general election the following year, standing again for the Liberal Party. In 1923 he fought a by-election as an Independent and lost again. Surely, this time, Churchill was down for the count.

In 1924, Churchill stood again as an Independent in yet another general election—and won his seat. A year later, he rejoined the Conservative Party, saying that, "Anyone can rat, but it takes a certain amount of ingenuity to re-rat." He was made Chancellor of the Exchequer by Stanley Baldwin and presided over the disastrous reintroduction of the Gold Standard and the return to the pre-war dollar exchange rate. This led—as predicted by many—to a full-blown depression and, ultimately, to the General Strike. Churchill is said to have favoured using machine guns on striking miners ("Either the country will break the General Strike, or the General Strike will break the country"[16]) and looked with some fondness on the activities of Benito Mussolini's fascists in Italy as being the best antidote to the dangers of creeping Bolshevism. He even had hopes that the emerging German fascist, Adolf Hitler, might "go down in History as the man who restored honour and peace of mind to the great Germanic nation and brought it back [...] to the forefront of the European family circle."

The Conservatives lost the general election in 1929. In the course of the 1900s, Churchill managed to antagonize most of the Conservative Party leadership over his vehement opposition to Home Rule for India and his support of King Edward VIII in the Abdication Crisis.[17]

In these 'wilderness years' Churchill nevertheless, and despite his self-confessed preference for fascism as the lesser of two evils as opposed to communism, saw more clearly than most the growing likelihood of a major conflict with Germany. He spoke consistently in the House of Commons for the development of the Royal Air Force and the need to create a Ministry of Defence. He fiercely criticized Prime Minister Neville Chamberlain for signing the Munich

Agreement, which granted Czechoslovakia's Sudetenland to Hitler's Germany (Germany had already annexed Austria) on the agreement that this would mark the end of Hitler's territorial ambitions. It gave Chamberlain the opportunity to declare, "Peace in our time:" Churchill's analysis was more accurate: "You were given the choice between war and dishonour. You chose dishonour and you will have war."

At the outbreak of World War II, Churchill was brought back to the cabinet as First Lord of the Admiralty. After Germany's lightning invasion of France in 1940, Chamberlain resigned and Churchill became Prime Minister and was asked to form an all-party government.

Churchill's success as a war leader was very mixed. His military chief of staff for most of the war, General Sir Alan Brooke, wrote that, "Winston had ten ideas every day, only one of which was good, and he did not know which it was." Several of them were really quite bad. He was obsessed with attacking Germany through Norway, which is probably a military impossibility. Despite his experience with Gallipoli, he continued to look for 'imaginative' ways of attacking the enemy's flanks: an attack on the Greek Dodecanese Islands ended in disaster. Churchill's experience of fighting the Boers, who waged such a successful 'hit and run' war against regular British troops, gave him a lasting belief in the effectiveness of behind-the-lines operations by groups of partisans. Churchill encouraged resistance in countries such as Greece and the former Yugoslavia; the Nazis crushed this resistance with appalling ferocity at little or no cost to their military machine. Churchill's fond memories of the relatively good behavior of British troops to their plucky Boer foes belonged to a different era.

But Churchill's constant search for a chance—almost any chance—to hit back at the enemy occasionally paid dividends: on the eve of the Battle of Britain—the battle for air supremacy prior to the planned German invasion of Britain—Churchill, remarkably, sent Britain's last significant tank force to Egypt to prevent Mussolini from seizing Egypt and the Suez canal; the vital link between the

Mediterranean and Britain's empire in the East. In December 1940, the British Western Desert Force drove Mussolini out of Egypt and captured 113,000 Italians. In a parody of Churchill's great speech about the Battle of Britain ("Never [...] has so much been owed, by so many, to so few"), relieved Britons joked that, "Never has so much been surrendered by so many, to so few." The Italian defeat prompted Hitler to despatch Erwin Rommel to North Africa with his *Afrikakorps*. Britain, having won the Battle of Britain by the skin of its teeth, and having prevented the loss of the Suez Canal and the oilfields of the Middle East, was still in the war.

The nation could not have come to this point without the inspiration offered by Churchill. After the fall of France, the defeat of the British Expeditionary Force and the humiliating evacuation from Dunkirk, a sensible nation might have sought terms with Germany. The Britain of Churchill's imagination was greater than its reality, but by his dogged insistence on resistance at all costs, Churchill brought the government, and then the nation—through the eagerly-awaited broadcast of his speeches via BBC Radio—to believe in Churchill's inspiring vision of their better selves.

> "I would say to the House, as I said to those who have joined the Government, 'I have nothing to offer but blood, toil, tears, and sweat'. We have before us an ordeal of the most grievous kind. We have before us many, many long months of struggle and of suffering. You ask, what is our policy? I will say: It is to wage war, by sea, land, and air, with all our might and with all the strength that God can give us: to wage war against a monstrous tyranny, never surpassed in the dark, lamentable catalogue of human crime. That is our policy. You ask, what is our aim? I can answer in one word: Victory—victory—at all costs, victory, in spite of all terror, victory, however long and hard the road may be; for without victory, there is no survival. Let that be realized; no survival for the British Empire; no survival for all that the British Empire has stood for, no survival for the urge and impulse of the ages, that mankind will move

forward towards its goal. But I take up my task with buoyancy and hope. I feel sure that our cause will not be suffered to fail among men. At this time I feel entitled to claim the aid of all, and I say, come, then, let us go forward together with our united strength."[18]

"Upon this battle depends the survival of Christian civilization. Upon it depends our own British life and the long continuity of our institutions and our Empire. The whole fury and might of the enemy must very soon be turned on us now. Hitler knows that he will have to break us in this island or lose the war. If we can stand up to him, all Europe may be free and the life of the world may move forward into broad, sunlit uplands. But if we fail, then the whole world, including the United States, including all that we have known and cared for, will sink into the abyss of a new Dark Age, made more sinister, and perhaps more protracted, by the lights of perverted science. Let us therefore brace ourselves to our duties, and so bear ourselves that, if the British Empire and its Commonwealth last for a thousand years, men will still say, 'This was their finest hour.'"[19]

3
DOING THE
PLANNING

One of the most underrated accomplishments of any manager is planning. Not in the obvious sense in which planning is one of the key functions of every managerial job specification (many managers' jobs consist of very little else than planning, that is ensuring that a certain result has been delivered by a particular deadline) but rather in planning the broad outline of what it is that you intend to achieve in your current role.

It is dauntingly easy to get bogged down in the details of any job. Sometimes simply keeping things running on a day-to-day basis seems like a pretty big achievement. In fact, that always feels like a pretty big achievement, because it is. But every manager needs also to find the time to plan exactly how they intend to achieve their broader objectives on the timescale that they have allowed themselves. The really great planners are the ones who seem able to hold huge amounts of information in their heads, who never for one moment lose sight of the objectives, or of the precise order in which they should be achieved. As a result, such managers seem to pull off a succession of miraculous successes. They are not, of course, miraculous; they are the product of meticulous planning.

The first two leaders from history in this chapter are brilliant examples of this technique: Napoleon's greatness as a military strategist was founded largely on the painstaking and detailed planning that he undertook for all of his projects. Napoleon had a mind like a filing cabinet—capable of storing and retrieving huge amounts of information, seemingly without effort—and this formidable machine ticked away at all times, tuning ideas over, seeing how they might work, thinking through the logistical implications of every possible course of action. When Napoleon set anything in motion, he had thought through how it would be accomplished, often in astonishing detail.

Lee Kuan Yew created the economic miracle of Singapore, the newly-independent and relatively insignificant island that had become the smallest nation in Southeast Asia and of which he had become Prime Minister. This miracle was the result of single-minded application and an extremely thorough planning process. Lee created an Economic Development Board to attract outside finance and to pull in any outside talent that was needed. He employed a Dutch economist, Dr Albert Winsemius, to advise him and the Board. Singapore developed a major oil-refining capacity and turned the old British dockyards into the most modern ship-building and repair facility between Europe and Japan. With no oil of its own, Singapore became a major refinery, shipping oil via the Persian Gulf and distributing refined products on to Indonesia, Australia, and other countries. Southeast Asia's first container-ship terminal was built, with 24-hour berthing. Lee passed new legislation allowing a crackdown on corruption: Singapore began to offer a low-wage, stable, and corruption-free manufacturing base for foreign investment. Housing developments sprang up alongside the factories and the office complexes. Singapore was transformed from a collection of swamp villages to a high-rise, modern city; its manufacturing services diversified into higher technologies. A program of education was started to supply the knowledge workers that Singapore needed for the future. Lee's one-party state ran Singapore like a corporation; Singapore at the time was not a model liberal democracy. But as an example of the way in which a substantial modern economy can be built virtually from scratch, Singapore is a stunning example of the power of planning.

Martin Luther King makes an unlikely bedfellow for Napoleon and Lee Kuan Yew. One thinks of King for his astonishing powers as an orator; for world-changing speeches such as his "I Have a Dream" speech, delivered on the steps of the Lincoln Memorial in Washington D.C. in August 1963. But it is useful to remind ourselves that figures like King do not emerge suddenly onto the world stage, make brilliant speeches, and change opinions overnight. They spend most of their lives doing far more mundane things—like planning. King's strategy to end racial discrimination in America was based on a carefully planned series of actions and events, all of which required great organizational skills and much tedious legwork—fund-raising, sitting on committees, writing letters, organizing demonstrations, registering black voters, spending time in jail. Whereas Napoleon's astonishing military victories changed the political face of Europe overnight, Martin Luther King's minor victories, his small steps forward, his little breakthroughs, the media coverage of unacceptable acts of violence against peaceful black demonstrators, all reached a tipping point in the major cultural shift marked by the passing of the Civil Rights Act of 1964—helped on its way by King's "I Have a Dream" speech after the March on Washington in 1963; all made possible by years of hard work and planning.

NAPOLEON BONAPARTE
(1769–1821)

Napoleon is known as one of the great military commanders of all time—possibly the greatest. He was also a remarkable leader in the most general sense. His leadership skills were based on a wide range of personal characteristics and strengths. He had a remarkable memory, able to store and recall huge amounts of information in great detail. He could focus on any issue for very long periods of time without losing concentration; his keen intelligence and his shrewd grasp of the key issues of the day gave him a commanding air of authority. He was personally brave, to the point of a kind of fatalism ("the bullet has not yet been made that has my name on it"); he had the ability to inspire others, and to drive them very hard. He had great breadth of vision; huge self-belief; and considerable personal charm when necessary.

Napoleon was a great showman. In both military and civic matters he liked to astonish, to dazzle. He was able to do this because he had always done the planning. Napoleon's agile mind was always turning things over, investigating the options, thinking of alternatives. He had a mind like a filing cabinet, but he also used some important tools to help his memory. He used a system of record books of key governmental and military information, constantly updated by clerks and all presented in precisely the same format. The internal organization of these books could not be changed without Napoleon's agreement; he knew exactly where he could find the information that he wanted.[20] He described his own mind as being like a cabinet, with information stored behind certain doors. If he wanted to think about a certain topic, he opened the relevant drawer in his mind—and there it was. When he wanted to sleep, he closed all of the doors and he slept.[21] One senses that the record books, laid out in their precise way, were uploaded into the compartments of his mind.

This astonishing mental resource meant that Napoleon was able to plan, not only in broad brush strokes, but in detail. When he conceived of a grand plan, he also supplied the logistics to deliver that plan, down to the last detail. Napoleons astonishing victories owed little to luck (though there is always fortune in battle, both good and bad). His victories—his success in many fields—owed almost everything to his meticulous planning.

𝒟

Napoleon Bonaparte rose from relative obscurity—the second son of minor Corsican nobility—to become Emperor of France. The scale of his achievements changed the face not only of France, but of Europe. Napoleon's first and greatest success, the one from which all others flowed, was as a military commander. He transformed the battlefield tactics of the late eighteenth century, using only the raw materials that had been available to any commander for most of the past 100 years. Napoleon's genius was to realize that the same military components—lines, columns, and squares of men, artillery, cavalry— could be used in a much more fluid way, rapidly changing tactics throughout a battle and looking always for the opportunity suddenly to concentrate forces at the opponent's weakest point.

Napoleon lent his military might to assist a coup d'état against the ineffectual government of the *Directoire* that had emerged after the overthrow of the extremists who had plunged the Revolution into the nightmarish Jacobin Terror. Napoleon then unexpectedly seized control of the coup itself and emerged as First Consul of the three new Consuls appointed to head up the new government. Napoleon began steadily to consolidate his powers: for the French he represented the strong hand that would safeguard the hard-won benefits of the revolution. In 1802, a plebiscite confirmed Napoleon as Consul for Life.

In the early days of his civic administration, in the short period of peace that France enjoyed after Napoleon had for the second time defeated the Austrian Empire and their allies in their attempts to undo the Revolution and restore the French monarchy, Napoleon demonstrated that his brilliance was not confined to military matters.

He set about rationalizing and modernizing France's archaic civil administration, started ambitious building programs, created the Bank of France to stabilize the currency and the economy, established an enduring system of secondary education, and reached a pragmatic entente with the Catholic Church. At this stage of his career, he was also able to delegate effectively, appointing the Second Consul, Cambacérès—a great legal brain and a brilliant administrator—to lead the team of lawyers that would create the *Code Civil des Français*; the so-called Napoleonic Code, which codified many of the civil rights for which the Revolution had been fought. The existence of the Code, now enshrined in law, gave the citizens of France a reason to believe that their hard-won rights and freedoms would not be snatched away from them. For many there were also concrete gains arising from the purchase of property belonging to the previous aristocracy, the crown, or the church. All of this gave France a good reason to support the man who seemed able to defend the new Republic from the monarchies of Europe, who regarded the very existence of republican France as a threat to their existence.

The peace between Britain and France foundered and Britain declared war, blockading French ports. A plot to assassinate Napoleon was uncovered and Napoleon seized the opportunity to have himself crowned as Emperor. With the risk that all of the revolutionary gains could be lost at a stroke if Napoleon were killed, the creation of a hereditary emperor of France was seen, perversely at first glance, as the best way of preserving the revolution.

Napoleon turned his attention on Britain, whose growing industrial wealth enabled her to become the paymaster of the allies ranged against France, stiffening their resolve with "British Gold." He built up a huge army and a fleet of barges at Boulogne. He devised an over-elaborate plot for the French navy to break out of British blockades, join up with the Spanish fleet in the West Indies and lure the British fleet to attack them there. The combined French and Spanish Fleet would then give the British the slip and return to control the English Channel. It was a strategy that Napoleon might just have been able to pull off on land, but he never did quite grasp that things are different at sea, that inconveniences such as winds and tides could interfere with the best-laid plans. The French and Spanish fleet finally ended up back in Cadiz, blockaded by the Royal Navy. Napoleon's plans to invade Britain were now unrealizable and were abandoned finally when Britain convinced Russia and Austria to join a new coalition against France. The combined armies of Austria and Russia began to mobilize against France.

Napoleon had already considered this eventuality and held an entire plan of campaign in his head. In an unbroken six-hour stint he dictated to his secretary a meticulous plan for the deployment of his *Grande Armée* (of nearly a quarter of a million men) in an unbroken six-hour stint. He was about to dispatch 210,000 troops from northern France to the Danube, collecting 25,000 Bavarian allies along the way: an unprecedented number of men traveling more than 200 miles in the remarkably short time of 13 days.[22] It was considered to be an impossible feat of logistics, and all of the plans for this deployment—down to the most remarkable detail of marches, supplies, river-crossings, timings, overnight stops—were held in Napoleon's head.

Napoleon now carried out one of his classic army maneuvers on a grand scale, surprising the Austrians with both the speed and direction of his attack, cutting them off in the fortress city of Ulm on the upper reaches of the Danube. The Austrian General Mack was forced to surrender his 30,000 men without any significant battle having been fought. At the same time, Napoleon, furious at the French navy's failure to implement his over-elaborate strategies for the invasion of Britain, had unwisely ordered the allied French and Spanish fleet to sail to the Mediterranean to support his land attack; an unnecessary risk. Villeneuve sailed out of Cadiz and was destroyed by Admiral Nelson in the battle of Trafalgar, two days after the surrender of Ulm. The French navy never recovered in Napoleon's lifetime; Britain had control of the oceans.

Napoleon turned his attention to the Russians; his plan to encircle them in turn was spoiled when the brilliant but impetuous commander of cavalry, Murat, was deflected from his goal by the understandable lure of seizing Vienna, the ancient capital of the Habsburg Holy Roman Empire. The wily Russian General Kutuzov withdrew his forces across the Danube while his rearguard created the impression that the Russians would, indeed, stay to defend Vienna. Murat was completely hoodwinked; he rode towards Vienna while Kutuzov escaped to the north. Napoleon was furious. He was now in a very exposed position; his troops were exhausted after eight weeks of campaigning. His lines of communication were very stretched. The Austrian armies in the Alps were marching towards the Danube; the Russians had met with the remnants of the Austrian Army in the interior and now numbered some 90,000 men. Napoleon was exposed between a rock and a hard place. He decided to attack.

Napoleon's overarching battle strategy was simple: he wanted to engage the enemy and to destroy their army, so that they no longer represented a meaningful threat. Now, from a position of apparent weakness, he lured his enemy toward the battle that was his best hope of success. It was a gamble, but not a desperate one: lines of retreat were still open to him.

Napoleon marched north from Vienna, deep into Moravia (Czech Republic). He left two army corps behind to defend against attacks from the south, making his apparent forces some 53,000 strong: the Russian and Austrian allies were nearly twice as strong, with 89,000 men. Napoleon was sure that they would not be able to resist the temptation to attack the outnumbered French army; once they had taken the bait he would call up the reserves from Vienna to bring his strength up to 75,000: a more reasonable match.[23]

The Allies watched as the French army seemed to walk into a trap. They proposed an armistice (to give the Austrian army in the Alps sufficient time to advance from the south). Napoleon seemed eager to agree.

Napoleon had chosen the ground for his battle very carefully: the apparently innocuous territory near Austerlitz, with various minor streams flowing north to south beneath a low plateau—the Pratzen

Heights. Every element of the terrain was to play its part; the battle was already being fought (and won) in Napoleon's head. "Gentlemen," he said to his officers, "examine this ground carefully. It is going to be a battlefield; you will have a part to play upon it."[24] Napoleon continued his grand deception: French troops had occupied the strategically valuable high ground of the Pratzen Heights; as the Allied forces approached, they were ordered to withdraw in apparent confusion. Napoleon requested a meeting with Tsar Alexander, but was fobbed off with a member of the Tsar's military staff. Napoleon allowed himself to be harangued by the young firebrand (probably one of the hardest things that Napoleon ever forced himself to do). The young Russian Count, bursting with pride at having browbeaten the mighty Napoleon, returned to the Allied headquarters convinced that he and his colleagues were on the brink of a great victory.

Napoleon now planned the destruction of the armies set against him. The French army corps left behind at Vienna were summoned to Austerlitz by forced marches. They covered 80 miles in 50 hours, snatching a few hours sleep and being fortified by huge allowances of wine. Napoleon deliberately extended the right wing of the French army, while his left wing was held securely by troops and cavalry. The Allies had seized the obvious strategic position of the Pratzen Heights after they had been abandoned, dramatically, by the French: as they looked down on Napoleon's dispositions it was obvious to the Austrian and Russian Allies that they should launch their main attack against the French right wing. Smashing through, they would both outflank the French line and cut them off from their line of retreat to Vienna.

The night before the battle happened to be the anniversary of Napoleon's coronation as Emperor of France. Napoleon issued an Order of the Day, encouraging the troops with a kind of reversal of the usual leading from the front: so secure was Napoleon in the loyalty of his troops that he promised to stay out of danger unless they faltered—at which moment Napoleon would join the battle and expose himself to danger.

"Soldiers, I shall in person direct all your battalions; I shall keep out of range if, with your accustomed bravery, you carry disorder and confusion into the ranks of the enemy; but if the victory is for a moment uncertain, you shall see your emperor expose himself in the front rank."[25]

Was any other commander so certain of the devotion of his troops that he could inspire them by threatening to appear in their front ranks if they should falter?

Napoleon was led through the camp by a torchlight procession of his troops, celebrating the anniversary of the Emperors' coronation. The army went into a kind of frenzied adoration of their great commander; this was their own celebration of his official coronation, so stiffly conducted one year earlier in Notre Dame Cathedral, with Napoleon overdressed in ermine. "This is the finest evening of my life," Napoleon said to his aides. It may well have been: never happier than when he was basking in the uncritical adulation of his army, Napoleon was on the eve of his greatest triumph. After Austerlitz, though there were many more victories to come, Napoleon began to limit access to his Imperial person, to ignore well-meaning (and well-founded) advice, and to start on the slippery slope toward full-blown megalomania, toward wars that were driven not by the need to defend France but by the desire to expand the empire. He was perhaps never again so much at one with his nation and with his beloved army.

The French troops from Vienna began to arrive at the French camp on the very eve of the battle after their astonishing march. The Allies attacked the apparently weak French right flank before dawn; the French were involved in a desperate and bloody struggle and fell back—this was no elegant feint; the troops on that wing took heavy casualties. So certain were the Allies that the route to victory lay through the French right flank that they poured troops from the center of their position—the Pratzen Heights—to attack the French right wing.

A heavy fog filled the valley beneath the Heights; it served to conceal the troops that Napoleon was gathering at his center. As the sun broke through the mist at nine o'clock—"the glorious sun of Austerlitz"—the French stormed the Pratzen Heights.

The Allies desperately tried to reverse the flow of troops from the wing back to the center; there was a fierce battle for control of the Heights, but the French eventually prevailed, moving artillery and troops and finally the Imperial Headquarters up onto the heights where they could command the entire battlefield. By the early afternoon, the whole Allied center had been pushed off the Pratzen Heights, and the Allied troops who had so recently been driving back the French right wing were now surrounded as new French troops poured off the Pratzen Heights to their rear. The Russians and Austrians lost 15,000 killed with 12,000 taken prisoner: nearly one third of their force. The remainder of the army was scattered: the Russians retreated through Hungary and Poland. The day after the battle, the Austrian Emperor asked for an armistice.

The Austrian and Russian armies had been destroyed at Austerlitz, which was always Napoleon's overriding goal: not simply to win a battle but to destroy the enemies' armies as a fighting force. Napoleon imposed punitive and humiliating terms on Austria, dismantling the Holy Roman Empire, a confederation of European states that had been ruled from Vienna for 500 years. This became increasingly the pattern for future Napoleonic victories: ignoring the advice of his Foreign Minister, the brilliant diplomat Charles Maurice de Talleyrand, Napoleon tended increasingly to impose peace settlements that left the enemy humiliated and resentful, but in a position to rebuild their forces and seek revenge.

In 1812 Napoleon invaded Russia, seeking his trademark rapid victory. After an unsuccessful attempt to destroy the Russian army in a maneuver near Smolensk, the two armies finally met in a bloody but inconclusive engagement at Borodino, near Moscow. The Russians retreated further, abandoning Moscow to the French but stripping it of supplies. Having taken Moscow, Napoleon expected the Russians to capitulate. Moscow was set on fire, probably by Russian saboteurs. Napoleon stayed in Moscow too long, finally ordering the retreat as winter temperatures plummeted. The Grand Armée was annihilated in the appalling retreat.

Napoleon started to raise a new army, but his enemies smelled blood. Napoleon was finally defeated at Leipzig in the Battle of Nations where half a million troops fought each other; the biggest European battle until the World War I. Napoleon fought on in a number of brilliant defensive battles as the Allies invaded France, but was completely outnumbered. Paris was taken by the Allies; Napoleon abdicated and was exiled to Elba. The hugely fat Louis XVIII was restored to the throne.

Napoleon escaped from Elba with a few hundred of the old guard whom he had unwisely been allowed to retain and began a triumphant procession to Paris; Louis XVIII and his aristocratic supporters fled the country. Napoleon promised a new constitutional government and an end to war; certain that the allies would move against him, however, he threw himself into financing and raising a new army, working non-stop, sleeping for perhaps three hours a day. His intellect was as sharp as ever; he was determined once more to drive events by the sheer force of his personality. But there was bitter resentment in the country at the new conscription and the threat of renewed war; many troops were required to keep down potential revolts. Napoleon flew into frequent rages and began to drive his Minister of War, the faithful Marshal Davout, to breaking point. The Prussian, and their British allies were massing in Belgium.

Napoleon showed all of his old strategic brilliance, attacking the Prussians before they could join forces with the British; destroying his enemy in detail before they could mass against him. He defeated the Prussian army, but some of the old fire seemed to be missing, both in Napoleon and in those of his Marshalls who had not deserted the Napoleonic cause—and the revolution—and gone over to the restored monarchy. Marshal Ney, the man who had heroically commanded the rearguard on the retreat from Moscow, was slow to attack Wellington's troops at Quatre Bras, losing vital time. The next day, heavy rain delayed the French attack; in the meantime the Prussian commander, Marshal Blucher, having given his word to support Wellington, had prevented his defeated troops from retreating back to the east. Fortified with gin and garlic, he marched to meet Wellington, as promised. Ney wasted the French cavalry in repeated charges against the stout defence of Wellington's infantry. The arrival of the Prussians sealed the French defeat.

The government in Paris deserted Napoleon; he attempted to escape to the United States but was prevented by a British naval squadron and finally surrendered formally on board one of their ships. He hoped to be allowed to settle in Britain, but was transported to his final exile in St Helena, where he died in 1821.

LEE KUAN YEW
(b. 1923)

Lee Kuan Yew created the city state of Singapore. He turned a small island that was significant only for its strategic importance as a naval base serving the British Empire's southeast Asian colonial interests, into one of the four Asian Tiger economies, alongside Hong Kong, Taiwan, and South Korea. There was absolutely nothing inevitable about this; it happened because of the vision of one man. Lee Kuan Yew's relationship to Singapore is perhaps best seen as that of a Chief Executive Officer to a corporation. If we were considering Lee's career as that of an executive rather than that of a politician we would say, without reservation, that his rise to power was brilliantly but ruthlessly orchestrated; that his sharp, legally-trained mind had a crystal-clear grasp of the issues involved and of the interests of the key players, whom he masterfully manipulated; that he made use of various factions to facilitate his own road to power, and that he then unceremoniously (and successfully) dumped them once power had been achieved. We would say that his vision for his corporation's future was equally single-minded, and that every obstacle to the fulfillment of that vision was brilliantly overcome. We would say, as analysts or as potential investors, that Lee's efforts on behalf of his corporation had led to unprecedented growth and financial success, to the great benefit of his workforce and his shareholders. Reservations about Lee stem from the fact that he created modern Singapore from the position of a politician rather than as an Executive Officer, and that what reads like firm action in the corporate world can translate as repressive behavior in the political arena. The cost of Singapore's Capitalist Statism, however—which has many similarities to the political regime and economic policies of the early Republic of Turkey, founded by Mustafa Kemal—can be measured only in lost liberties and in degrees of state interference.

The island of Singapore was acquired for the East India Company—the quasi-governmental trading organization for the British Empire—by the marvellous eighteenth-century figure of Sir Thomas Stamford Bingley Raffles, in 1819. The island became a British colony in 1824 and became a British Crown Colony in 1867. All of which glosses over the fact that the island had been a significant trading post for the local people for a thousand years or so before a decline in the fourteenth century, and long before the rise of the British Empire.

Singapore became an important trading post on the spice route from Indonesia to the west, and then a significant British naval base, built particularly to counter the threat of rising Japanese influence in the region. Unfortunately, when the Japanese did attack Singapore in 1942, during World War II, having fought their way down through Malaya, the British contingent collapsed within days, leading to the largest surrender in the history of the British Army—80,000 surrendered at Singapore, joining the 50,000 troops who had already been captured on the Malaysian mainland. Winston Churchill called it the "biggest disaster and worst capitulation in British history."

The fall of Singapore had a two-fold effect on young Lee Kuan Yew and his contemporaries. Lee, whose Chinese great-grandfather had emigrated to Singapore in the late 1800s, and who was 19 years old when Singapore was captured by the Japanese, would never forget the effects of foreign domination:

"[The Japanese] made me, and a generation like me, determined to work for freedom from servitude and foreign domination. I did not enter politics. They brought politics to me."[26]

The second effect on Lee and his contemporaries was the vivid realization that the mighty British Empire was not all-powerful. Even after Britain, in the magnificently-uniformed person of Lord Mountbatten, accepted the surrender of Japan alongside representatives of the other Allies, Britain's humiliating defeat by the Japanese still resonated.

Lee learned Japanese and became a translator for the official Japanese news agency. He fled from Singapore in the last days of the war and hid in the Malayan interior until the British arrived. Lee, a fearsomely bright student, was in a hurry to get on with his studies. His parents found him a civilian berth on the troop-ship *Britannic*; he arrived at Liverpool, traveled to London and spent one term at the London School of Economics before winning a place at Fitzwilliam College, Cambridge, where he took a double first in law. He returned to Singapore and started work as a lawyer in a well-known firm before setting up his own practice with his wife, with whom he had studied at Cambridge, and his elder brother. The politics of Singapore were changing rapidly; it was not a question of whether Singapore would become independent but when, and who would benefit most. Lee set out to ensure that he would emerge in a position of political control. His vision never wavered, though events took various turns that even the clear-sighted Lee could not have predicted.

Communism was an inescapable part of the post-war politics of Singapore, Malaya, and Southeast Asia as a whole. When China had emerged from the World War II and its own war with Japan, the Communist Party of China had defeated their Nationalist opponents to emerge as the new rulers of China. The Singaporean Chinese had been significant fund-raisers for both parties—Communist and Nationalist—during the Sino-Japanese War.

Communist groups in Malaya had fought a war of resistance against the Japanese. The Malayan Communist Party, formed in 1930, demanded an end to British Colonial rule. After the Japanese invasion, the Party formed the Malayan People's Anti-Japanese Army, and were supported with British arms. At the end of the war, they were legally ratified in recognition of this wartime collaboration against the Japanese. Later, the Communist Party used violent action in support of union demands. As increasing violence led to the threat of a full-scale rebellion, the British colonial government declared a State of Emergency in 1948 that would not be lifted until 1960. The Malay Communist Party was suppressed once more; their anti-Japanese forces re-emerged as the Malayan National Liberation Army (MNLA) and fought a guerrilla war against Commonwealth forces. Support for the MNLA came substantially from Malaya's three million Chinese. Elsewhere in Southeast Asia, the war against the French in Vietnam would end in 1954, with communist forces, backed by China and the USSR, driving the French out of Indochina. The Second Indochina War—The Vietnam War—would begin in 1959.

Britain was determined to avoid a communist government in a newly independent Singapore. Ironically, since Lee Kuan Yew would eventually emerge as the leader of one of the bastions of capitalism in Southeast Asia, Lee initially tied his flag to left-wing causes in order to harness their popular support. He later comprehensively severed all ties with his former allies, arresting some and exiling others.

Lee made a name for himself in Singapore as legal counsel for two left-wing issues. He represented the Postal Worker's Union during a strike and was rarely out of the local papers, issuing a barrage of statements and letters to editors. Lee helped to win significant concessions for the Union from the colonial government. Student activists who were backing the strike turned to Lee to defend them against charges of sedition for the publication of a student journal. Lee—ironically, given his later repressive dealings with the Singaporean press—argued for the inviolable right of the students to freedom of speech. The charges against the students were dismissed; the high-profile case established Lee as a champion of the left.

Lee began to focus on a political career—the goal of all of his previous efforts. He and a group of like-minded friends formed a new political party, the People's Action Party (PAP). Lee became secretary-general. The new party had solid Trades Union support. The elections in 1955 were fought on a limited franchise—the bulk of the Chinese population was still disenfranchised, but those Chinese with dual citizenship of both the United Kingdom and of the Colonies were entitled to vote for the first time. Lee knew that to attract the Chinese vote he needed a left-leaning, communist-friendly agenda. He was about to play a remarkably subtle political hand: harnessing pro-communist support without being taken over by them, while remaining the leader of choice for anti-communist supporters.

The new party's platform was unashamedly populist: repeal of the State of Emergency imposed after the Communist insurrection in Malaya; independence for Malaya and Singapore; Malayans (and Singaporeans) to take on the running of the civil service; universal adult suffrage. At this point, Malaya and Singapore saw themselves as one nation, though Singapore was predominantly Chinese, while Malaya was a mixture of ethnic Malay, Chinese and other ethnic groupings. Prominent Malayan politicians joined Lee and his colleagues on electioneering platforms. The relationship would later fall apart.

Lee continued to play both sides of the electorate. With several prominent left-wing members of the PAP in jail (conveniently enough for Lee's leadership) the PAP nevertheless needed the section of the vote that these imprisoned figures represented. The PAP campaigned on a platform promising that they would refuse to assume power unless the Trade Unionists were released from prison. In the elections, the PAP won 43 of the 51 constituencies with 54 percent of the total vote.

There was one last-minute hurdle. When the executive committee came to choose a Prime Minister, Lee was shocked to find that he had a serious rival. Ong Eng Guan had been elected with an impressive 77 percent of the vote in his constituency. He was popular, larger-than-life, and had been a very successful mayor of Singapore. He had the popular touch: on the day of his inauguration as mayor, he had set off firecrackers outside City Hall and got himself arrested. He refused to wear the colonial wig and regalia and performed his mayoral duties in his shirt sleeves. It is hard not to like Ong's way of handling people whom he felt to be wasting time in meetings at City Hall. To encourage committee members to be more concise, Ong would make tactful suggestions, such as, "Shut up," "Sit down," "Get out," or "Blab, blab, blab, blab."[27] The vote between Ong and Lee was split down the middle; Lee was saved when his ally, Toh Chin Chye, exercised his casting vote, as Party Chairman, in Lee's favor. Lee Kuan Yew, at the age of 36, was Prime Minister of Singapore.

Lee began to lobby for Singapore to be united with an independent Malaya—Malaya had become an independent state in the British Commonwealth in 1957. Lee argued that Singapore, left on its own, could fall into the hands of the communists. One of the most compelling reasons for Malaya to accept Singapore into the greater Federation of Malaysia was the fear of a communist state off the southern tip of Malaya. In fact, Lee cracked down so hard on communists in Singapore that, over the next year or two, this threat was soon proved to be non-existent. Lee worked hard to have his Singaporean political party, the PAP, accepted into the Federal Government, but was rejected. He almost certainly had plans to become Prime Minister of Malaysia. The two sides fell out over Lee's political ambitions, exacerbated by the issue of race: Malaysia's population was almost equally split between Malay and Chinese citizens, with about 20 percent made up of other ethnic groupings. When Lee formed an opposition grouping in Malaysia based on his predominantly Chinese PAP, this polarized politics between Malay and non-Malay groupings; there were riots between Malays and Chinese. It seemed possible that Lee wanted to form a rival Federation based on the predominantly Chinese states of Singapore, Sarawak, and Sabah (the latter two being Malaysian states on the island of Borneo). Singapore was ejected from Malaysia in 1965, and became the Republic of Singapore.

With Singapore unexpectedly independent and thrown onto its own resources, Lee set about planning the development of the economy with impressive single-mindedness. He established the Economic Development Board, which set out to attract both foreign investment and any necessary outside expertise. The Board itself was staffed with experts in every necessary field. Lee employed a Dutch economist, Dr Albert Winsemius, to help develop the country's national economic strategy. Singapore had traditionally relied on entrepot trade—its geographical location gave it the perfect position from which to buy goods from shippers who did not want to undertake the full journey between, for example, east and west, and to sell them on, at a profit, to more distant customers in both markets (the French word *entrepôt* translates as "between two places"). The developing plan was to transform Singapore from an entrepot economy to an industrialized manufacturing base within ten years.

Lee was conscious that his neighbors, Malaysia and Indonesia, would be increasingly keen to cut out the middle man and that, with the world shrinking daily, shipment direct from supplier to customer on a world-wide basis would become increasingly common. This did not mean that Singapore's location on the main shipping route from the Far East to Europe was a shrinking asset: Singapore built Southeast Asia's first container-ship terminal, offering a 24-hour berthing system to speed-up turnaround. In the first ten years of Lee's Prime Ministry, the volume of cargo handled by Singapore doubled. The island, with no oil resources of its own, developed a major oil-refining capacity; crude oil was imported via the Persian Gulf, and shipped on as refined products to Indonesia and Australia.

When the British decided to close their huge naval base in Singapore, it was a potentially devastating blow. Lee turned it into a tremendous opportunity: he persuaded British Prime Minister Harold Wilson not to destroy the base, which was normal practice (to prevent naval facilities from being used by a hostile power) but to allow Singapore to develop it for civilian use. Singapore became the best-equipped shipbuilding and ship-repair yard between Japan and Europe.

New legislation gave the Corrupt Practices Investment Bureau substantial powers to investigate and prosecute anyone suspected of corruption. Civil Service salaries were improved and reviewed regularly to remove the incentive for corruption. An Employment Act guaranteed an absence of labor disputes and wage restraint by making arbitration compulsory. Singapore could offer foreign investors relatively inexpensive industrial labor costs with a stable and corruption-free administration. Equally important were Singapore's strong work ethic and can-do attitude. Singapore was beginning to emulate the other 'tiger economies' of Southeast Asia. Unemployment fell dramatically between 1965 and 1973. Huge housing developments sprang up on land reclaimed from swamps or from the sea itself. Slums disappeared. Industrial, shopping, and office complexes were built.

Lee decided that Singapore should be "Clean and Green". Teams of gardeners appeared and began planting. Shop owners were obliged to keep their shop fronts clean and tidy; littering became a relatively serious offence.

By the end of the 1960s, Singapore was ready to offer more than a stable and low-cost manufacturing base; a new industrial development was planned to deliver sophisticated and capital-intensive factories producing high-technology goods: cameras; electronics; machine tools. The country could afford to be more selective about its inward investment—new criteria looked at investment proposals that developed worker skills, offered technological growth and had guaranteed export potential. Singapore began to develop as a financial market. By the end of the 1960s there were more than 20 foreign banks on the island; Asian dollar deposits were tax-free (compared to the 15 percent tax on deposits in Hong Kong); hard currencies were exchanged free of charge. Growing American interest in Southeast Asia made Singapore a vital part of the flow of American capital towards the region—and later of European capital also. Dr Winsemius, the economic advisor, encouraged new investment in further education: the unemployment issue had been effectively solved, what was needed now were higher-level skills and knowledge-based services.

Singapore ranked 19th on the World Bank's 2007 list of GDP per capita. The United States ranked 10th. Japan ranked 20th.[28] It is amazing what planning can achieve.

MARTIN LUTHER KING
(1929–1968)

Martin Luther King, a Baptist preacher, developed an emotionally charged style of address that led, in time, to his being proclaimed as one of America's greatest orators. His themes were constant and fundamental: the obvious injustice of a system that created a form of second-class citizenship for citizens of a nation built on the premise that all men are created equal, and the call for non-violent protest as the morally acceptable means of confronting injustice.

It would be tempting to focus on King's inspirational speeches as his best claim for greatness as a leader. But the speeches were what brought King to international acclaim once he had worked his way onto a national and international platform: his hardest work as a leader had been undertaken, years before, in the arduous, unglamorous, and unrewarded efforts to organize local action—in the hard graft of the committee room; in the raising of funds and the distribution of leaflets; in the finding of allies, supporters and well-wishers; in the encouragement of groups of people faced with violent intimidation and under the constant strain of fighting the establishment without any of the weapons of power. Like the great generals whose dramatic victories are the result not only of hard-fought battles, but also of all the detailed strategic and logistical planning, so King's later speeches should be seen in the context of a life dedicated to a cause; of two decades of planning and hard work. His "I Have a Dream" speech has gone down in history as a defining statement of black Americans' struggle for equality. It would not have the resonance that it does without the long history of hard-won minor victories and significant milestones that King's movement had achieved previously on the long road to freedom.

King's own activism was sparked by the apparently mundane actions of one black woman from Montgomery, Alabama: Rosa Parks. One day in 1955, Rosa had taken her seat in the 'colored' section of a

Montgomery bus as usual, but as the bus filled up the driver moved the 'colored' sign further back, asking Rosa and other black passengers to give up their seats for white passengers. Something in Rosa snapped. She refused to give up her seat and was arrested and convicted of violating a local ordinance. Black churches organized a one-day boycott of local buses. Following the success of this day of action, an organization known as the Montgomery Improvement Association (MIA) was formed. The Association elected as their President a relative newcomer to the area, the Reverend Dr Martin Luther King. The bus boycott was resumed and was to continue for over a year; buses stood idle; the bus company's finances began to suffer. Black churches were burned and bombed by segregationists; King's own home was firebombed. King's MIA negotiated special rates with black taxi drivers to help black people to travel about town (taxis were also segregated); when the city declared these reduced fares to be illegal, they organized car-pools. Legal activists took up other cases of racial discrimination on buses: in December 1956 the United States Supreme Court declared racial segregation on buses to be unconstitutional.

In order to sustain the momentum of the Montgomery civil rights victory, King, with other black leaders, founded the Southern Christian Leadership Conference (SCLC) in 1957. He established himself as its leader; toured, gave speeches, wrote about the events in Montgomery.

King was more than a great public speaker. He did the hard and unrewarding work that created an organization that could bring about the dreams that he spoke about so eloquently. He also put his life in danger.

Martin Luther King was born in Atlanta, Georgia, in the Southern States of the United States of America, in 1929. His father was a Baptist minister, as was his mother's father. King grew up in a middle-class family in the most affluent society the world had ever seen. In the 1920s, America severely restricted the tide of immigration from

Europe that had populated the vast continent and settled down to the business of creating wealth via industrial-scale farming and the mass production of consumer goods. Great swathes of America entered the middle-classes; it was a time of radios and electrical appliances, of suburbs and cars: by the year of Martin Luther King's birth, there were nearly 30 million motor vehicles on the road—one for every citizen in five. For the one in ten citizens who were black African-Americans, however, the American dream proved to be elusive, especially in the Southern States, where segregation was a legally-sanctioned facet of everyday life. King studied theology, philosophy, and ethics at theological college. He was introduced to the non-violent activism of Mahatma Ghandi that was to have such a profound influence on him. He went on to take his doctorate in Theology at Boston University.

Thirty-four years after his birth, King was to write a letter in response to a statement in which white, liberal clergymen—people sympathetic to the Civil Rights cause—had called for a halt on protest marches aimed at ending the racial segregation of stores in Birmingham, Alabama. Direct action incited hatred and violence, they argued, no matter how peaceful the actions might be in themselves. King's written response to these clergymen spells out the difference between the white and the black perspective, and the reason why black Americans "find it difficult to wait." King was in jail in Birmingham at the time, for defying a court injunction banning further demonstrations in the city, and his response was later published as his *Letter from Birmingham Jail*. Although King makes reference to the violence—sometimes fatal—that was still commonly inflicted on blacks by whites in the southern states, with virtual impunity, it is the more widespread and commonplace insult, the everyday humiliation, that King tries to bring home to his white colleagues.

"We have waited for more than 340 years for our constitutional and God-given rights. The nations of Africa and Asia are moving at jetlike speed toward gaining political independence, but we creep at horse and buggy speed toward gaining a cup of coffee at a lunch counter [...] when you have seen hate-filled policemen curse, kick, and even kill your black brothers and sisters; when you see the vast majority of your 20 million negro brothers smothering in an air-tight cage of poverty in the midst of an affluent society; when you suddenly find your tongue twisted and your speech stammering as you seek to explain to your six-year old daughter why she can't go to the public amusement park that has just been advertized on television, and see tears welling up in her little eyes when she is told that Funtown is closed to colored children, and see the depressing clouds of inferiority begin to form in her little mental sky [...] when you take a cross-country drive and find it necessary to sleep night after night in the uncomfortable corners of your automobile because no motel will accept you; when you are humiliated day in and day out by nagging signs reading 'white' and 'colored' [...] when you are forever fighting a degenerating sense of 'nobodiness' [...] then you will understand why we find it difficult to wait."[29]

Four years after the Supreme Court's decision that segregation on buses was unconstitutional, it further ruled that any racial segregation in transport facilities was illegal: interstate movement and commerce was vital to the economy of the United States, passengers of any race should not be forced to accept segregated facilities in states even where law or custom enforced general segregation. The "Freedom Rides" began. Mixed-race teams of students traveled from Virginia, through the Carolinas, Georgia, Alabama, and Mississippi, ending in New Orleans. The Freedom Riders insisted on using the "Whites Only" facilities at bus stations where segregation was in force. In Anniston, Alabama, the bus was attacked and its tyres slashed. As the crippled bus ground to a halt out of town on the highway, it was firebombed. A mob attempted to barricade the doors, intending to burn the occupants alive. An under-cover agent drew his gun and forced the mob back from the door. The escaping Freedom Riders were beaten by the mob; Alabama state troopers arrived to see off the attackers.

At Birmingham, the riders were again set upon by a mob, apparently aided by the police under the Commissioner for Public Safety: Bull Connor. The attackers used baseball bats, lead pipes, and bicycle chains. Two riders were hospitalised, one white, one black. With all of the riders injured, and the bus companies unwilling to provide drivers, the rides were nearly discontinued. Many of the original riders flew on to the planned rally in New Orleans. Diane Nash, leader of the Student Nonviolent Coordinating Committee, sent more riders.

It was now May 1961. The government of President Kennedy (just five months into his presidency and fresh from the Bay of Pigs disaster, a calamitously bungled invasion of neighboring communist Cuba, intended to overthrow the government of Fidel Castro) began to take an interest through the office of the Attorney General, Robert Kennedy, the President's younger brother. In Birmingham, with the bus station surround by a violent mob, the Greyhound bus driver refused to travel further. Robert Kennedy put pressure on both the bus companies and the Alabama Governor, John Patterson. Patterson was able to play a tricky and legally consistent game: he was the elected Governor of a state that had chosen a segregationist policy. If the government wanted to send in troops to support the "outside agitators" who were in Alabama to "foment disorders and breaches of the peace" and, for example, the state police and fire brigade were to strike in protest at this federal intervention, then would the government be responsible for any subsequent damage to the city?

President Kennedy, soon to meet the Russian President Nikita Khrushchev in Europe and on the point of asking Congress to increase spending on nuclear weapons to strengthen his hand in the escalating Cold War, did not want to walk into the negotiating chamber on behalf of the free world with embarrassing pictures splashed over the international media of Federal troops trying to prevent American citizens from assaulting their black fellow-citizens. The need for the

President to call in the Army to help get a bus out of a station in Alabama could also raise fundamental questions about Kennedy's competence and his ability to deliver on recent sweeping promises to take the country into a new era of civil rights for all. The fact that the President had depended heavily on southern votes for his recent election may also have been at the back of his mind. His brother, Robert Kennedy, the Attorney General, assembled a makeshift team of Marshalls from Federal bodies such as the US Border Patrol, the Bureau of Alcohol, Tobacco and Firearms, and even prison officers.

Greyhound Buses put pressure on their unfortunate drivers to get back behind the wheel; Patterson supplied a police escort, sirens wailing, to the city line, where the convoy was picked up by the police. With a highway patrol plane in the air and a posse of reporters following, the convoy sped on to Montgomery. At Montgomery city limits, the protective convoy disappeared. The bus drew into Montgomery station and into the hands of a waiting mob. Black and white Freedom riders, news photographers and reporters, and Attorney General Robert Kennedy's negotiator, John Seigenthaler, who had driven to meet the bus and had gone to the aid of a female Freedom Rider being attacked by the mob, were viciously beaten.

The next day, people began to gather in the Montgomery church of King's lifelong associate, Ralph Abernathy. (Abernathy was to join King in jail on 19 different occasions; King was to claim that jail held no terrors for him more fearful than Abernathy's snoring.) Freedom Riders, pointedly not identified by name, were recognizable in the church by their bandages. King had flown into Montgomery, raising new government fears about the legal complications of protecting King himself. He went to Abernathy's church. There were some 1,200 people in the church by nightfall. A huge mob of some 3,000 had gathered outside. Robert Kennedy mobilized his makeshift army of Marshalls, a handful of whom made a fragile barrier against the mob. King insisted on going outside to address the mob, but was hauled back inside as bricks and missiles were hurled.

Petrol bombs were thrown over the Marshalls' line, burning in the streets short of the church. A car was set on fire. The ministers inside the church led the congregation in hymn-singing, interspersed with appeals for calm. Some men in the church reached for weapons with which to defend themselves and their families. King made a dramatic telephone call to Robert Kennedy, pleading for federal aid to prevent a massacre. Kennedy knew that further Marshalls were on the way, but could offer no assurance as to when they would arrive: they arrived before the phone call ended and fired tear gas at the crowd. The crowd regrouped; someone threw a brick through the church windows. Tear gas began to fill the church itself. Robert Kennedy decided to call his brother, the President—but John F. Kennedy was in Virginia: would it be legal to move troops before papers could be got to the President for signing?

In the end Governor Patterson forestalled the need for Federal troops by sending in the Alabama National Guard. King preached to the besieged congregation, blaming Governor Patterson's pronouncements about the Freedom Riders for having created the atmosphere of violence in which such terror could thrive.

The Kennedy government began to feel that the Freedom Riders had made their point, and that to persist was to tarnish the reputation of America abroad. They struck a deal with the governors of Alabama and Mississippi: the states would protect the riders from mob violence, but the government would not prevent them from arresting riders who violated state laws on the use of segregated facilities. The riders kept coming and the jails filled up. Eventually, in 1961, the Kennedy administration leaned on the Interstate Commerce Commission to end segregation of all interstate transport.

King's campaign continued on every front: he organized action for black voters' rights, for labor rights, and for equality of education. Throughout the 1960s the Federal Bureau of Investigation (FBI) spied relentlessly on King in an attempt to prove that his organization was infiltrated by communists (it would have been so much easier for the American conscience to accept that King's activities were driven by subversive forces, rather than being driven by the unpleasant realities of American society).

When jailed in Birmingham in 1963, King was campaigning for the de-segregation of downtown city stores. After his release from jail on appeal, High School students joined the marches as the enthusiasm of their elders waned. There were scenes of schoolchildren being attacked by police dogs; the nation began to demand an end. Birmingham's businessmen agreed to de-segregate their stores; in the wake of the agreement, King's hotel and his brother's home were bombed. Blacks rioted in response.

In 1963, as the culmination of the 'March on Washington' in which black and white leaders called for the speedy passage of the promised civil rights bill, a crowd of a quarter of a million Americans heard King deliver his electrifying "I Have a Dream" speech. Two weeks later, white supremacists in Birmingham bombed a Baptist church, killing four black girls attending Sunday school.

In 1964, King was awarded the Nobel Peace Prize. By then, President Kennedy had been assassinated. It was President Lyndon Johnson who passed the historic Civil Rights Act of 1964, guaranteeing equal access for all citizens to public facilities, to employment, and to education. The Voting Rights Act of 1965 extended the vote to previously disenfranchised African-Americans in the South. In 1968 King was killed by a sniper's bullet on the balcony of his hotel in Memphis, Tennessee.

4

LEADING FROM
THE FRONT

Nothing is more impressive in a manager than to lead from the front. This can take many forms, the most obvious of which is the traditional concept of not asking anybody else to do what you wouldn't do yourself—of exposing yourself to danger along with your troops. The military analogy is not so far-fetched: it is inspiring when a manager picks up the phone to talk to a key client if there is a problem; when they step in to mediate a dispute; when they stick their neck out to make the case to senior management for the needs of their own team or division; when they take on a difficult interview with the media; when they are seen to be out and about promoting the organization to the outside world. The first leader from history in this chapter, Admiral Lord Nelson, personifies this ideal. A brilliant strategist famous for building a unique rapport with his colleagues —his "band of brothers"—Nelson inspired because he always led from the front. He was the first to put himself in the way of danger.

The other two leaders personify different ways of leading from the front. Mutafa Kemal—the founder of modern Turkey—was brave in an entirely Nelsonian way, leading his troops fearlessly from the front in both World War I and the subsequent battle for Turkish independence. But Kemal also demonstrates another way of leading from the front: by the strength of your conviction, the passion of your vision, and the depth of your commitment. Kemal was determined that an independent Turkey would survive the dismantling of the Ottoman Empire. He had no real grounds to hope that this could be achieved, but he did it anyway. His conviction, his belief, and his sheer industry inspired a nation to follow him.

The last example, Muhammad Ali, is similar, but with the striking difference that Ali did not set out to lead anybody to any particular destination. What Ali did was to insist on his right to be his own man—to refuse to conform to the expectations that society had for him. "I know where I'm going and I know the truth, and I don't have to be what you want me to be." It is a difficult example for a manager to follow—sometimes even a dangerous one—but there are times when you need to make a stand on an issue simply because you are absolutely convinced that it is the right thing to do, regardless of the opinions of everybody else. If you are right (and let's hope you are) then people will begin to follow you.

Nelson had become famous throughout the Royal Navy for his audacity and his personal bravery. At the battle of St Vincent, Nelson broke out of formation to attack Spanish ships that he feared would escape if the fleet continued with the maneuver that the admiral had commanded. He risked being court-martialled, but hoped that there was sufficient leeway in the interpretation of the admiral's signal to justify his actions, if necessary. Being Nelson, he probably did not agonize over this decision: his burning ambition was always to engage the enemy. His 74-gun ship, HMS *Captain*, broke away from the British line and engaged three much larger Spanish ships, exchanging broadsides for an hour, inflicting much damage and being hit hard herself. Nelson then led his crew to board one of the Spanish ships, crossing over from that ship to another that had become entangled with it. Nelson accepted the surrender of both vessels. It was actions such as these that created real devotion in the men who served with Nelson. They would follow him anywhere and they were prepared to die for him. His most famous victory, at Trafalgar, involved an unusual and dangerous maneuver: Nelson led his ships—and those of his vice admiral, Collingwood—at a right angle to the enemy's line of ships, instead of sailing parallel to them for the traditional exchange of broadsides. He meant to break through and split the French and Spanish line, and knew that as they passed through the line they could fire their cannons down the entire length of the enemy ships, inflicting great damage. He intended to destroy the allied flagship and, having broken the line, utterly to destroy, piecemeal, the French and Spanish Fleet. But Nelson knew that his ships would take heavy fire as they approached the enemy in this formation, and would be unable to bring their own broadsides to bear. Nelson, in breach of all tradition, put his own flagship at the very front of the line.

Mustafa Kemal created modern Turkey. He salvaged the nation from the wreckage of the Ottoman Empire at the end of World War I, when the ailing empire—"the sick man of Europe"—was being carved up by the victorious Allies. He then transformed the nation, economically and socially. He abolished the Sultanate and established a secular state. He set up a one-party state and a kind of state-sponsored capitalism, but he also established universal suffrage for both men and women (enfranchising women before, for example, France or Italy), and laid the foundations for the multi-party democracy that would emerge after his death. Kemal had always led from the front. He showed conspicuous bravery and great leadership skills during the Allied invasion of Gallipoli at the start of World War I. As the Allies prepared to divide up the Ottoman Empire between them, Kemal became determined to save Anatolia—the peninsula between the Black Sea and the Mediterranean that was the homeland of the Turkish-speaking people—and create the Republic of Turkey. With a few remnants of the army that had fought in the Great War, he set up a new Nationalist Party and an alternative government in the interior and, by single-handedly bombarding the Sultan's government with telegrams, brought about the resignation of the Sultan's chief minister, the Grand Vizier, and the promise of new elections. The Nationalist Party won a majority; British troops invaded Constantinople and dissolved the new Parliament. Kemal retired to the interior again and built up the army, fighting a stubborn resistance against Greek forces that began to spread throughout Anatolia to claim territory for Greece. Kemal inspired a heroic resistance and finally forced the Greeks to abandon Turkey. The British signed an armistice and a new treaty recognized the independence of the Republic of Turkey. Kemal was honored with the name of Atatürk—Father of Turkey. Few leaders have featured quite so prominently at the forefront of an entire movement: Kemal had decided that a Republic of Turkey should be established; he brought it into being by the force of his will and his inspiring leadership.

Muhammad Ali is an unusual example in this context, because he was not a leader and never set out to be one. In the process of his remarkable career, however, Ali became the hero of a generation. Having won the title of heavyweight boxing champion of the world, Ali converted to Islam and joined the radical Nation of Islam—an organization that seemed to set itself against everything that the white establishment held dear, and had been declared to be "un-American" by the state of California. Later, at a time when the war in Vietnam still had broad popular support, Ali refused to be drafted into the United States army. He succeeded in making the point that black Americans didn't have to fit the stereotype of what constituted "a good representative of their race." In doing this, Ali proved simply that he would be his own man whatever the cost—and for a time that cost was severe; he was stripped of his title and banned from boxing. Ali finally won his court case against the government and was recognized as a conscientious objector; he regained his license and fought his way back to becoming heavyweight champion of the world once more. Ali shows how it is possible to lead from the front by having faith in yourself and your own convictions.

HORATIO NELSON
(1758–1805)

Horatio Nelson—Lord Nelson as he became—was an odd-looking, likable, passionate, and intelligent man with many human frailties, including sea-sickness, vanity, and an ill-considered and very public adulterous affair with the wife of the British Envoy to Naples. Nelson inspired huge confidence and fanatical loyalty amongst his officers and crew. In July 1797, during the Napoleonic wars, Nelson was leading an attack in small boats on the town of Cadiz, when they were boarded by Spanish defenders. Nelson was at the forefront of the hand-to-hand fighting: his life was saved on two occasions by his coxswain, John Sykes, who parried one sword blow to Nelson's head with his bare arm. "Thank God, sir, you are safe," said the badly-wounded Sykes.

Nelson's effect on morale is shown in his officers' letters. When he arrived off Cadiz in September 1805, shortly before the battle of Trafalgar, one captain wrote, "Lord Nelson is arrived! A sort of general joy has been the consequence, and many good effects will shortly arise from our change of system." The last point is interesting: it is not just Nelson's presence that is an inspiration to his men; Nelson's methods are known to be effective—he knows his stuff. Nelson was constantly experimenting and innovating. "He possessed the zeal of an enthusiast," wrote Nelson's second-in-command at Trafalgar, Admiral Collingwood, after Nelson's death, "and everything seemed, as if by enchantment, to prosper under his direction. But it was the effect of system, and nice combination, not of chance."[30]

Nelson is often thought of as being a shining example of a leader who genuinely empowers his team, which he was. In the Mediterranean, with his first fleet, he wrote in a letter home: "Such a gallant set of fellows! Such a band of brothers! My heart swells at the thought of them!"[31] Nelson had indeed cultivated the captains of his fleet with regular meetings and suppers on board his flagship. Nothing is more independent than a fighting ship at sea, not simply because any warship was expected to be a self-contained unit, re-supplying itself and even repairing itself during tours of duty that could last for years, but also because, in the smoke and chaos of battle, signalling (by flags) was utterly unreliable and sometimes impossible. Before an action had started, a commander needed to be certain that the captains under his command understood the general plan of attack—the broad strategy and the most likely tactical developments. By spending time with his "band of brothers" discussing strategies and tactics, outlining possible plans of attack, discussing the enemy's strengths and weaknesses, Nelson brought his fellow captains to the point where they began to think like him—to the extent that, in a sudden, unplanned engagement, they could be hoped to react exactly as he would himself.

Like any great leader, Nelson had many strengths. Perhaps his most defining characteristic, one which he demonstrated throughout his career, was his outstanding personal bravery and his habit of leading from the front. Nelson was always in thick of it. He had lost an arm and an eye on separate occasions leading attacks on the enemy on shore. He never asked his crew to do anything that he would not do himself and, as a result, he could be certain that they would follow him.

Nelson was born in 1758 and enrolled in the Royal Navy at the age of 12 quickly becoming a midshipman. He saw action in the American War of Independence and by the age of 20 was captain of a 28-gun frigate. By 1798, he was in charge of his own fleet, in the Mediterranean. Britain, with other European Allies, was at war with the new, revolutionary French Republic. France's most formidable general, the young Napoleon Bonaparte, had assembled an expedition to Egypt; his success there could lead to a threat to British interests in India.

Nelson's primary objective was to prevent the French expedition from sailing. He failed utterly in this when his flagship, Vanguard, was dismasted in a storm; the French fleet of warships and troop carriers passed by while Nelson carried out repairs to his ship in Sardinia. Nelson then sailed to Alexandria; the French arrived in Alexandria the day after Nelson left the port. It took Nelson another month of fruitless searching before he received confirmation that the French were indeed in Egypt.

It was during this time, in command of his first fleet, that Nelson began to develop his unique leadership style. Some of the captains in his fleet were known to him from other, earlier campaigns. Others were entirely new faces. Nelson set up a series of suppers on board his flagship. The various captains began to come together as a genuine team. Nelson encouraged a free-ranging discussion of the means by which the French Fleet could be discovered and engaged; the team began to absorb the ideas and attitudes of their admiral—one of the great 'natural' leaders of all time.

The concept of the "band of brothers" was mentioned explicitly by Nelson for the first time after the coming Battle of the Nile, as he strove—like any good manager—to ensure that each of his captains was recognized for their part in the event. Nelson, again like any good manager, reserved the right, in private, to assess and weigh more critically the contribution played by each captain. Some of the "band of brothers" off the coast of Egypt were not called upon again. But Nelson's notion of the admiral and his captains as a "band of brothers" was more than just window-dressing. He knew that his own success depended on the individual and unpredictable contribution of each of his commanders as events unfolded. Nelson gave his men the cause, the commitment; he bound them up with his own zeal. He shared his thoughts on strategy and tactics with them in depth. He ensured that they fully understood their mission. And then he let them loose.

The English fleet found Alexandria full of French transport ships, but not the French warships. The next anchorage was Aboukir Bay, to the north. With evening approaching, they found the French fleet anchored in line in the Bay, protected on the landward side by shallows. Nelson immediately decided to attack and ordered the ships to form a line of battle. As they approached the anchored French fleet, his commanders seized the initiative. Captain Foley, in HMS *Goliath*, spotted that the French ships were anchored at their bows only; if they had enough water to swing at anchor then there was enough water for Foley to sail between them and the shore. The French, believing themselves protected to landward, had not even cleared for action on that side. More ships followed Foley, one of them running aground; the rest attacked from the seaward side. The British ships had the wind at their backs; the last ships in the French line were not able to sail up, against the wind, to help the defence. The English ships worked their way down the line, pouring shot from both sides into the French fleet. The French flagship was the massive *L'Orient*: 120 guns; the biggest warship of her day. *L'Orient* inflicted serious damage on the English HMS *Bellerophon*, but then caught fire. Other English ships joined the attack. The French Vice-Admiral, de Brueys, lost both his legs. With his stumps tourniqueted, he directed the action from a chair until a cannonball destroyed what was left of him. Later that evening *L'Orient*'s magazines blew up. The stunning explosion stopped the battle for some 30 minutes, after which it resumed, though less forcefully. When fighting stopped at dawn the next day, 11 French battleships and two frigates had been taken or sunk. The French navy in the Mediterranean had been destroyed.

Nelson became a national hero. Three things stand out from this action. Firstly, Nelson never lost sight of the need to engage the enemy. It may seem obvious, but many other commanders in similar situations failed to do so. Secondly, Nelson saw his objective as the need to destroy his opponent: to make them no longer a fighting force; many commanders lacked his will for total engagement and settled for an honourable result. Finally, Nelson expected his captains to act on their own initiative and put them in a position to be able to do so.

Nelson was also prepared to disobey orders—or at least, not to follow them—if his instincts told him that the route to victory lay elsewhere. One year before the Battle of the Nile, in 1797, Nelson was under the command of Admiral Sir John Jervis when the British fleet attacked a much larger fleet of Spanish warships. Jervis ordered the British fleet to form a line of battle ahead and astern of his flagship *Victory*. Nelson's ship was near the end of the line. The British fleet split the Spanish fleet in two, allowing the British to fire on them in both directions. Passing through the Spanish position, the fleet began to turn through 180 degrees to renew their attack.

Nelson—at the end of the line—was close to the half of the Spanish fleet now sailing in the opposite direction; he did not believe that the whole fleet could stay in line and make the turn in time to prevent the Spanish from escaping. He decided that he could interpret a second signal of Jervis ("Take suitable steps for mutual support and engage the enemy as coming up in succession") as an excuse to disobey Jervis' previous instruction to form a line. He broke away and attacked the passing Spanish ships, including the massive Spanish flagship, the four-decker, 130-gun *Santisima Trinidad*. Other British ships came quickly to Nelson's aid. With his ship now so badly damaged as to be almost unmanageable, Nelson managed to put her alongside the Spanish *San Nicolás*, which had also become entangled with another Spanish ship, the *San José*. Nelson and his marines boarded the first vessel, and then went across her to board the second. The engagement was an emphatic victory for the British, who had been outnumbered by 27 ships to 15. Nelson reported to Admiral Jervis on board *Victory* and reported that, "The Admiral embraced me, said he could not sufficiently thank me, and used every kind expression that could not fail to make me happy."

Had he failed, Nelson could have been court-martialled for disobeying orders in the face of the enemy. He had risked his entire career. But it is worth noting that the Navy was not so hidebound by discipline that it insisted on court-martialling Nelson, even if only to exonerate him. Nelson had good reason to believe that success would bring reward—not criticism. At the Battle of Copenhagen (1801) Nelson more flagrantly ignored a command from his superior officer. Nelson's ships had carried out an audacious attack on the Danish fleet through narrow and treacherous channels and were beginning to overwhelm Danish defences when Admiral Parker ordered a general recall, believing that the battle was going badly. Not only would this have wasted the initiative, but Nelson's ships would have been forced to retreat across the line of fire from a still-active section of the Danish defences. Nelson turned to his flag-captain and said, "Foley, you know that I have lost an eye," (Nelson had lost his right eye in Corsica in 1794, when a cannonball impact threw stones and sand into his face; he lost his right arm in 1797, leading an attack on Santa Cruz in Tenerife), "and have a right to be blind when I like; and damn me if I'll see that signal."[32] Nelson was victorious. The phrase "to turn a blind eye" had entered the English language. In the event, Admiral Parker was ordered to hand over his command to Nelson. To some extent, the navy expected and encouraged independence of mind in its commanders. More importantly, it encouraged success.

Nelson's final moment of glory came, of course, at Trafalgar in 1805. The British had been blockading the combined French and Spanish fleet in Cadiz when the French Admiral Villeneuve finally left the safety of the harbor in response to a foolish and perhaps spiteful command from Napoleon, ordering the fleet to sail to the Mediterranean to assist the land attack on Austria. When Nelson arrived with the fleet, it would be wrong to imagine that he was rejoining his "band of brothers." Of the captains of the 27 ships of the line that Nelson commanded, only eight had served with him before. Nelson's success did not depend on the support of a closely-knit team; it depended on the brilliant use that he was able to make of any team put at his disposal. Nelson circulated his plan of attack. It contained the apparently laconic order: "In case signals can neither be seen nor perfectly understood, no captain can do very wrong if he places his ship alongside that of an enemy." This was in fact a precise instruction as to the tactics that Nelson wanted his captains to employ. French and Spanish ships tended to fire high, attempting to dismast the opponent. British gunners fired faster and more accurately than their opponents and were instructed to fire low. Nelson knew that firing into ships' hulls at close quarters could do immense damage to men and guns, putting a ship out of action more effectively than destroying her rigging. This was the kind of pell-mell action that Nelson wanted.

Nelson and his second-in-command Collingwood broke with all convention by sailing at the head of their two columns: flagships were traditionally placed at the center of the line of battle. The two British lines attacked at right angles to the line of enemy ships rather than passing alongside them to exchange broadsides in the traditional way. Nelson meant to split the French and Spanish line of ships into three sections and to destroy the enemy fleet piecemeal. Attacking the enemy in this manner meant that the leading British ships were exposed to fire for a desperately long time as they approached, without being able to return fire with broadsides of their own. Nelson, sailing at the head of his own column in HMS *Victory*, had placed himself in the position of most danger: he would not ask another captain to do anything that he was not prepared to do himself. Once the British ships had engaged with the enemy, passing through the enemy line at right angles, the British gunners were able to fire, one by one, through stern or bow of the enemy ships, inflicting terrible damage as cannonballs ricocheted through the whole length of gun-decks, smashing guns and men alike. The center and rear of the enemy line was destroyed. Nelson was hit by a musket ball, fired by a French sharpshooter from the rigging of one of the enemy ships that he had so closely engaged, and died below decks three hours later.

What sets Nelson apart as a leader is his refusal to accept qualified success. He wanted victory. He was prepared to override his orders and ignore his superiors in order to achieve this. He seemed to want fame and to enjoy it, but he was prepared to risk his career and his life to pursue what he saw as his role in the navy: the destruction of the enemy. He also knew that his fellow commanders were not there to follow his detailed orders but to achieve the common end by whatever means they saw fit. There are no detailed orders for victory. At the end, far more than most commanders, he was able to say, with every justification: "Thank God, I have done my duty."

MUSTAFA KEMAL ATATÜRK
(1881–1938)

Not many leaders get to create a nation state. Mustafa Kemal did just that as the tottering Ottoman Empire was being dismantled at the end of World War I by the victors; especially by Great Britain, France, and Italy.

Mustafa Kemal had distinguished himself during the war, especially in the defence of Gallipoli against British and Allied forces. He had shown himself to be a man who would lead from the front in the most extreme circumstances, showing great bravery and also considerable military acumen. After the war, with the Ottoman Empire about to be carved up in the most cynical way by the victorious powers, Kemal decided that the Turkish nation would be independent. He had little reason to believe that this could be achieved. In conversation with an American General who was about to report back on the political situation in the remnants of the Ottoman Empire, Kemal stated that he intended to make Turkey an independent state. The General pointed out that this was beyond hope, that there was no military or political logic that could justify such a faith. "What you say, General, is true," said Kemal. "What we want to do, in our situation, is explainable neither in military nor in any other terms, but in spite of everything, we are going to do it, to save our country, to establish a free and civilized Turkish state, to live like human beings. If we can't succeed," he continued, "we prefer, being the sons of our forefathers, to die fighting."[33] The general was impressed.

This could, of course, have been the wild talk of any idealist, but Kemal was no mere dreamer. He organized what meagre materials he had; he used the few legitimate tools of political power at his disposal to get himself into a position of authority, from which he negotiated, with considerable success. When fighting began, he created an army out of nothing and defeated his enemies. Starting from nowhere, Kemal persuaded both the outside world and his own countrymen that his vision was achievable, and then he made it happen: he led from the front and brought people with him. Since Kemal's vision of modern Turkey was radically different from that of many of his compatriots, he brought them with him, in many cases kicking and screaming. He also established a one-party state. However it is fair to say that Kemal's vision was always that Turkey should move towards the modern democracy that it has since become. In 1934, Turkey, still a one-party state, granted full voting rights to women, a decade before France and Italy.

Mustafa Kemal always wanted to be a soldier. He went to military high school and then on to military college. In 1905 he graduated from the War Academy. In 1908, Kemal had some involvement in a minor rebellion—the Young Turk Revolution—that forced the Sultan of the Ottoman Empire to reinstate the Parliament that he had suspended. Kemal had far more involvement in various other nationalist secret societies that he helped to found, such as "Fatherland", which eventually became part of the Committee of Union and Progress (CUP). Soon after his graduation he was arrested for political agitation and banished to the State of Damascus, Syria, and was lucky to escape a second arrest before being sent to organize resistance among the Libyans against the Italian invasion of North Africa in 1911.

The first Ottoman leader to call himself "Sultan" had been Murad I, in 1359. With the conquest of Constantinople in 1453, the Ottoman state became an Empire; in 1517 the Ottoman Sultan also became the Caliph—the head of the whole Islamic community. The Caliphate had moved from Baghdad in 1258 after the city had fallen to Hulagu Khan, grandson of Genghis Khan. The Caliphate had been taken on by the Mamluk Sultans of Cairo, but after their defeat in 1517, had been passed on to the Ottoman Sultan, Selim I (father of Suleiman the Magnificent). The Sultan was the all-powerful head of the mighty Ottoman Empire; as Caliph, he was head of all Muslims. These ancient titles, embodied in Sultan Mehmed VI, were about to be overturned in a remarkable revolution.

Kemal fought in the various minor wars that preceded World War I. Having been involved in Libya against the Italian invasion of Libya in 1911, he again saw action against Bulgaria in the Balkans in 1912. By 1914, he was a lieutenant colonel. At the outbreak of war, the Ottoman Empire sided with the Central Powers—Germany, Austria-Hungary and their empires—and Kemal was posted to Gallipoli to resist the Allied landings, following Churchill's failed naval expedition to attack the Dardanelles and open the Black Sea to Allied shipping. The Ottoman army mounted a brave and well-organized defence. Opposing the landing of Australian troops at an unexpected location to which the current had carried the Australian boats, Kemal exceeded his authority by ordering his best regiment, the 57th, to move up to some high ground that would command the landing area. In his order of the day he wrote, "I do not order you to attack, I order you to die. In the time it takes us to die, other troops and commanders can come and take our place." Most of the 57th did die in that battle, and the Anzacs were so shaken that their commander asked that night to be evacuated. They were instructed to hold on and dig in because other attacks would take the pressure off their beachhead. The Turks also dug in.

A German commander was impressed by Kemal: a "clear-thinking, active, quiet man who knew what he wanted. He weighed and decided everything for himself, without looking elsewhere for support or agreement to his opinions."[34] What Kemal wanted was for his troops to push the invaders back into the sea or die in the attempt. Kemal demonstrated his own readiness to die with conspicuous bravery and *sang froid*. As a succession of shells dropped in a pattern ever-closer to his trench until it was a certainty that the next would be a direct hit, he refused to take cover: "It's too late now. I can't set my men a bad example." By chance, there was no next shell.[35]

Kemal went on to fight the Russians in the Caucasus Campaign: for centuries the Russians had wanted control of the Bosporus and the Dardanelles (and, by definition, of Constantinople), to give them access to the Mediterranean from the Black Sea. They planned to settle Cossacks in the area. Early defeats by German Armies in Prussia, on Germany's Eastern Front, compelled Russia to withdraw half its troops from the Caucasus; when the Russian revolution broke out in 1917, the Russian army began to disappear altogether. One of the few Turkish successes of the Caucasus war had been a briefly successful counter-offensive by Mustafa Kemal. The end of the war found Kemal in Aleppo, in northern Syria, facing the advancing troops of British Field Marshall Allenby. Kemal established a defensive line on the Jordan that became the territorial basis for the eventual armistice.

The Ottoman Empire had sided with the losers of World War I and was greatly weakened by the war itself. The Triple Entente of Britain, France, and Italy had been planning the carve-up of the ailing empire since early in the war. The oil deposits of the Middle East were the main focus, and there were other territorial interests in the Empire's previous territories from Italy, France and, in particular, Greece. The finances of the empire were to be controlled by the Allies. The straits between the Black Sea and the Mediterranean—the Bosporus, the Sea of Marmara, and the Dardanelles—were to be international waters; certain ports including Constantinople were to be international Free Ports. Britain was given a mandate in Mesopotamia, with an oil concession granted to the Turkish Petroleum Company (later renamed as the Iraqi Petroleum Company). Britain was also to administer Palestine.

Territory around Smyrna on the western coast of Anatolia (the peninsula between the Black Sea and the Mediterranean that makes up most of modern Turkey) was to be occupied by Greece but nominally owned by the Ottoman Empire. At the end of five years there was to be a plebiscite to ask if the local population would like to become a part of Greece. Italy had occupied the Dodecanese during the wars of 1911–12 and would keep these islands; southern and western Anatolia would be a "Zone of Italian Influence"; Syria and southeastern Anatolia would be a Zone of French Influence. Nobody was quite sure about where Kurdistan's borders should be (not even, to be fair, the Kurds themselves). A referendum was planned, but the issue was never settled, leaving that contentious issue completely unresolved. The whole arrangement was an imperial carve-up with a distinctly nineteenth-century flavor. This Treaty of Sèvres, as the proposed agreement was known, would surely have been ratified if it were not for one man: Mustafa Kemal.

Sultan Mehmed V had died just before the end of World War I. His successor and brother, Mehmed VI, offered no resistance to the victorious Allies' plans for the dismemberment of his empire. The Ottoman Parliament had been dismissed once again. The Turkish army was disbanded. Kemal, already a general without a job, found his rank and responsibilities (and salary) reduced. The Sultan launched a wave of British-supported arrests of political figures. It became increasingly likely that Kemal would be arrested soon. He began to talk to like-minded allies about a movement of national resistance. The nationalist mood was stronger in the interior than in Constantinople and was being encouraged by local actions against the Greeks now moving into the Anatolian mainland: Greece, with the increasing support of the British Prime Minister, Lloyd George, was pursuing the 'Grand Idea' of an expanded Greece that would include all of the areas that had come under Hellenistic influence across the ages. This included a significant area of the western coast of Anatolia, on the Aegean coast.

The Grand Vizier was the Sultan's Chamberlain and head of the government, whose offices were known as the Sublime Porte. (The courtyards inside the gates of palaces and cities in the Middle East were traditional gathering places, and the gate (*porte*) to the Grand Vizier's Palace in Topkapi, Constantinople—where foreign ambassadors to the Ottoman capital were welcomed—was known as the Sublime Porte.) The Grand Vizier now looked for an officer who could restore order and allow the British Authorities to pursue their plans. A minster who was supportive of nationalist aims put Kemal's name forward for the job; another well-wisher in the ministry helped to extend Kemal's powers. Despite the Grand Vizier's suspicion of Kemal, he was glad to get him out of Constantinople: Kemal was despatched as Inspector-General with two army corps at his disposal, with direct control over five provinces and indirect control over five others. The Sultan's Grand Vizier had been encouraged to hand substantial powers to the man who was about to destroy them both.

In May 1919, 20,000 Greek troops landed at Smyrna. The local Greek population took to the streets in welcome. Turkish troops surrendered and were marched to the waterfront. As they passed they were struck and their fez snatched from their heads. The fez had been the traditional headgear of the Ottoman Empire since medieval times; its lack of a brim allowed the wearer to press his forehead to the ground during prayer as required by the Muslim faith. To the Christian Greeks, the fez was a symbol of their ancient enemy, the Turks, and their Islamic faith. One Turkish colonel refused to take off his fez and stamp on it; he was shot. Later, the Greek troops lost control and shot hundreds of Turkish troops, whose bodies were thrown into the sea.[36]

Constantinople was in uproar; the Sultan wept—though if he had paid any attention to the plans of the Allies, he should not have been surprised. Kemal sailed for the port of Samsun, in northern Turkey, ostensibly to take up his Inspectorate. The British had woken up, too late, to the danger that he represented. Kemal ordered the boat to stay close to the Turkish coast in case the British tried to intercept them, but they made their landfall safely. He began to rouse the locals, who were largely unaware of the Greek landings at Smyrna. Meetings were held at mosques. Kemal made contact with all Turkish army units surviving in Anatolia.

The telegraph system was much more widespread than the telephone, and Kemal made full use of it. He bombarded the War Ministry with complaints about British activities: unauthorized troop movements; support for Greek partisans. The British demanded his recall. Kemal moved inland. He sent a circular to all local provinces requesting their attendance at National Congresses at Sivas in the west and at Erzurum in the east. The British tried to round up all armaments in the region, but were met with cheerful obstruction. There were "a suspiciously large number of accidents on the railway" —the British official was forced to take to a camel caravan when the railways were at one time out of action for several months. An artillery park with 40 modern guns was discovered. The Turks smote their foreheads: these guns had, most regrettably, been "overlooked."[37]

Telegrams to Kemal came thick and fast, calling on him to return to Constantinople, where his life and freedom were guaranteed by the Sultan. He was called on to resign his office as Inspector-General. Kemal did finally resign before he might be dismissed, but was very anxious about the effect that his lack of a formal role would have on his followers. His Chief of Staff declared that he could no longer report to Kemal, since he had no military capacity, and asked to whom he should now deliver his documents. It was only when a senior officer saluted Kemal and told him that the officers and men still accepted him as their commander that Kemal knew that his prestige had survived his official rank. His carriage was delivered, complete with cavalry escort. It had been a dangerous and significant moment.

The Congresses at Erzurum and Sivas drafted what was to become the National Pact, which insisted on the preservation of Turkey's existing frontiers and called for the election of a provisional government. The Sublime Porte issued a warrant for Kemal's arrest. Kemal hit the telegraphs again, making contact with military commanders and civil authorities around Anatolia. He was given a mandate to act on their behalf. He telegraphed an ultimatum to the Grand Vizier, signed in the name of the Congress, declaring that the cabinet was coming between the nation and its Sultan. It declared that Congress would now deal only with the Sultan.

The General Assembly of the Sivas Congress announced that a Representative Committee would act as a provisional government and maintain order in the country in the Sultan's name until a new government could be formed that had the confidence of the nation.

The Committee had never in fact met. Kemal signed all documents on the Committee's behalf with a seal. The Congresses had been real enough: with some semblance of a democratic mandate, Kemal was now waging war on the government virtually single-handed.

Kemal's control of communications was his key strength. Telegrams continued to arrive at the Sublime Porte from Kemal's network of military commanders and regional civic authorities, demanding the resignation of the government. The British knew that only a withdrawal of the Greeks from Smyrna would placate the Nationalists, and this was not an option. To commit troops to suppress the Nationalist uprising would be to start a new civil war with an uncertain outcome. The British began to withdraw troops from flash-points in Anatolia to avoid escalating the conflict. The Sultan forced the resignation of his Grand Vizier, and installed a Ministry of Conciliation to organize elections for a new parliament. Kemal had brought down the government.

The promised new elections returned a predominantly nationalist parliament which ratified the National Pact—the document spelling out commitment to an independent Turkey. British warships arrived at Constantinople under cover of darkness. British troops occupied the city and the ministries; parliament was dissolved. Kemal convened the first Grand National Assembly of Turkey at Ankara, in central Anatolia. The President of the previous parliament was persuaded to make way for Kemal by becoming Vice-President to Kemal's President. The Assembly drafted a Constitution Act, which struggled with the issue of establishing the sovereignty of the people while retaining the sovereignty of the Sultan, which the Assembly was committed to preserving. This played well in the country, which was not ready to envisage a nation without a Sultan. Kemal, however, managed to sideline discussions on the future of the Sultanate, while the Assembly confirmed the unconditional sovereignty of the people: a fundamental conflict that Kemal would soon resolve.

The Nationalists had continued to acquire arms; most were smuggled by nationalist supporters, but the country's enforced multi-nationalism began to play its complicated part—the Italians, who did not like the Greeks, began to sell arms to the Nationalists. The French seem simply not to have been too bothered; they allowed a large cache of arms to be stolen by Nationalists in Gallipoli, apologizing that they had been "outnumbered" by the raiders.[38] In August 1920 the Sultan's Grand Vizier signed the Treaty of Sèvres, confirming the Allies partition of the Empire. Greek troops began to move out through Anatolia. The Grand National Assembly voted through legislation authorizing the raising of a National Army that counter-attacked, finally stopping the Greeks at the Battle of Sakarya, which lasted for 21 days. During the battle, Kemal, as Commander-in-Chief, had said, "You will no longer have a line of defence, but a surface of defence [...] all of Turkey shall be our surface of defence."[39] This determined defensive strategy led the Greeks to decide that their losses were too heavy to sustain; they began a retreat to Smyrna on the coast. They asked the Allies for assistance, but the Allies had begun to see that the Treaty of Sèvres was unenforceable. They offered the Nationalists a modified version of the treaty, but Kemal rejected it. An all-out attack by the Nationalists drove the Greeks out of Smyrna. In October 1922, the British signed an Armistice with the Nationalists and it was agreed to settle the remaining issues at Conference in Lausanne the following month. Before the conference could begin, the National Assembly passed a motion instigated by Kemal to abolish the Sultanate. The last Sultan left Constantinople for Malta on a British battleship. The Ottoman Empire had ended. The Treaty of Lausanne recognized the republic of Turkey as an independent state. Kemal was elected President and began a series of dramatic reforms.

Kemal began to secularize the state, abolishing the Caliphate. The powers of the Caliphate were transferred to the Grand National Assembly and, despite sporadic attempts to recreate the institution elsewhere, the title has been inactive ever since. Kemal also abolished religious orders such as the Dervishes, along with religious courts and the practice of polygamy. A rebellion against this secularization was put down, allowing Kemal to repress all political opposition through a Maintenance of Public Order Act. The original Grand National Assembly had been replaced by a new parliament consisting almost entirely of Kemal's new People's Republican Party. An assassination attempt allowed him to remove some old political enemies from a rival political party, the Committee of Union and Progress (of which Kemal had once been a member) by the effective expedient of having them hanged. This was Kemal's only major purge. Thereafter the new republic was essentially a one-party state.

Kemal's reforms continued and included the social and political emancipation of women, and the creation of a thoroughly modernized education system, drawing heavily on the advice of American educationalist, John Dewey. In the absence of foreign investment or oil reserves, Atatürk established a statist economy that carefully nurtured the tobacco and later the cotton industries. He helped to create a national rail system and a modern banking and finance system. Kemal had not only established an independent Republic of Turkey from the collapsing Ottoman Empire in the face of the intentions of the victorious allied powers and of the territorial ambitions of Greece, he had revolutionized the new nation's administration, and set it on the road to becoming a modern, democratic, industrialized state.

MUHAMMAD ALI
(b. 1942)

Muhammad Ali is a leader who did not set out to be a leader. He was never a leader of men, but he became a role model and a hero; he allowed people to think that they could behave in a different way. He did this by being his own man, despite the fact that this brought the weight of the whole American establishment down on his head.

In the 1960s, to be the professional heavyweight boxing champion of the world seemed more important than it does today. The sport, the championship, the fighters themselves, all seemed more significant than they do now. When Cassius Clay, as he was then called, took the title from Sonny Liston and said, "I am the greatest," it didn't seem like a foolish boast. Boxing matches of the time were shown live only on close-circuit TV. When Muhammad Ali—Clay's then-new Islamic name—fought Sonny Liston for a second time, millions of Americans watched the rebroadcast of the fight. It seemed to matter; it was a big thing. And, in America, in the 1960s, this big thing was inevitably tied up with money, politics, and race.

When Clay had declared his conversion to Islam and his membership of the radical black Nation of Islam, it was like a slap in the face for the white boxing establishment. Cassius Clay, a young black kid, was supposed to be grateful for the opportunities that professional boxing had offered him, and for the rewards that would now be showered on him as Champion of the World. He was also not supposed to make a fuss about being black; in fact, the good-looking pale-skinned Clay had looked like being a black boxer that white America could welcome: clever, funny, non-threatening. When Cassius Clay declared that he was abandoning his 'slave' name of Clay and that he would now be known as Cassius X (the Nation of Islam later gave Cassius the honor of his own "original" name of Muhammad Ali) he said a simple but powerful thing. He said, "I know where I'm going and I now the truth, and I don't have to be what you want me to be. I'm free to be what I want."

Ali later refused to be drafted for the Vietnam War. He challenged the establishment. He lost everything for a time, and then he won it all back. He became a hero for a generation of Americans, black and white—and for people around the world, especially in Africa. Now, American Presidents are keen to be seen alongside Ali and non-governmental organizations are grateful for his support for programs of hunger relief and conflict resolution.

The lesson for modern leaders is difficult. There are times when you have to be your own person: when you have to ignore all of the pressure and stick to what you want to do. It's dangerous, but it can't be wrong. As Ali said, "I have lost nothing. I have gained the respect of thousands worldwide. I have gained my peace of mind."

On the eve of Cassius Clay's big moment—his fight in 1964 against Sonny Liston, heavyweight champion of the world—there were rumors that Clay, as Ali was still known, was involved with the Nation of Islam: a radical black group. President John Kennedy had been assassinated in November 1963 and the Civil Rights Act, introduced by Kennedy in an attempt to end racial discrimination, had not yet been passed by his successor, President Johnson. The bitter riots in Birmingham, aimed at ending racial segregation in the southern American states, had happened the previous year, as had the March on Washington and Martin Luther King's epoch-changing, "I Have a Dream" speech. When young Cassius Clay got home to Louisville from the 1960 Rome Olympics four years earlier, having won the light-heavyweight boxing gold medal, he had been refused service in a 'whites-only' restaurant: "With a gold medal round my neck, I couldn't get a hamburger in my home town." [40] Racial tensions in America were still high and race was a big political issue. Now Clay, with a chance (though it was seen at the time as a very small chance indeed) of winning the greatest individual prize in American sports, was flirting with a group that had been declared 'un-American' by the state of California: a black organization that seemed to stand against everything that America held dear.

America had got used to the idea of black boxing heroes, but only relatively recently. Jack Johnson became the first black heavyweight champion in history in 1908, when he beat the Irishman, Tommy Burns, in Sydney. The *New York Times* made the politics of the situation crystal clear: "If the black man wins, thousands of his ignorant brothers will misinterpret his victory as justifying claims to much more than mere physical equality with their white neighbors."[41] You can't state a racist claim any more clearly than that. Johnson beat a succession of Great White Hopes and became the most famous black man in America. He went out with white girls and was eventually nailed on a trumped-up charge under the notorious Mann Act for the prohibited "transport of women across State lines for immoral purposes"; he went into exile in Mexico to avoid a prison term. In 1915 he was persuaded back to face the latest Great White Hope, Jess Willard, and was counted out in the 27th round. Jackson said he stayed on the canvas to give himself a better chance of getting back to the States. He returned five years later and served a year in prison. It was more than 20 years before another black sportsman had a shot at the heavyweight title.

In the 1920s, the white champion Jack Dempsey had simply refused to fight any black opponents; nobody thought that this reduced his claim to be champion. In the 1930s came Joe Louis: talented, black, and very conscious of the historic precedents for black fighters in America. His team coached him to win every contest by a knock-out, if possible, to avoid the bias of white judges, and never, ever, to be caught alone with a white woman.

Ironically, Louis' balancing act as a successful black boxer was made even more precarious by the burden of politics that was laid on his shoulders. He beat the Italian boxer, Primo Carnera, in 1935, when Mussolini was preparing to invade North Africa. The two boxers struggled unsuccessfully to avoid the pre-match build up of Africa versus Italy. Louis won in the sixth round. In 1936, Louis was beaten by the German, Max Schmeling, in a contest that the Nazi party was keen to portray as a triumph of Aryan superiority. Louis won the world title in 1937 from James Braddock ("The Cinderella Man") and in 1938 he faced Schmeling in a rematch. The black athlete Jesse Owens had dismayed the Nazis by his success at the Berlin Olympics of 1936: Louis' fight with Schmeling was equally laden with political symbolism. It was made crystal clear to Louis by the full weight of the American establishment that it was expected—as his patriotic duty, in the cause of anti-fascism and as an example of the decent behavior expected from his race—that he should beat the living daylights out of Schmeling. Louis did exactly that within two minutes of the first round.

For the first time in American history, the black guy had won and everybody was delighted. The black man had done the right thing by his race and by his nation. This was a victory for freedom against fascism. The distinct lack of everyday freedoms for American blacks would not be allowed to cloud the issue. Louis fought nearly 100 exhibition bouts for (segregated) American troops around the world during World War II—getting no reward above his GI's pay. Back home, after the war, he was pursued by the federal government for back taxes. He took up wrestling to pay the rent, and ended up being wheeled out at Las Vegas to meet and greet the high rollers.

The role-models for future black fighters had been cast. From the establishment's point of view, there were the bad guys like Johnson, and the "good representatives of their race," like Louis. Floyd Patterson fitted well into the latter mold, but at least he managed to do well from it. He was the youngest man ever to win the heavyweight title; he got rich and was invited to the White House. He married a white girl and moved into a white neighborhood: a perfect example of integration. Sonny Liston was not a good representative. He learned boxing in the state penitentiary, came out, and made a living as 'muscle' for debt collectors. He was convicted again for the offence of assaulting a police officer outside his own home—what, exactly, the police officer was doing outside Liston's house was not raised in court. The conviction made it harder to get fights; he became more dependent on backing from organized crime. In Philadelphia, Liston was arrested 19 times, once—surprisingly—for impersonating a police officer. When he left Philadelphia for Denver, Liston said, memorably, "I would rather be a lamppost in Denver than the mayor of Philadelphia."

Liston got to fight Patterson. The establishment made it very plain which side they were on: Patterson got messages of support from JFK, Ralph Bunche and Eleanor Roosevelt. The president of the National Boxing Association said, in the well-worn phrase, that Patterson was, "a fine representative of his race."[42] Liston knocked Patterson out in the first round to become heavyweight champion of the world. In the rematch, ten months later, he did it again.

In the perverse logic of racism, when Cassius Clay fought Liston in 1964, Clay was another 'Great White Hope'. An Olympic amateur boxing champion, pale-skinned, well-behaved, articulate, playing the marketing game, hyping the fight, going with the money, Clay lambasted Liston as "a big ugly bear": "I'm gonna give him to the local zoo after I whup him […] I'm young, I'm handsome, I'm fast, I can't be beaten […] He's too ugly to be the world champ. The world champ should be pretty like me."[43] For "big ugly bear" the white establishment could happily substitute "big ugly black man." Clay was sounding like a champion they could do business with.

The promoter of the fight nearly cancelled the match when he heard the rumor of Cassius Clay's involvement with the Nation of Islam. Clay had been seen with Malcolm X, a Nation of Islam firebrand who was in fact temporarily suspended from the organization for making inflammatory remarks about the recently assassinated President Kennedy. The Nation of Islam wanted to distance itself from moderate Christian leaders like Martin Luther King. The Nation was everything that white America didn't want them to be; black, proud, African, non-Christian, anti-integration. But, in the fight world, money talks. Sonny Liston was the seven-to-one favourite to win the fight; the only interest in the match was to see exactly how the loud-mouthed, boastful young Clay would get beaten. Clay managed to avoid admitting an involvement with the Nation but also promised there would be no public confirmations or denials about the Nation before the fight. The match went ahead. Clay beat Liston in seven rounds.

Clay was now the heavyweight boxing champion of the world. Huge wealth, fame, and the warm embrace of the establishment all beckoned. Clay announced his conversion to Islam and his membership of the Nation. He would now be known as Cassius X —discarding the surname that some African slaves took on from their white owners after emancipation. It was seen, though it should not have been, as a kick in the teeth for white America, for boxing, and for the establishment.

Clay set out his case for being seen as a "good boy" to the press. "I'm no troublemaker [...] I'm a good boy. I have never done anything wrong. I have never been in jail. I have never been in court. I don't join any integration marches. I don't pay attention to all those white women who wink at me [...]." It was all sounding quite hopeful until the sting in the tail: a simple but searing statement of individuality: "I know where I'm going and I know the truth, and I don't have to be what you want me to be. I'm free to be what I want."[44] The establishment didn't miss the message. The one thing that Clay was not supposed to be was his own man, let alone declare a different allegiance: non-American; non-Christian; African; Islamic. It got worse.

Malcolm X took Cassius X to the United Nations to meet African delegates. Cassius X said, "I am the champion of the whole world," and I want to meet the people I am champion of."[45] He then announced a tour of Africa and Asia, accompanied by Malcolm X. Suddenly, two African-Americans were acting as diplomatic representatives of their fellow black citizens of America and bypassing all normal diplomatic channels. Cassius X had only recently flunked the qualifying test for eligibility for the US Armed Forces because of his writing and spelling skills. Cassius insisted that he had tried his hardest to pass. Then the Nation of Islam bestowed a rare honor on Cassius: an "original" name. He was to be known as Muhammad Ali—a name more in keeping with the new champion's role as an international ambassador for the faith. Few American sports journalists used the name at first, though the British press did.

In 1966, with the American war in Vietnam intensifying, the required pass-rate in the qualifying test for the armed forces was lowered: Ali retrospectively passed the test and was eligible for combat. He made it plain that he did not intend to be drafted. Ali's off-the-cuff remark at the time was, "Man, I ain't got no quarrel with them Vietcong." With this simple statement, Ali had done it again. The individual was not supposed to question the state. If the man said you were at war with the Vietcong, then you were; your personal opinion was not a issue. Ali had raised the spectre of the popular consensus for the war (or the lack of it). In the case of his refusal to fight, it was difficult to cast the traditional slur of cowardice on the heavyweight champion of the world. At the time of Ali's outburst against the Vietnam War, he was a lone voice within the establishment of sportsmen or popular performers, other than those few with long-standing connections to the political left. Most people still supported the war. *Life* magazine had run a special issue entitled, "Vietnam: the War is Worth Winning." TV and newspaper coverage supported the war effort.

As the war progressed, both the toll in American lives and the disproportionate cost that the black community was being asked to bear also became clear: a far higher proportion of blacks eligible for the draft were actually drafted than was the case for whites. Black casualty rates in Vietnam were also disproportionately higher; blacks were far more likely to get killed in combat than their white comrades because they were more likely to be given frontline roles. Ali's stance resonated increasingly strongly with both black and white citizens as America became increasingly less confident of the war's moral justification. In 1967, Ali refused to step forward for his induction into the US Armed Forces and was warned that he was committing a felony. On the same day, his license to box was suspended and he was stripped of his world title.

Ali filed for deferment as a conscientious objector. Judge Lawrence Graumann ruled that Ali was "sincere in his objection on religious grounds to war in any form." The Justice Department argued that Ali's objections were "racial and political" and overturned the recommendation. At the retrial two months later, the jury convicted Ali after deliberating for only 21 minutes. The judge imposed the maximum sentence. The case went to appeal, but the sentence was upheld. The case was referred to the Supreme Court. Ali was looking at a long jail sentence.

In 1970, the New York Supreme Court judged that Ali had been unfairly denied a boxing license; at least he was able to box again. Ali stopped Oscar Bonavena in the 15th round at Madison Square Gardens, giving him a chance to regain the heavyweight championship from Jo Frazier, who had gained the title in Ali's absence. Frazier was undefeated. In March 1971 Ali met Frazier in an epic attempt to regain his title. He lost on points, and was knocked down by Frazier in the 15th and final round. It was his first professional boxing defeat, but later that year the Supreme Court reversed Ali's conviction for refusing the draft. He was a free man.

Ali fought his way back to a title fight; he lost to Ken Norton (who broke Ali's jaw) and then beat Norton in a rematch. George Foreman won the heavyweight championship from Frazier, and Ali subsequently beat Frazier in 1974. In October that year, Ali got his shot at the new world champion, and regained the heavyweight championship of the world from George Foreman in the world-famous "Rumble in the Jungle" in Zaire.

By taking a principled stand on matters of individual conscience, Muhammad Ali became, unintentionally, a great leader. Ali helped to establish the right of America's black citizens to be citizens on their own terms, without having to conform to a particular set of expectations. Ali became an iconic leader for a generation of people, black and white, across the world. Ali never asked that everybody should follow him or adopt his philosophies, he merely asked for the right to hold his own opinion. His simple statement of where he stood and of what he intended to be shook the establishment into recognizing that there were different ways of being an American citizen. Though this had special resonance for African-Americans at the time, it had an equally strong impact on their white fellow-citizens, uncertain as to how to respond to an establishment that they felt had lost touch with their own values. Few people who have set out to be leaders have been as successful in changing hearts and minds as was Ali in his un-chosen role as an opinion-leader for 1960s America.

5

BRINGING
PEOPLE WITH
YOU

There is no hierarchy of talents for management; some managers have certain strengths, others have other strengths. Nevertheless, it is hard to imagine a successful manager who is not able to bring people with them.

Bringing people with you is not one skill, but a set of skills. Some managers bring people with them because they are good speakers. They may or may not be good at motivating people face to face, but if you put them on a podium, or behind a microphone, then they are able to inspire an audience to follow them to the ends of the earth. Others achieve the same ends, more painstakingly, through their actions. They keep on doing the right thing, consistently, until people can see the intention that runs through their actions. At that point, like-minded people tend to come on board and to follow that leader.

The third kind of manager, probably the rarest of all three, is the genuine diplomat. These managers, the diplomats, highlight the inevitable tension that lies in the concept of bringing people with you. With their own team, leaders want to set out the real facts of the matter as persuasively as possible and to have their team members wholeheartedly buy-in to the proposed plan of action. In the wider context within which an organization works, managers must also try to bring along their various constituencies—customers and suppliers; the local community; the media; the industry—without them having bought into the plan in the same way. These constituencies may be brought with you by a combination of factors, including appeals to self-interest and common interest. They may come with you, but only because there is something in it for them.

History has plenty of examples of great leaders who were not great diplomats. Often they had shown great diplomatic skills at the beginning of their career in bringing together interested parties and placating hostile factions—but forgot these skills or the need for them once they had established themselves in a position of power. The perfect manager, the master of every technique, will combine the rhetorical skills of a Pericles, the persistent tenacity and transparent decentness of an Abraham Lincoln, and the seductive diplomatic finesse of a Talleyrand.

Charles Maurice de Talleyrand-Périgord—or plain Talleyrand, as he has fortunately come to be known—seemed to possess the devilish skill of persuading people to do the exact opposite of what they had intended to do, by bringing them to the realization that it was in following Talleyrand's proposals that, after all, and surprisingly, their true interests lay. People didn't wake up the next day hating Talleyrand and wondering how they had let themselves be talked into doing something that they now regretted; they woke up the next day wondering why they had been so slow in coming to the right conclusion. Talleyrand was self-serving in the extreme, and yet his actions were more in the interests of France than were those of his master, Napoleon. Talleyrand saw the world of European politics as a subtle and shifting pattern of allegiances and favors; a world in which deals had to be struck in the constant attempt to serve everyone's self-interest as well as one's own. Napoleon saw Europe as a collection of enemies that needed to be subdued and bent to his will. Talleyrand's approach was better, and more sustainable.

George Washington is almost too large a figure from whom to draw small conclusions. It is interesting—and alarming—to speculate what might have happened if a man of a lesser stature than Washington had taken up the presidency of the new United States of America, and indeed, whether the collective states would have been happy to elect anybody else as their President (Washington was elected twice with 100 percent of the electoral college votes; something that has never been repeated). Washington, as a General, had delivered victory against the British colonial powers; the 13 states huddled on America's eastern seaboard were now independent. Army officers, alarmed by the weakness of the Continental Congress during the war, urged Washington to become the head of state, the king of the new nation, to prevent another foreign power from quickly overpowering it.

Washington refused, with sincere indignation. He had been as keen as any man to shake off a foreign government that sought to put limits on what George Washington and his fellow Americans could do, without him—or they—being able to influence the actions of that foreign power in any significant way. If George Washington now became the new king in the land, then other people's liberties would be restricted in the same way that his had previously been restricted by the British. He and his fellow colonists had fought a war of independence to establish a republic; a republic it would be.

By refusing the chance to become king of the new country, Washington proved that he was the man most fitted to become its elected president. After his unanimous election, he at first refused a salary, but then recognized that a presidency without pay would only be open to rich men, like himself. President Washington was given remarkable powers by the 1st United States Congress, which he quickly restrained in practice by establishing what was, and was not, the role of the government's Executive. By proving that it was possible for a president to run a country without becoming a dictator —something that neither England's Oliver Cromwell had managed a century earlier, nor would France's Napoleon Bonaparte some 20 years later—Washington was instrumental in establishing a successful republican form of government: of the people, by the people, for the people, as Abraham Lincoln would later write. You can't bring people with you much more than that.

John Churchill, Duke of Marlborough, rose to great wealth from a position of relative poverty: his father had fought for King Charles during the English Civil War and had been heavily fined by a victorious Parliament for his pains. Young Churchill was given a place at court by the newly-restored but impecunious Charles II; he became a page to James Stuart, the younger brother of Charles II, and learned the skills of a courtier. Churchill quickly proved himself to be a brave fighting man and a great general. His loyal support of James, a Catholic, during plots to prevent James' accession to the throne (because of his Catholicism), earned Churchill his first ennoblement. He was later to desert his master when James was overthrown by William of Orange and his wife Mary (James' sister), in England's Glorious Revolution. The new king and queen never quite trusted the turncoat Churchill; it took all of his diplomatic skills to stay in a position of influence and he was briefly imprisoned in the Tower of London on suspicion of plotting to restore James to the throne. After the death of Mary, and then William, Queen Anne came to the British throne and the Churchill family fortunes improved. Churchill was put in overall command of the Allied Dutch, Austrian, and German forces, fighting against Louis XIV of France. Marlborough's diplomatic handling of the Allied forces enabled him to win a great victory despite, in effect, the wishes of his Dutch allies—though his diplomatic skills were such that the Dutch probably didn't even notice that Churchill had acted entirely unilaterally.

CHARLES MAURICE DE
TALLEYRAND-PERIGORD
(1754–1838)

Talleyrand was Napoleon's Foreign Minister and later Grand Chamberlain and Vice-Elector of the Empire. Mannered, devious, gammy-legged, a consummate diplomat, Talleyrand's aristocratic background led during the French Revolution to the issue of a warrant for his arrest, but he had wisely absented himself—first to England and then to America—and survived when so many of his peers were executed. He has been described, variously, as 'the Prince of Diplomats' (which he was) and as a cynical and opportunist racketeer and traitor (which he also was, but in the most distinguished way).

Talleyrand was a contradictory figure, in many ways. Everything about Talleyrand was redolent of pre-revolutionary France, of the old regime: his elaborate, old-fashioned style of dress; his habit of rising late in the morning and greeting visitors in his dressing room as the whole elaborate Talleyrand façade was created; his languid manners; his view of politics. "Those who did not know the years before 1789," said Talleyrand, "do not know the true sweetness of life." And he expressed his disdain of generals rather neatly: "War is much too serious a thing to be left to military men."

Talleyrand watched with growing horror as Napoleon moved from the successful defence of France's borders against the monarchies of Europe—who wanted to undo the effects of the French Revolution—to expansionary wars that gave Napoleon great glory (and much-needed cash in the form of war reparations from conquered territories), but that did nothing for France's long-term security, and disturbed the delicate diplomatic balance of Europe: something that Talleyrand had helped to cultivate for all of his adult life. Talleyrand felt so strongly about Napoleon's alliance with Russia that he resigned as Foreign Minister. Napoleon saw the alliance (at least for a few moments) as a coming together of the great Emperors of East and West and hoped to persuade Russia to join his great scheme: a Europe-wide embargo on trade with England—that "perfidious Albion" who had disturbed all of Napoleon's plans. Talleyrand saw the alliance as a gross disturbance of the balance of European power. He began to accept payments from both the Russian Tsar and the Austrian Emperor to advise them how best to deal with Napoleon. Talleyrand also kept up his relations with the exiled Bourbon King and was, eventually, to welcome the restored Louis XVIII back to his throne after Napoleon's final defeat. "Treason," said Talleyrand in a different context, "is a matter of dates."

Talleyrand's diplomacy, though self-serving, was undertaken in the best interests of France, as Talleyrand saw them, and Talleyrand was usually right. He was one of the great persuaders; someone who led others not by being in a position of command but through influence, reason, and an exceptionally acute understanding of human nature. Talleyrand, always an opponent of violence, was a master of the subtle art of achieving a balance of self-interests in order to bring about settlements with real foundation, in stark contrast to the settlements imposed by Napoleon by force of arms. "The art of statesmanship," said Talleyrand, "is to foresee the inevitable and to expedite its occurrence."

Born into the aristocracy in Paris in 1754, a deformed foot prevented Charles Maurice from taking up a career in the army. Talleyrand himself ascribed the limp to a childhood fall, but it seems certain that he suffered from a congenital 'club foot'. This led the young Talleyrand towards the other traditional career for minor aristocrats—the church—despite a rather obvious lack of any significant faith. In 1789, thanks to paternal influence, he became Bishop of Autun. Surprisingly—or in Talleyrand's case, probably presciently—he supported the revolutionary cause at the outbreak of the Revolution, assisting in writing the Declaration of the Rights of Man and proposing the Civil Constitution of the Clergy, which nationalized the church. He was excommunicated by Pope Pius VI for his pains and resigned his bishopric, a self-defrocking that also allowed him to marry.

Talleyrand was apparently extremely attractive to women, which seems to have been due more to his wit than his looks. A Scottish peer remarked at the time that Talleyrand was, "the most disgusting individual I ever saw. His complexion is that of the corpse considerably advanced in corruption." This seems to have been a reasonably fair comment since, when Talleyrand died, the restored King Louis XVIII commented, on being informed of the death, "But there is no judging from appearances with Talleyrand." This excellent *bon mot* may have been as much a reference to Talleyrand's famous immobility of face as to its complexion; his face never betrayed his thoughts, nor his emotions.

Returning from America in the safer political climes of 1796, Talleyrand became Foreign Minister for the *Directoire* (the revolutionary government that emerged after the Terror) but subsequently aided Napoleon in his 1799 coup against the *Directoire*, a charge that Talleyrand vehemently but unconvincingly denied —Talleyrand had cultivated the obviously talented Napoleon from the early days, throwing a magnificent ball for him on his return from Egypt. Later, Talleyrand was made Napoleon's Grand Chamberlain and Vice-Elector of the Empire, but he resigned after the Franco-Russian Alliance made at Tilsit in 1807, in despair at Napoleon's continued and increasingly megalomaniac drive towards the domination of Europe. Prior to his alliance with Russia, Napoleon had smashed the Russian ally, Prussia, whose great military reputation from the glory days of Frederick the Great concealed a rigidly disciplined but outmoded military organization. Napoleon went on to defeat the Russian forces in turn, but charmed the young and impressionable Tsar Alexander and offered both reasonable terms and a vision of Napoleon and Alexander as Emperors of the whole world, divided into East and West. In contrast, Napoleon imposed humiliating peace terms on Prussia, including the payment of massive war reparations. Great swathes of

Prussian territory west of the river Elbe were ceded to become the Kingdom of Westphalia, of which Napoleon's brother Jerome was to be King. Prussian territories in Poland became part of the Grand Duchy of Warsaw. The beautiful Queen Louise of Prussia (described by Napoleon as "the only real man in Prussia") broke down in tears—and was consoled by the ever-solicitous Talleyrand. It helped greatly to confirm Talleyrand's position with the aristocracy of Europe as a man they could deal with. Talleyrand, for entirely sound diplomatic reasons, was set against the new alliance with Russia and the treatment of Prussia. The latter's humiliation, in fact, spurred Prussia on to modernize not only its army but its entire state. A resurgent Prussia was to be a key factor in Napoleon's ultimate defeat.

Talleyrand had continued to keep in contact with all of France's enemies—with the exiled Bourbons, with Emperor Francis of Austria, and Alexander, Tsar of Russia—accepting, indeed demanding, payments from all parties. Talleyrand had never had any scruples about acquiring wealth along his diplomatic path. He made a killing when the Treaty of Amiens was signed in 1802, bringing a temporary peace between France and Great Britain, by buying Belgian bonds very cheaply—because he was one of the very few people in the world who knew that a condition of the treaty was that Belgian bonds would, indeed, be honored.[46] He also accepted payments from various German rulers during Napoleon's reorganization of German princedoms in return for protecting or enlarging their territories.

Talleyrand's continued intriguing led Napoleon famously to denounce him to his face in 1808 as "a shit in silk stockings." Talleyrand limped out of this dressing- down saying merely and, one likes to believe, languidly, "It is a pity that so great a man should have been so poorly brought up."[47]

What had led to Napoleon's rage was Talleyrand's plot, in partnership with Fouché, Napoleon's sinister Chief of Police (a man who knew where all the bodies were buried, in many cases literally), to carry out a coup to replace Napoleon with Murat, the charismatic cavalry commander whom Napoleon had first made Marshal, then

Duke and, finally and recently, King of Naples—an impressive career path for the son of an innkeeper. To face down the coup, Napoleon had left the war in Spain at a time when his continued presence could have been critical; with Napoleon gone, his marshals failed to smash the retreating British army under Sir John Moore, which was able to fight a tenacious retreat to Corunna and be evacuated by the Royal Navy, though without Sir John, who was killed in the defence of Corunna.

It is surprising that Napoleon did not have Talleyrand shot. There does seem to have been something of a personal bond between the two men; Talleyrand's charm was famously hard to resist. On his side, Talleyrand constantly acknowledged his (sometimes reluctant) admiration of Napoleon's drive and ambition, and of the bonds that had been forged between them in their common efforts for the revolutionary cause: "There are bonds that last a lifetime, and those I have contracted with the Emperor will last to my dying day."[48] Napoleon always acknowledged enjoyment of his late-night conversations with Talleyrand in the early days of power, as the two men—so brilliant in their very different ways—plotted and planned to defend the new Republic against the hostile monarchies of Europe. Later in Napoleon's career, after Talleyrand had resigned as Foreign Minister, the Emperor would feel the lack of his old friend's uncanny knack of getting things done, of oiling the wheels of international diplomacy. When Talleyrand's successor was taking too long to negotiate the essential cash reparation from Austria, after the Austrian Empire had suffered yet another defeat at the hands of the French, Napoleon lost his temper with his new minister. "In Talleyrand's time," said Napoleon, "we would have taken perhaps 60 million, and he would have had ten million," (that is to say, ten million francs would have been quietly siphoned off as a reward for Talleyrand's efforts), "but it would all have been finished two weeks ago. Now do it."

Talleyrand was indeed a born intriguer, but one who arguably had the greater interest of France more to heart than did Napoleon, who was beginning to become dangerously megalomaniac. "He is intoxicated with himself," said Talleyrand, who believed that France, having stabilized the revolution and regained her natural borders of the Pyrenees, the Rhine, and the Alps, should hold back from any further expansion of empire and work instead to form powerful alliances with the old European powers. Talleyrand saw the war in Spain for the pointless diversion that it was; he felt even more strongly—with even more vindication—about Napoleon's later invasion of Russia.

It is probably dangerous to take anything that Talleyrand said of himself as anything other than self-serving, but this passage from his memoirs seems believable: "I therefore served Bonaparte when Emperor as I had served him when consul: I served him with devotion so long as I could believe that he himself was completely devoted to France. But when I saw the beginning of those revolutionary enterprises which ruined him, I left the ministry, for which he never forgave me."[49]

It was Talleyrand who, after Napoleon's defeat and exile to Elba, would lead the Provisional Government under the restored Bourbon King Louis XVIII, and who negotiated for France at the Congress of Vienna, achieving an extremely lenient peace settlement for France. The victorious Allies had not even intended for France to be represented at the Congress. Talleyrand suspected, quite rightly, that the Allies intended to knock France back into a secondary position in European politics. As the representative of King Louis, Talleyrand inveigled his way to the conference table and began to play the four major powers off against each other, while subtly creating discontent among the minor powers of Europe who, also quite rightly, were mistrustful and resentful of the intentions of the big four: Austria, Prussia, Russia, and Great Britain. Talleyrand's first action was to unravel the Alliance. What could this word "Allies" mean when the alliance had existed only in order to defeat Napoleon, who was now successfully deposed? For his part, Talleyrand represented the interests of his patron, King Louis whom, after all, the erstwhile Allies had fought a war to reinstate.

Talleyrand not only completely unravelled the Allies' plans to force a settlement on France that would weaken her future position in Europe, he outrageously brokered a secret deal between France, Austria, and Great Britain agreeing that each would supply 150,000 men to aid the others in the event of aggression from Russia or Prussia. Talleyrand had exposed the secret fears at the heart of the old Alliance. France, far from being sidelined, was back at the heart of European politics, restored to her 1792 borders.

Napoleon's return from Elba undid much of Talleyrand's good work, leading as it did—after Napoleon's final defeat and exile to St Helena—to the far more stringent second settlement of 1815, which reduced France further to within her boundaries of 1789.

The last word should go to Talleyrand:

> "We have learned, a little late no doubt, that for states as for individuals, real wealth consists not in acquiring or invading the domains of others, but in developing one's own. We have learned that all extensions of territory, all usurpations, by force or by fraud, which have long been connected by prejudice with the idea of 'rank,' of 'hegemony,' of 'political stability,' of 'superiority' in the order of the Powers, are only the cruel jests of political lunacy, false estimates of power, and that their real effect is to increase the difficulty of administration and to diminish the happiness and security of the governed for the passing interest or for the vanity of those who govern [...]"[50]

GEORGE WASHINGTON
(1732–1799)

George Washington, the first President of the United States, led the revolutionary army that was to defeat the British Empire, and turned the 13 east-coast colonies—from Massachusetts and New Hampshire in the north to South Carolina and Georgia in the south—into the 13 "United States" of America. In the late eighteenth century, outside of the original 13 colonies, the majority of the land west of the Appalachians belonged to American Indians, and the land west of the Mississippi was claimed by Spain. The modern United States of America was still a long way in the future.

A man of commanding personal presence, Washington came to personify the struggle against the British. As commander-in-chief of the Continental Army, as it was known, he fought a dogged war for eight long years, suffering some heavy defeats but also some occasional victories of great psychological significance. His true genius lay simply in keeping the Continental Army intact as a fighting unit. The army survived a terrible winter in the second year of the war, losing a quarter of its strength (it had been only a meager 10,000 men to begin with) to starvation and disease. Washington seemed to hold the army together by sheer willpower and force of personality. Morale improved; men re-enlisted, and new recruits arrived. Eventually, aided by the French, the colonists wore the British down; after a decisive American victory at Yorktown, the British granted the 13 colonies their independence. A new nation had been born. A group of senior officers from the victorious American army, concerned at the weakness of the Continental Congress (delegates from each of the colonies who had been running the war effort and were now running the country), were determined to install Washington as an effective monarch to guarantee the stability of the new nation. Washington refused.

It takes a man of rare moral fibre to turn down a kingship. Great leaders are prone to decide that, come to think of it, they probably are the one person best-placed to assume complete control after all. Oliver Cromwell had failed the test in England in the middle of the seventeenth century, and turned the fledgling English republic into a military dictatorship, which soon lapsed back into a monarchy. Leaders with their hands on the levers of power at times of great revolution tend not to let go of those levers. Washington did.

Washington fervently believed in the republican virtues for which he had fought. He had come to have a great distaste for being a second-class citizen—a colonist—subject to laws and taxation imposed by a distant king and parliament. He had a pretty high estimation of his own worth; as a land-owning aristocrat he had always struggled with the notion that anybody else was better than him, but he had the moral rigor to understand that everybody else had the right to feel the same way as he did. Washington—the man who could have been king—chose instead the correct path of empowering other people. He brought the nation together under his careful Presidency at a time when it could so easily have fragmented, or been hijacked by a lesser man than Washington. He served his first term in office, and reluctantly accepted a second term—and then he went home.

Washington was born into a relatively prosperous plantation-owning family in Virginia. His brother married a daughter of Colonel Fairfax, one of Virginia's most powerful landowners, and when his brother died of tuberculosis, he inherited the substantial estate (with its 18 slaves) when he was 20 years old.

Washington joined the Virginia militia and was sent by the Governor of the colony (a British appointee, of course) to French territories in the north, to warn the French not to stray across the borders, near Lake Eyrie, onto land occupied by Britain. The French laid claim to a vast region of territory, known as Ohio Country, west of the Appalachian Mountains and east of the Mississippi, running the length of the sub-continent from the great Lakes to the Gulf of Mexico. One hundred years earlier, the great French explorer, La Salle, had claimed the whole of the Mississippi basin for France, and had explored the Ohio River Valley. The French declined to retire as requested and moved further south. Washington reported back on French movements; the French and Indian War was about to begin—a war between Britain and France, with American Indians fighting on both sides.

Washington acquitted himself relatively well in the wars against the French, and showed conspicuous bravery. He rose to the rank of Brigadier and fought alongside regular British troops. In 1758 he resigned his commissions and returned to his plantations in Virginia, marrying a wealthy widow of his own age and acquiring considerably more land. He became a prominent citizen of the colony, just at the time when Britain decided that the colonies in North America should contribute to the cost of the war that had recently been fought against the French in order to maintain the colonists' territories and freedoms. Parliament passed a Stamp Act in 1765, raising money by taxing all official documents, such as legal documents, wills, and permits. It was not expected to be a controversial measure, but the colonists had extremely strong opinions about the difference between taxation with their consent—taxation by their local, elected government—and taxation without their consent, imposed on them by a distant Parliament in London, in which they had no representation. "I think the Parliament of Great Britain has no more right to put their hands into my pocket, without my consent," wrote Washington, "than I have to put my hand into yours, for money."[51] "No taxation without representation!" became a popular rallying cry.

Washington had, like many colonists, already been offended by the Royal Proclamation of 1763. This attempted to consolidate British ownership of the territory won from the French in the war, and banned anyone from the 13 colonies from buying land or settling west of the Appalachians. Washington, like many others, had already laid claim to lands in the Ohio valley. Washington's growing anti-British conviction was more economic and personal than ideological. He had always had an aversion to authority and, as a wealthy landowner and a man of some standing in Virginia, he was deeply averse to the notion that a distant Parliament that he could not influence could affect his wealth, his opportunities, or his status.

Resistance to the Stamp Act spread, with secret societies threatening violence on anybody who sold the stamps; Washington supported a boycott of British goods. The Stamp Act was in fact repealed (Benjamin Franklin eloquently argued the American case in the British Parliament) but Parliament retained the right to raise further taxes and in 1767 imposed a tax on paint, lead, paper, glass, and tea. Although the taxes on items other than tea were also repealed (as British exports of these taxed items to the colonies sharply declined), the tax on tea remained. It led to widespread smuggling of tea by enterprising Americans who, naturally, also encouraged a boycott of British tea, imported from China. Stocks of unsold tea built up in the warehouses of the British-owned East India Company; the British government passed an Act allowing the Company to sell tea without payment of any tax to Britain, enabling them to undercut even smugglers' prices. A group of Bostonian businessmen (and smugglers) dressed themselves up entirely unconvincingly as Mohawk Indians and dumped a shipment of East India Company tea into the waters of the city's harbor—the Boston Tea Party. Nothing else was stolen. A padlock that had been broken was anonymously replaced with a new one a little later.

Ironically, the great Benjamin Franklin himself—hero of the repeal of the Stamp Act—had proposed the tax break for the East India Company, which was struggling not only because of the American boycotts but also because of war and famine in India and an economic slowdown in Europe. It was thought that the colonists would benefit from (and be grateful for) the lower price of tea. In fact, since the smuggling of tea into North America was so widespread as to constitute a significant local industry, the tax break to the giant East India Company was seen as another example of oppression by the British.

This colorful act of economic sabotage, however, shocked even those British politicians who had been well-disposed to the colonists. It was not merely a symbolic gesture: the tea was worth at least £10,000 at the time—equivalent to around £1m today. Parliament closed Boston port until the cost of the dumped tea was repaid (Benjamin Franklin spoke in favor of repayment), imposed martial law on Massachusetts and passed other Acts felt to be repressive.

Washington had been a member of the Virginia 'House of Burgesses' (a kind of locally elected parliament) when it was disbanded by the British Governor. He was instrumental in setting up unauthorized meetings that called for the boycott of British goods and was elected as a delegate to the First Continental Congress in Philadelphia, 1774, which supported the boycott and proclaimed their opposition to the "Intolerable Acts" that the British Parliament had passed after the Boston Tea Party. Conflict was rapidly approaching. The British occupation of Boston was a watershed for Washington; when Washington attended the Second Continental Congress, he wore his Virginia Militia uniform—the only man to do so.

By this time (May 1775) the first shots of the war had been fired. The month before, the British had moved to seize weapons stockpiled by local militia in Massachusetts, but riders (including the famous Paul Revere) had roused the countryside. In a clash at Lexington, British troops fired on 'minutemen' (militia men ready to respond 'at a minute's notice'), killing several. At Concord, the British met a large force of minutemen and retreated back to Boston, where they were besieged. When the Second Continental Congress met in May, it was known that British forces were on the way by sea to relieve Boston. Congress voted for the formation of a Continental Army and, the next day, George Washington was elected as Commander-in-Chief. Virginia's support for the revolution—as the richest and most populous colony—was essential, and Washington was the most eligible Virginian. His protests that he was not equal to the task may have been genuine—Washington had commanded nothing bigger than a regiment, and his military experience told him that a motley army of colonial militiamen was unlikely to defeat one of the most powerful professional armies in the world.

Washington took control of the Continental Army in July 1775 and continued the siege of Boston, eventually forcing the British, under General Howe, to withdraw by moving heavy artillery (and a number of dummy cannons) to a commanding position above the city. The British withdrew south to New York, and Washington moved after them. Congress issued the Declaration of American Independence and a British expeditionary force of 33,000 troops set off across the Atlantic. The first set-piece battle (and the biggest of the entire war) took place at Long Island, where the Continental Army of about 20,000 men was heavily defeated by a British force of similar size, and driven back to Brooklyn Heights. Washington managed to withdraw to Manhattan, but Howe later landed a force to recapture New York City and drive the colonists back to Harlem Heights. Washington was eventually forced to retreat to New Jersey and then across the Delaware River into Philadelphia. The Americans had lost 5,000 men killed or captured; with desertions running rife, Washington's army in New Jersey in November 1776 numbered around 6,000. The revolution was on the point of extinction. Fortunately, General Howe subscribed to the eighteenth-century notion that wars could not be fought in winter (he had also notably failed to destroy the Continental Army when it was trapped in Manhattan). His troops retired to their winter quarters around Trenton. At Christmas, Washington launched a daring attack across the Delaware and captured 1,000 British troops at Trenton. The British despatched General Cornwallis with 8,000 men to crush Washington, but Washington outflanked Cornwallis by means of an overnight march to attack his rear-guard at Princeton, winning another vital victory.

These victories were small, but they had immense psychological advantage. Everything had seemed lost, but now there was hope. But in both of these separate attacks, Washington had effectively risked the entirety of his tiny revolutionary army. From this point, he decided that the route to success was survival and doggedness (two very

Washingtonian attributes) and that the best way to win the war was not to lose it. Washington took his army into winter quarters at Morristown, New Jersey. Most of the revolutionary army had been enlisted on one-year contracts. As enlistments expired in January 1777, the strength of the Continental Army was probably a derisory 3,000.[52] Washington asked Congress for the power to raise a standing army. Standing armies were, of course, anathema to republican revolutionaries, but these were desperate times. Washington got his powers to raise troops—but was left with the laborious task of dealing directly with each individual state in order to do so.

The British government proved the depth of their resources by continually resupplying the British Army in America; they could do this because they were a sovereign nation, able to raise taxes and fund a national debt. The Continental Congress, in stark comparison, was hamstrung by the very principles that had caused the rebellion against Britain. If the colonists did not want to be taxed or legislated for by a parliament in London, no more did they want to be governed by a Continental Congress—which also operated on the basis of one state one vote, and could not therefore claim to fairly represent the nation as a whole. Washington sent his Circulars to each individual state, asking for men, supplies, and money to help the war effort. As the war progressed, he became more and more convinced of the need for a central body that could coordinate and fund the war effort. Despite his increasing frustrations with Congress, Washington never lost sight of the essential need for civilian control of the war effort, nor did he challenge their authority: the Continental Army must be subordinate to the Continental Congress.

In the following year, 1777, General Howe set out to take Philadelphia, seat of the Continental Congress, the revolutionary government. Washington put his army—now up to 11,000 men —between Howe and Philadelphia, but was outmaneuvered; British troops walked into Philadelphia unopposed, the disgruntled Members of Congress having fled the city, muttering about Washington's failure. Washington had, in fact, cleverly extricated his army from the defeat, a war-saving maneuver for which he got no thanks. In the north, however, one of Washington's generals had won a deeply significant victory: a British army marching out of Canada heading for Albany, New York, was successfully ambushed and harassed by American militia, and finally defeated at the Battle of Saratoga. Morale, much battered by the loss of Philadelphia, revived. The French, who were keen to strike back at the British after their disastrous losses in the French and Indian Wars, came into the war on the revolutionaries' side.

Washington and his army survived the terrible winter at Valley Forge, Pennsylvania, to emerge greatly reduced but intact and highly motivated, with Washington now established as the leader of the Army and, increasingly, as father of the nascent nation.

The British left Philadelphia and retired to New York, now potentially at risk from attacks by the French navy, where Washington kept them pinned down. The French navy were in fact more interested in capturing British possessions in the Caribbean than in attacking the mainland. The Royal Navy moved south to protect British interests in the Caribbean, making combined operations easier in the south than in the north. After initial successes under General Cornwallis, the British found themselves unable to win a decisive victory or to pin down the opposing army. The British moved back north to Yorktown, from where they planned to be shipped by the Royal Navy to New York. A crucial French naval victory against the Royal Navy at Chesapeake Bay meant that Yorktown could now be neither evacuated nor resupplied; Washington and his French ally Rochambeau raced south and besieged Yorktown. The surrender of Cornwallis in October 1781 marked the effective end of the war, as support in London for a continuation of the conflict in America evaporated.

It was at this point—with victory apparently won but far from secure—that the army, unimpressed by the behavior of the Continental Congress during the war, sought to make Washington a monarch, to prevent the new nation from succumbing sooner or later to some foreign power. A meeting was called to coordinate strategy amongst dissident officers; Washington cancelled the meeting on the grounds that only he had authority to order such an event, and convened instead a meeting of all officers. He spoke eloquently and forcefully against any notion of creating a king, monarch, or dictator. He identified himself with the revolution and with the struggle of the army, but drew the conclusion that any attempt to enthrone him would be a repudiation of all that they had fought for together, and as an assault on his personal integrity:

> "Let me conjure you, in the name of our common country, as you value your sacred honor, as you respect the rights of humanity, as you regard the military and national character of America, to express your utmost horror and detestation of the man who wishes, under any specious pretences, to overturn the liberties of our country [...]"[53]

Washington did not believe—demonstrably—in the desirability of kings. Happily, he did believe in the need for strong government. Even more happily, he believed that this government must be civilian and not military. Washington had demonstrated these beliefs time and again during the war of independence.

Washington retired from the army and went back home to his plantations in Virginia. By showing that he chose not to assume the mantle of absolute power, Washington, of course, proved that he was precisely the man who should be at the head of the new nation. When the new Constitution was thrashed out, Washington was elected as the first President of the United States, winning 100 percent of the electoral votes (something that no future president ever achieved). The Presidency was designed with Washington in mind; he was given considerable freedom of action, because he was trusted not to abuse that freedom. It is fortunate that he lived up to people's great faith in him. Many of the revolutionaries had an inbuilt distrust of any form of central authority, which reminded them of the bad old days under British rule. The new Constitution was much more concerned with how Presidents were to be elected or removed than it was with spelling out the Presidential powers. Washington had no illusions about the need for central control, but knew that this should be within the framework of a democratic system whose power derived from the will of the people which, in turn, would guarantee its citizen's essential freedoms, rights, and wellbeing. He was convinced that the United States had to be a nation, and not merely a confederation of states, or it would rapidly succumb to the influence of the other great nations—Britain, France, Spain—who were still controlling, or seeking to control, vast swathes of North American territory. Washington was the perfect embodiment of the kind of leader who could govern a people who were very reluctant to be governed at all. He turned the Constitution into a workable instrument of government. It is entirely possible that, without Washington, the great American republican experiment might have failed, as it was widely expected to do.

Washington at first declined a salary ($25,000 per annum) on the grounds that his was a public service that should not be rewarded, but then accepted the salary so that the future presidency should not become a rich man's preserve. He opposed the idea of party politics. He reluctantly accepted the second term of office to which he was elected in 1792, and then refused a third, establishing the practice that would become law when the 22nd amendment was passed in 1947. He retired gratefully to his home in Virginia and died in 1799. He caught cold, having failed to change his clothes after inspecting his farm on horseback, in freezing rain. He developed a sore throat and pneumonia, but probably died because of excessive blood-letting by his doctors, leading to dehydration. The British Royal Navy lowered its flags to half-mast in his honor.

JOHN CHURCHILL, DUKE OF MARLBOROUGH
(1650–1722)

John Churchill lived in one of the most turbulent periods of English and European history. He was born during Cromwell's Protectorate —England's brief flirtation with Republicanism. Charles II was restored to the throne when Churchill was 16, marginally improving the family fortunes. John's father, Winston Churchill (an ancestor of the British Prime Minister, Winston S. Churchill), had fought on the Royalist side in the English Civil War and been fined by Parliament as a result. Charles, though relatively impoverished, recompensed Winston for his losses and found him a minor government position—though Winston still died a debtor. Winston's son, John, became page to Charles' younger brother, James, Duke of York, while John's sister became Maid of Honour to James' wife, Anne Hyde, the Duchess of York—a gesture that had the advantage of not involving Charles in the expenditure of any hard cash, a commodity of which he was rather short. It seems likely that the young John Churchill decided at an early age that he would never be poor again, and he would not let matters of mere principle stand in the way of his first objective if he could possibly help it.

Thanks to his wits, charm, courage, and military prowess, Marlborough rose to the very top of English society. He became one of England's greatest generals and lived through the reign of five British monarchs: Charles II, James II, William and Mary (joint monarchs), Anne, and George I. In Europe, Churchill fought in the complex struggles between the various European powers of the time, including Spain, France, the Dutch Republic, the Holy Roman Empire, and the German princedoms. Having grown up at court as page to the young James, Duke of York, Churchill became the consummate courtier. He was handsome, charming, subtle and discreet: a natural diplomat. His great success in command of Allied forces in Europe owed as much to his diplomatic skills in keeping the various elements of the alliance more or less on-message as it did to his considerable military skills. Churchill was also prepared to act unilaterally if he felt that his diplomatic skills would not persuade his colleagues to take the necessary course of action—relying, of course, on his ability to make everything all right again after the event.

Like probably all great diplomats, Churchill was loyal to his masters right up to the moment when it became obvious that they were no longer on the winning side. Later in life, he deserted his old master James, who had then become King James II on the death of his brother, Charles II, and sided with the Dutch Prince, William of Orange, a grandson of Charles II and the husband of James' own daughter, Mary. William and Mary, both Protestants, were invited by Parliament to rule as joint monarchs in place of the Catholic James II, who was deposed in what became known as the Glorious Revolution. Churchill, probably the one commander who could have defeated William's invading forces, switched sides at the vital moment, ensuring William's victory.

Although Churchill was an outstanding general, his achievements in life were due mainly to his ability to thread his way through the minefields of political favor (he was imprisoned in the Tower of London for suspected treason at one point in his life) and to master the complicated command structures of the various European alliances for which he fought. Churchill's greatest skill lay in bringing people with him.

When Charles II married his Portuguese wife, Catherine of Braganza, she brought with her a substantial dowry, including £300,000 in cash, and the cities of Bombay and Tangiers. The Earl of Clarendon, father of Anne Hyde, Duchess of York, and a key counsellor to both Charles and his father, noted that when Charles first heard of Catherine's dowry, he "seemed much affected." Young Churchill had made the most of his position at court. At the age of 17 he obtained a commission as an ensign in the King's Own Company of the 1st Guards (later called the Grenadier Guards). He was posted to the newly acquired city of Tangiers and gained useful military experience fighting the Moors. There is a suggestion that the handsome young Churchill had already caught the eye of one of Charles' many mistresses, the beautiful Barbara Villiers, Duchess of Cleveland (who was also Churchill's second cousin). What is certain is that, on his return from Tangiers, Churchill was soon sharing his favors with the notorious Barbara, who was to bear six illegitimate children acknowledged by Charles as his own—hence the "Fitzroy" surname that they were allowed to adopt. One of these children may, in fact, have been young Churchill's. There is a marvellous story that the king nearly surprised the two in bed together, but that either Churchill leaped out of a window and escaped or that he hid in a wardrobe and was discovered. If the second story is true, then it is said that Churchill and Villiers begged the king's forgiveness on their knees and that Charles, with the moral realism of a man who knows that he is standing in a glasshouse holding a handful of pebbles, declared merely that Churchill was "a rascal," and forgave them both. Villiers gave Churchill the handsome sum of £5,000, which gave the young rascal a useful start in life.

Despite Churchill's father's wish that he should marry into money, he later married for love. However, his wife, Sarah Jennings, was the childhood friend of Princess Anne, daughter of Churchill's boss, James, Duke of York. Sarah became Anne's most trusted friend and confidante and when Anne became Queen (after the death of her older sister, Mary, and Mary's husband William), Sarah was to become one of the most influential women in the country. The queen did finally tire of the strong-willed Sarah and banished her from court, but by that time Sarah Churchill was Duchess of Marlborough and she and John were amongst the wealthiest of Queen Anne's subjects. The route to such fame and fortune was, however, far from straightforward.

In 1672, Churchill saw action at sea with his master, James, against the Dutch Provinces. A year later he fought with the Duke of

Monmouth for the French against the Dutch at the siege of Maastricht. In return for this support, Charles had received a useful payment of cash from the French. The Duke of Monmouth, James Scott, was another illegitimate son of Charles (by Lucy Walter, who by this time was dead). Charles recognized James as his son, but not as his heir. There were rumors that Charles and Lucy had secretly married, in which case Monmouth would be the rightful heir to the British throne. Churchill fought alongside Monmouth at Maastricht with a "forlorn hope" of 30 men who captured part of the citadel and held out all night against Dutch attacks. Churchill is reputed to have saved the Duke's life; certainly his bravery was commended by Louis XIV of France ("The Sun King") and noted by Charles II.

Some years later, Churchill gained his first diplomatic experience as part of an English delegation, seeking to negotiate a treaty with the Dutch provinces and Spain against France; Churchill impressed William of Orange with his negotiating skills. On his return to England, Churchill found that his Catholic master, James, had been excluded from London as hysteria grew about a "Popish Plot", supposedly discovered by a man called Titus Oates, and said to reveal plans by the Catholic Church to assassinate Charles II. Charles was distinctly unimpressed and unfazed by this tale, but his more anti-Catholic ministers were keen to believe the story, which was designed to prevent James from ascending to the throne. Churchill stayed with his master, James (in exile in Brussels and then in Scotland). When the plot was proved to be a fabrication, allowing James to return to London, Churchill was rewarded with a Scottish peerage and the Colonelcy of the King's Own regiment of Dragoons. (Dragoons were mounted soldiers carrying firearms—originally a primitive kind of flintlock musket called, in French, a *dragon*.)

At the death of Charles in 1685, James became King James II. Churchill's old commander and comrade-at-arms, the Duke of Monmouth, led a rebellion against the new king, pursuing his own claim to be the rightful heir. One supporter of Monmouth's claim was a young Daniel Defoe, author of *Robinson Crusoe*. The revolt was defeated at the battle of Sedgemoor and the victory was seen (with justice) as being due to the efforts of Churchill rather than to his unimpressive commander, the Earl of Feversham.

Monmouth was captured and beheaded, and a witch-hunt against Monmouth's supporters was conducted via the "Bloody Assizes" of the infamous Judge Jeffreys. No distinction was made between passive and active support of the rebellion (the charge being one of treason). Over 1,400 people were convicted and sentenced to death. In the end, 320 people were hanged (or, far worse, hanged, drawn, and quartered) and the remainder were deported to the plantations of the West Indies as indentured servants (a form of slavery). Many more died of typhus in England's filthy gaols before they could be transported.

There is an argument that the brutality of this repression was the first step in Churchill's growing disenchantment with his old master, James. He had also seen, during James' exile in Scotland, his master's disturbingly vicious suppression and persecution of a revolt by radical Protestant Covenanters, often using Catholic Highlanders to defeat and purge their Protestant fellow countrymen. What is certain is that Churchill was to abandon his King during the coming revolution —the Glorious Revolution.

James, a man of far more rigid principles and far less common sense than his brother Charles, continued to demonstrate an alarmingly single-minded tendency to divide the country on sectarian lines. He commissioned a large standing army, staffed predominantly by Catholics, in both England and Ireland. When Parliament sought to challenge this, he prorogued Parliament. Recent English history had led to a well-grounded fear both of Kings with a belief in the divine right of the crown (like James' father, Charles I) and of standing armies—like the Parliamentarian New Model Army of the English Civil War, which had refused to disband after the Civil War and which came, briefly, to run the country under Cromwell. Matters came to a head when James' second wife, the Italian Mary of Modena (his first wife, Anne Hyde, had died in 1671) gave birth to a son, James Stuart—a Catholic heir to the throne.

Before that birth, James' older daughter Mary had been heir to the throne. Mary had been raised as a Protestant at the wise insistence of Charles (who had almost certainly been a Catholic throughout his life and who 'converted' quietly on his deathbed). Mary had married William, Duke of Orange in 1677: they were both the grandchildren of Charles I and first cousins (which meant that William's father-in-law, James, was also his uncle). Mary would have been first in line for the throne of England on James' death, and William third. The birth of James Stuart tipped the balance in their favor: Parliament invited William to become joint monarch of England with his wife, in a constitutional monarchy based on the Bill of Rights—a revolutionary document that laid the basis for Britain's modern constitutional monarchy, and ensured that future monarchs would be governed by Parliament.

William landed at Torbay at the head of some 14,000 elite Dutch mercenary troops—rather in conflict with Parliament's initial suggestion that a token force would be sufficient. James faced the invaders at Salisbury. Churchill argued for an attack; the unimpressive army commander (Feversham again) advised a retreat. James himself was suffering from one of the nosebleeds to which he was notoriously prone, and took this as a bad omen. It may be that Churchill would have fought for James had the King shown any semblance of resolve, but Churchill only ever wanted to be on the winning side; he must have seen that his old master was doomed. He defected to William. On the following day, James' daughter, Anne, firm friend of the Churchills, did the same, deserting her own father's cause.

James fled to the continent; William and Mary were crowned. Churchill was rewarded by being made Earl of Marlborough, but neither William nor Mary really trusted him, partly because of his previous attachment to James II and partly because of the Churchill family's close relationship to Princess Anne, Mary's sister. Churchill—we must now call him Marlborough—spent several years campaigning in France (England had declared war as part of a Grand Alliance against Louis XIV's expansionist plans) and, as ever, acquitted himself well.

The Glorious Revolution was so-called because it was a bloodless affair, at least on English soil, but blood was to be shed in Ireland. In 1690, James attempted to regain his throne but was defeated in Ireland at the Battle of the Boyne. Marlborough went to Ireland after the battle and won victories, but was not given any command independent of William. Marlborough lobbied against William's appointment of Dutch commanders in the English army and planned to move two resolutions in the House of Lords, proposing that foreign officers could not hold commissions in the English army and that all Dutch troops would be sent home. This was both brave and rash of the usually cautious Marlborough. It can only be that he felt very strongly about the presence of foreign officers within the British Army and the presence of foreign troops on British soil—something dangerously close, for Marlborough, to a matter of principle.

In 1692 Marlborough was suddenly dismissed from all his army and government posts. It does seem certain that Marlborough had remained in contact with his old master, James. With Marlborough, this is less likely to be evidence of subversion and more likely to be an insurance policy against the far from unthinkable restoration of a Stuart monarchy. Suddenly, amid rumors of a Jacobite invasion supported by France, a treasonable letter was produced, apparently signed by Marlborough amongst others. (The term Jacobite refers to a supporter of James Stuart, and has no connection with the later radical French revolutionary Jacobins, named after their meeting place in a monastery in the rue St-Jacob in Paris.) Marlborough and the rest were sent to the Tower of London. The great Marlborough languished in a traitor's prison.

The letter was soon shown to be a forgery and the alleged plotters were released. Marlborough's return to full favor was a slower process. Queen Mary—who had taken against Churchill from the first—died in 1695, and he returned to court. Some years later there was a reconciliation with William, but William himself was to die in 1702. Queen Anne—that great friend of John and Sarah Churchill—was on the throne and war on the continent had escalated. Marlborough's moment had come.

The Habsburg Spanish King, Charles II, sickly from generations of Habsburg in-breeding, died childless and left his kingdoms to the grandson of the Bourbon Louis XIV of France. The Habsburg Holy Roman Emperor, Louis I, was keen to protect his dynasty. The Grand Alliance, formed earlier to resist Louis XIV, was reconvened to resist this new threat of French aggrandisement. Marlborough was put in charge of Allied British, United Provinces (Dutch), and German forces against the French in support of Austria and the Holy Roman Emperor, Leopold. It cannot have seemed long ago that he was fighting with the Duke of Monmouth for the French against the Dutch.

Churchill's powers of command were hedged by limitations: it took all of Churchill's considerable diplomatic powers of tact and persuasion to manage the operation with any success. He could not, for example, give direct orders to Dutch troops unless they were actively fighting alongside British troops; in every other situation he had to consult with Dutch political advisors.

Marlborough's main brief was to defend the Dutch territory against the French. He performed well, capturing Liège and several other towns from the French, for which he was rewarded with a full Dukedom. But the French also planned a direct attack on Vienna, capital of Leopold's Holy Roman Empire, across the Alps from northern Italy, supported by their Bavarian allies in the west and helped by a Hungarian revolt against the Empire in the east. Success would force the Emperor Leopold out of the war and see the collapse of the Alliance. If the French were successful, the war was lost. Marlborough saw the danger, but knew that he could not convince the Dutch to fight on the Danube, so far south of their immediate concerns. He got permission from the Hague to march to the Moselle river but, once there, wrote to the Dutch to say that the situation impelled him to take his troops into Germany to join their German allies in order to protect the Empire and the Alliance. A letter could, after all, take some time to arrive. Marlborough reassured the nervous Dutch that in the event of a counter-attack by the French in Marlborough's absence, he could ferry troops down the Rhine at speed in barges.

The French Marshall, Villeroi, stationed in the Low Countries near Brussels, was intended to pin down Marlborough's army in the region of Maastricht. As Marlborough set off for Coblenz, where the Moselle River meets the Rhine, he was shadowed all of the way by Villeroi. Marlborough crossed the Rhine, but turned south along its eastern bank, suggesting that his target might be Strasbourg, to the south in Alsace. Marlborough finally swung his army east, towards the Danube, and his destination was finally in no doubt: Bavaria, and on to Vienna. Along the route, Marlborough had been joined by Allied Hanoverian, Prussian, and Danish troops as he marched to join forces with the Austrian commander, Prince Eugene. The French quickly attempted to devise a strategy to counter Marlborough's unexpected line of attack but, in a recurring lesson from history, the centralized French line of command prevented the one man who knew what was actually happening on the ground—Villeoi—from taking independent and speedy action. Any change of plan had to be authorized by Versailles.

Marlborough had brought his army 250 miles from the Low Countries to the Danube in five weeks. It was a masterpiece of logistical planning. When the army reached its chosen destination, it pitched its tents, boiled its kettles and sat down to rest; Marlborough had managed his lines of supply so that everything they needed was to hand. The French, in contrast, had faced a tough march through the passes of the Black Forest in an attempt to head Marlborough off at the Danube. The difficult roads had proved treacherous for the supply wagons; local peasants, the victims of French foraging, managed to do away with several thousand French soldiers as they passed through the forests.

As the Franco-Bavarian armies sought to avoid a battle until sufficient forces could be brought up, Marlborough started to lay waste to the Bavarian countryside in order to force the issue. In the final, hard-fought Battle of Blenheim, Marlborough and Eugene inflicted a crushing defeat on the French and Bavarian armies. Vienna and the Alliance were saved, and Bavaria passed into the hands of the Allies. There were more battles to come, but Blenheim is seen as the pivotal victory that prevented what might have been a subsequent domination of Europe by France, and an entirely different future for Europe.

Marlborough was rewarded by a grateful Queen Anne, and a grateful nation, with the grant of the Royal manor of Woodstock, in Oxfordshire, and a huge grant of £240,000 to build a palace. Marlborough contributed to the building works, which were to finally cost in the region of £300,000 (about £17.5m in modern terms). The rest of Marlborough's life was not plain sailing. Despite further dramatic successes against the French, politics at home became ever more fraught. His wife, Sarah, finally fell out of favor with Queen Anne, partly for her vigorous support of the Whig Party, of whom Marlborough was a favorite and supporter. The Whigs finally lost power to the Tories; Marlborough was relieved of his post as commander-in-chief in 1711 and accused of various charges of embezzlement, all of which failed on the basis that the (very substantial) monies that Marlborough had earned during his tenure of senior military positions were based on long-established and common precedent (or in some cases had been explicitly provided for under the Queen's signature), and that most of the money so earned had been spent on creating an intelligence network in the interest of the nation's security. Some of the payments were nevertheless declared to be illegal, but these were overlooked. It can never be denied that Marlborough was particularly interested in the potential financial rewards of his many official titles and posts.

Marlborough and his family spent some years in exile on the continent but, after the death of Queen Anne and the accession of the Elector of Hannover as King George of England, Marlborough was welcomed back and restored to the role of Captain-General of the armed forces. The years, however, had taken their toll. Marlborough suffered a series of strokes, and died in 1722.

6

MAKING
THINGS HAPPEN

One of the most basic things that a manager has to do is to make things happen. As a junior, or even a middle manager, it will do you no harm at all to be seen rolling up your sleeves and sorting out whatever mess you may have inherited: whether it be completely revamping the training program, overhauling the bonus system, or making sure that everybody really understands the provisions of the Health and Safety Act. But, interestingly, each of the three leaders from history in this section illustrate the subtle point that the really effective managers are the ones who make things happen by means of good strategy and direction—by employing top-class team members and empowering them to take action—rather than by personally taking a problem by the shoulders and shaking some sense into it.

Oliver Cromwell and General George Patton were archetypical men of action. They were constitutionally unable to see things in a mess and not to sort it out themselves. Oliver Cromwell famously, but entirely unconstitutionally, threw the remnants of the English Parliament out of the House of Commons. Eventually, and to his great discredit, he ended up running the country himself, rather badly. Cromwell had helped to create a remarkable army for the Parliamentarians in their fight against the injustices of which they felt King Charles was guilty; Cromwell built up and commanded the best-organized cavalry troop in the country and went on to be a highly successful general. With King Charles arrested and Parliament uncertain as to how to proceed, Cromwell seemed oblivious to the fact that by leading the army to London in order to force Parliament to take the right (Cromwellian) course of action, he was guilty of behavior as high-handed and absolutist as any of which King Charles stood accused.

George Patton, like Cromwell, couldn't stop himself from sorting things out by personal and physical intervention. After the D-Day landings and the subsequent bitter fighting in the narrow hedgerows of Normandy, the Allied forces struggled to get their troops and armor out of the Cotentin Peninsula and found themselves snarled up in the little town of Avranches. Faced with a potentially invasion-threatening traffic jam in this small provincial French town, Patton jumped out of his jeep and onto a traffic policeman's box in the town center and started personally to direct traffic; it began to flow. Patton went on to lead his troops in an unstoppable dash across occupied France toward Germany. If the petrol hadn't run out, Patton might well have driven straight to Berlin (though, being Patton, he hadn't really thought through whether he would have any sort of back-up or support when he entered German territory). Neither Patton nor Cromwell could help themselves. They had to make things happen; themselves; straight away. They were both, as it happens, cavalrymen; possibly addicted to the exhilaration of the charge—the decisive moment in which the opposition is swept away. As a manager, you may want to have a cavalryman in your team: every army needs its cavalry, for quick, decisive action that strikes terror into the heart of the opposition. There is room for a bit of the cavalryman in every manager (male or female) but the clever manager never allows the urge to change things to override the strategic issue. Most importantly, if you can delegate the necessary action, then you should. You are supposed to make things happen, not to do it all yourself.

Zhou Enlai is a different example of a manager who made things happen. Zhou, actually, is the perfect example of a manager who spends his or her working life sorting out the messes that their bosses' madcap schemes have landed them in. That sort of problem, obviously, no longer arises in modern management, but it used to be quite common. Tragically, the madcap schemes of Zhou's boss, Mao Zedung (also often written as Mao Tse Tung) led to the deaths of millions of people, which Zhou was unable to prevent. When Zhou showed Mao the figures that showed how production had slumped during the pointless and vicious Cultural Revolution—the last paroxysm of unbridled Maoism—Mao had enough sense remaining to call a halt. Zhou himself was nearly "purged", but Mao knew that it was Zhou who kept China running. Zhou worked phenomenally hard; he established a routine of working until five in the morning and then sleeping until ten. The things that he had wanted to make happen for China were spelled out in the Four Modernizations that he got to the forefront of the agenda toward the end of his life: the modernization of agriculture, of industry, of defense, and of science and technology. A sound agenda for any national leader.

OLIVER CROMWELL
(1599–1658)

Oliver Cromwell proved himself to be, above all else, a man of action; a man who lived in remarkable times who, when called upon, found himself capable of remarkable deeds. Cromwell was a country squire from a Cambridgeshire family that had seen better times. His father died when the young Cromwell was still at University; his studies were cut short and he could have expected to spend the rest of his life tending his fields and raising children. Instead, he became a highly proficient cavalry leader; invented the concept of a professional standing army (as opposed to an army of regiments raised by wealthy men, or troops of foreign mercenaries); toppled and executed a King, and then rose to reign, in effect, in the King's stead. The fact that becoming the ruler of the nation was in direct opposition to everything that Cromwell had stood and fought for during the Civil War seems to have been lost on Cromwell himself. Presumably he would argue that he was a decent and godly man doing his best to run the country as it should be run (something that, sadly, could not be left to other, less reliable folk), whereas Charles I had been an unprincipled tyrant serving only his own ends.

Oliver Cromwell was that most dangerous of men: he believed that he could see God's intentions here on earth and was convinced that he knew what God wanted men to do. When things weren't going the way that God and Oliver wanted, he would lose patience, tip over tables, bundle people out of rooms, call in the troops—and take over. Cromwell would have made a good medieval baron (just as he was a very good military commander); but he made a very bad parliamentarian. As a result, Cromwell unfortunately makes a bad role model for leaders in modern consensual organizations, except in one sense: if you wanted somebody who could make things happen—somebody who would sort things out when the going got rough—then Cromwell would be your man. And in that sense, there is still much to be admired about him.

When Cromwell was born in 1599, Elizabeth I was still on the throne (she died in 1603). Cromwell was born into a moderately prosperous family of country gentlemen. Oliver's great grandfather was knighted by Henry VIII; his grandfather was knighted by Elizabeth I. Cromwell's uncle, another Oliver, entertained King James I so lavishly at Hitchinbroke (granted to the family by Henry VIII) that James returned several times for more. The expenditure nearly ruined the older Oliver, who was eventually forced to sell the great house. Young Oliver, though from the poorer side of the family, grew up in the classic tradition of minor English gentry, loyal to King (or Queen) and country. It would have seemed a monstrous notion in the early 1600s to imagine that this young gentleman would grow up to overthrow and execute his King, Charles, the eldest son of the King James whom Oliver's uncle had entertained too well.

Oliver was educated at Huntingdon Grammar School. The master of the school, Thomas Beard, was also a friend of the family. A fiercely anti-Catholic protestant, Beard believed strongly in "Providences" —the visible signs of God's will at work on earth, brought about by his chosen instruments, in order to reward the just and punish the wicked. It was a belief that the young Cromwell seems to have taken to heart.

Cromwell continued his education at Cambridge University. He was always more physical than intellectual; a man of action rather than a deep thinker. His studies were cut short by the death of his father. He returned home to look after his mother and sisters and seems, during this period, to have been given to drinking and brawling. "Here comes young Cromwell," the landladies of the local taverns would call, "Shut up your doors!"[54] Cromwell married in 1620, at the age of 21, and said goodbye to those rowdy days. Some years later, after a period of depression, he experienced a religious conversion to a radical form of

Protestantism. Cromwell became the Member for Huntingdon for the Parliament of 1628–29. Parliaments were summoned by the king only when he had need of them—almost always when he had need of their agreement to raise further taxation, in this case to fund a war with Spain. Parliament was becoming increasingly dissatisfied with this one-sided arrangement. Great religious and ideological shifts were taking place in Britain in the seventeenth century; a questioning of all forms of authority—religious and secular. Unfortunately, Charles Stuart, King of England, Scotland, and Ireland, was the monarch least well-equipped to handle such shifts with any political acumen.

The 1628 Parliament put to the king a "Petition of Right" raising fundamental questions about the relationship between monarch and subject on issues such as taxation without the consent of Parliament, and arbitrary imprisonment contrary to the ancient rights enshrined in Magna Carta. Charles' financial straits forced him to accept the Petition, but he argued that it only confirmed ancient rights and did not affect his royal "prerogative." The king, answerable to God alone, retained the right to make laws without Parliament and to raise taxation without Parliament in times of national emergency. When the Parliament of 1628 was dismissed, less than a year later, Charles ruled without Parliament for more than a decade.

The embers of conflict were smouldering on several fronts and Charles managed to fan each one into flame. The most contentious area was religion: Charles, married to the Catholic Queen Henrietta Maria of France, favored a more ceremonial Church of England at a time when any suggestion of 'popery' was abominated by most Protestants. Many Protestants were also keen to move from a church controlled by a hierarchy of bishops and clergy to a Presbyterian church—one controlled by elders of the church community. Some, the Independents, held the more radical view that individual communities could interpret scripture for themselves without any church hierarchy.

Parliament was finally recalled in 1640, promptly dismissed, and then recalled once more. In August 1642, Charles raised the Royal Standard at Nottingham—a feudal call for men to rally to their king.

Parliament also began to raise troops. Charles declared that he fought for "the Protestant religion, the laws of England, and the liberty of Parliament," Parliament issued a commission to raise troops "for King and Parliament." Charles had succeeded in provoking a civil war with subjects who still favored a monarchy. It wasn't the idea of a kingship that they objected to; it was Charles himself.

Cromwell went home to Cambridgeshire and raised a troop of soldiers for the Parliamentary cause. Like the majority of the Parliamentary army, Cromwell had never seen any form of military service. He had been a good "committee man" in Parliament and a forceful, though rambling and inelegant speaker. His main interest had been the rooting out of "popery". He now found himself at the head of a troop of cavalry.

Cromwell proved to be a quick learner and a forceful leader of men. He watched the early successes of the Royalist cavalry, led by one of the King's German nephews, the dashing Prince Rupert. At the Battle of Edgehill in 1642, early in the Civil War, Rupert's cavalry had overwhelmed their opposition. In the exhilaration of success, however, Rupert's cavalry swept on beyond the battlefield, chasing fugitives and plundering baggage trains, returning to the field to find that the battle had turned against them in their absence. Cromwell knew that he needed "men of a spirit that is likely to go on as far as a gentleman will go"—that is to say, men committed to the Parliamentary cause, in the way that the aristocracy were committed to the Royalist cause.[55] He looked for these amongst men like himself—"godly" men. Cromwell trained them hard and imposed strict discipline. They enjoyed some early successes, which Cromwell ascribed to God's favor.

His troopers' discipline was demonstrated in the significant battle of Marston Moor in July 1644. After a successful clash with Rupert's cavalry, Cromwell restrained his troop from the traditional hot pursuit; they regrouped and charged unexpectedly into attacking Royalists on the far wing of the battle, turning a deteriorating position into a significant Parliamentarian victory. For Cromwell, it was not only the discipline, but also the godliness that created success. Without it, one could not expect the Lord's favor. There are reports of Cromwell's "wild glee" on the eve of battles, certain of the Lord's support: "I could not, riding alone about my business, but smile out to God in praises, in assurance of victory, because God would, by things that are not, bring to naught things that are."[56]

Cromwell's troops had proved their worth against experienced and professional cavalry, led by a highly talented commander, Prince Rupert. Cromwell, however, complained about the rest of the Parliamentarian army—the "profaneness and the impiety and the absence of all religion, the drinking and the games". "Until the whole army were new modelled," he wrote, "and governed under a stricter discipline, they must not expect any noticeable success in anything they were about."[57] The army was indeed "new modelled": the New Model Army was created, with Thomas Fairfax in command and Cromwell his second as Lieutenant General of Horse. The army quickly showed its worth, despite being lampooned by one Royalist commander as the "New Noddle." It was a good joke, but one that turned sour for the King's forces as the disciplined and well-trained army showed its worth in battle. By 1646, the King had fled from his temporary capital of Oxford, which later fell to a siege by Cromwell. Charles later surrendered to a Scottish Parliamentarian army.

It was all over, or it should have been. Cromwell retired to civilian life—a mere MP once again. His sole concession to his greater eminence was to move his family to London. The years that followed could so easily have had many different outcomes. Parliament was now predominantly Presbyterian. The Army was predominantly Independent (like Cromwell himself). Some more radical Independents believed in complete individual liberty of conscience —a dangerously anarchical idea for the times. The Presbyterians in Parliament were now keen to disband the New Model Army. The Army had many grievances, primarily about the substantial arrears in their pay. When asked to discuss disbandment, the Army countered with a petition for the payment of arrears and indemnity against any future prosecution. A leading Presbyterian Member of Parliament,

Denzel Holles, proposed a resolution that would make protesting Army officers "enemies of the state." Battle lines were being drawn up. The King began to play all sides off against the other. He had already set in motion a plot to use Scottish support to regain his throne in return for the establishment of a Presbyterian Church. The Presbyterians in Parliament were now actively considering this option. Many soldiers and officers would also have favored the restoration of Charles if the right to follow their own religious beliefs had been guaranteed. Parliament voted to disband the Army in stages.

As events unfolded, on every occasion Cromwell seemed undecided as to his true role as he tried to represent both Parliament and the Army. The King, in captivity at Holdenby, was seized by the army and brought to Newmarket, in the Army's heartland. Cromwell was suspected of being responsible and fled from London in the early hours after hearing that Parliament planned to arrest him: at this point, Cromwell was seen as being the Army's man, and a threat to Parliament. The Army then marched toward London with Cromwell at their head. Cromwell had initially been reluctant to take this action, but persuaded himself that the Army would march anyway and that he could be a moderating influence. The Army demanded the impeachment of 11 Members of Parliament who had been active in calling for the disbandment of the army. The 11 MPs fled from London.

Army officers, including Cromwell, approached the King with moderate proposals: they wanted freedom of religious observation; Parliament was to meet every two years; there would be a better distribution of Parliamentary seats; the bishopric would be abolished—but Charles would be restored to his throne. Charles seems to have missed the point that the New Model Army was at that point the most powerful force in the land and that it was offering him a very moderate deal in exchange for the retention of the monarchy. Charles prevaricated, thinking that there were better deals to be done. In London, Presbyterian supporters mobbed Parliament in protest against the growing predominance of Independents in Parliament and in support of the reinstatement of the King, in exchange for the promised Presbyterian Church. The 11 Presbyterian MPs who had earlier fled from the Army returned to Parliament; the Speaker and some 60 Independent MPs fled in their turn. The mob demanded the King's return to London. Charles now firmly rejected the Army's offer of a settlement, believing that events were moving in his favor.

Members of both the House of Commons and the House of Lords appealed to the Army for protection from the mob. The Army, led by Oliver Cromwell riding at the head of his own regiment, marched on London. The Speaker was restored to Parliament. The 11 Presbyterian members, condemned by history to an increasingly farcical role, took themselves off again. Cromwell did not emerge from this episode as a fully-fledged military dictator. The significance of the Army's involvement seemed, if anything, to have been lost on him. Attendance at Parliament dwindled and the Army Council became increasingly the power in the land.

At this point, Cromwell appeared to be attempting to moderate opinion. The Army, still trying to decide what constitutional settlement should result from its recent sacrifices, met near their headquarters in Putney for a series of debates, and proposed several sweeping political innovations such as the introduction of universal male suffrage (one man one vote) and even free schooling and health care, all of which were seen as dangerously radical at the time. One group, known as The Levellers, proposed an extreme egalitarian form of social model. Cromwell made increasingly vague and meaningless speeches and generally tried to calm the tone of the debate. In Parliament, however, Cromwell argued that the soldiers, having conquered a kingdom, surely had the right to give that kingdom laws—though only by submission to Parliament.

The machinations of Charles finally came to fruition: there was a Royalist uprising in Wales and a Scottish invasion of England in the north. Cromwell, now commander of the Army, put both rebellions down. At Preston, Cromwell crossed the Pennines to make a surprise attack on the much larger Scottish Army moving south into England. This was Cromwell, the man of action, at his forceful best.

This new outbreak of war spelled the death of Charles Stuart. Elements in Parliament were still prepared to negotiate with Charles, but the Army had had enough. The Army marched again on London, and as Members arrived at the House of Commons on December 6th 1648, they found the House surrounded by troops. They were met by a certain Colonel Pride, with a list in his hand. Some members were arrested, others barred; some were allowed through after signing a declaration disavowing the continued negotiations with the King; some had been Army loyalists all along. It was a full-blown military coup. Parliament was now controlled by the Army.

Cromwell managed to delay his return to London from the north until the evening of that same day, to announce that he had no idea about the purge, but that, "since it was done, he was glad of it, and would endeavor to maintain it."[58] Charles I was speedily tried and executed for treason, despite the absence of any legal basis for either the court or the charge of treason, a crime that could only be committed *against* the monarch.

After the King's execution, Cromwell became a Member of the Council of State—a powerful member, but no more than that. He was sent by the Council to pacify Ireland, which he did so bloodily that by many he is remembered primarily for this brutal action. He went on to defeat a Scottish uprising in support of Charles' son, the man who would be Charles II.

Cromwell returned to London as a conquering Caesar. The Rump Parliament (the remnants of the purge by Colonel Pride—'Pride's Purge') had failed to offer any new constitutional solution for the country or to establish a new, tolerant national religious framework. Cromwell had demanded that the Rump give way to a new Council, but it suddenly emerged that the Rump had gathered to pass an Act prolonging its own sitting. Cromwell came to House, listened for a time, and then began to speak. As he spoke, his anger mounted; he began to pace the floor. He abused the members, calling them whoremasters, drunkards, corrupt and unjust: "Perhaps you think this is not Parliamentary language; I confess it is not, neither are you to expect such from me […] it is not fit that you sit at Parliament any longer. You have sat long enough unless you had done more good." As one brave soul protested, Cromwell exploded: "I will put an end to your prating. You are no Parliament. I say you are no Parliament. I will put an end to your sitting." He called in his musketeers and pointed at the speaker: "Fetch him down."[59]

Even after the expulsion of the Rump Parliament, Cromwell did not emerge with supreme power, the Council of Officers proposed that the functions of parliament should be carried out by a Nominated Assembly of 140 "godly" men, with the laudable intention of representing a broad range of religious opinions. Still essentially puritan in character, and with several extreme opinions represented, it was alarmingly referred to as the "Parliament of Saints"; Cromwell was exhilarated: this was surely what God had intended. The "Saints" failed to agree any new religious or constitutional agreement and voted for their own dissolution. Cromwell was invited to become Lord Protector.

As Protector, Cromwell was most impressive in his attempt to find a religious settlement that would tolerate broad differences of religious opinion. He could not, however, restrain himself from trying to improve the morals of the nation. After a Royalist uprising, he imposed a form of direct military rule by Major Generals: committed puritans who also tried to improve the nation's manners and prohibit their more dubious pastimes, such as bear-baiting, horse racing, cock-fighting, and stage plays. "Unruly" taverns were closed. There were penalties for adultery, swearing, and blasphemy. Matters such as adultery and fornication had previously been dealt with by church courts as sins; now they were crimes. The Adultery Act of 1650 made these crimes punishable by death, though this was never enforced.

The rule of the Major-Generals lasted for only one year. Parliament was recalled and offered Cromwell the kingship and a revised constitution. Cromwell refused the crown, on the biblical grounds that the Lord had seen fit to allow him to remove a king, and that therefore he should not seek to restore the office: "I will not rebuild

Jericho." In 1657, Cromwell was re-installed as Lord Protector, this time with greater powers and much pomp and ceremony. He died in 1658. The Protectorate had not been made hereditary, but Cromwell had been allowed to name his successor. His son Richard, perhaps fortunately, was no Oliver. With heavy irony, Richard was deposed by an Army coup, which ushered in the restoration of King Charles II.

GEORGE S. PATTON
(1885–1945)

"I don't want to get any messages saying,'I am holding my position.'
We're not holding a goddamned thing. We are advancing
constantly and we are not interested in holding onto anything,
except the enemy's balls. We are going to twist his balls and kick
the living shit out of him all of the time. Our basic plan of operation
is to advance and to keep on advancing regardless of whether we
have to go over, under, or through the enemy. We are going to go
through him like crap through a goose; like shit through a tin horn!
From time to time there will be some complaints that we are
pushing our people too hard. I don't give a good goddamn about
such complaints. I believe in the old and sound rule that an ounce
of sweat will save a gallon of blood. The harder we push, the more
Germans we will kill. The more Germans we kill, the fewer of our
men will be killed. Pushing means fewer casualties. I want you all to
remember that."[60]

George S. Patton was in command of the US Third Army in the lead-up
to the Allied invasion of northern Europe in 1944, as the final effort to
defeat Nazi Germany got under way. Patton knew where he was headed.
Not for Normandy; that was just the jumping-off point. He and the
Third Army were going to Berlin, and when he got to Berlin and found
Hitler, he was "going to personally shoot that paper-hanging goddamned
son of a bitch just like I would a snake."[61] But there was much more to
Patton than his blood and thunder speeches and his deliberate use of
profanity. Patton believed above all things in training and discipline, in
being prepared to meet the enemy. "If men do not obey orders in small
things, they are incapable of being led in battle. I will have discipline—to
do otherwise is to commit murder."[62] Patton trained his men hard and
insisted on tight discipline: sloppiness, lack of alertness, waiting in
foxholes for the enemy to come to you—these were what got you killed.

"No bastard ever won a war by dying for his country. He won it by making the other poor dumb bastard die for his country."

Patton, as his superiors were well aware, was not a well-rounded leader. He was, as you may have guessed, no diplomat. His aggression, his will to fight, and his determination to instill the same fighting spirit in his troops and officers often spilled over into inappropriate treatment of his subordinates. Alan Brooke, the British Chief of General Staff, thought that Patton was, "a dashing, courageous, wild and unbalanced leader good for operations requiring thrust and push but at a loss in any operation requiring skill and judgment."[63] It is a harsh but not entirely inaccurate picture. On the other hand, it is interesting to consider which Allied commander the German High Command most feared. The answer? George S. Patton.

Patton was a cavalryman at heart. He received his commission as a cavalry officer in 1909. He even developed a new type of sabre —the Patton Sabre—for cavalry use and felt obliged to explain why he had not been able to use a sabre when pursuing and killing three of Pancho Villa's Mexican bandits in New Mexico in 1916: Patton couldn't use a sabre because he was on foot, not on horseback. He and his men had driven to a suspected bandit hideout in their cars and jumped straight from their vehicles into a gunfight. If anyone exemplifies the quite sudden switch in warfare from cavalrymen on horseback with sabres to cavalrymen in vehicles with guns, it is Patton. He saw action in World War I with the new United States Tank Corps; was wounded and decorated. Patton's experience of World War I forged his passionate belief in the pointlessness of holding positions. After the war he and an army colleague, Dwight D. Eisenhower, both lobbied for the further development of armored warfare, but with little success. Patton returned to the cavalry.

In August 1944, the Allied invasion of Normandy after the D-Day landings was becoming bogged down in the deadly hedgerows and lanes of that region, in what a German corps commander at the time called "a monstrous bloodbath." The Allied commanders had become embroiled in a bloody battle to gain and hold territory, slowly pushing forward on an extended front and securing their lines of communication. There was a real risk that the war would degenerate into static lines of battle, horribly reminiscent of World War I. The one man whose every instinct was against this—Commander of the Third Army, George S. Patton—was currently in the doghouse and not keen to step out of line with his commanding officer, Omar Bradley, or with Bradley's boss, Patton's old friend Eisenhower. Patton had suffered a succession of PR disasters—a harsh welcome for the outspoken old warrior to the new world of media exposure and the sensitivities of the folks back home.

Patton had an unholy love of battle and the enterprize of war. "Compared to war, all other human endeavor shrinks to insignificance," he said. "God, how I love it."[64] Patton was intensely emotional about the bond between fighting men and about the courage of the ordinary soldier. It got him into trouble in Sicily in 1943 where he was commanding the Seventh Army. Visiting wounded soldiers in hospital he was, as ever, deeply moved. When he found an uninjured soldier suffering from what we might now call shell-shock, he was incensed. In his rage he struck the man; the press got hold of the story, and it cost Patton his command of the Seventh Army. It could easily have also cost him any future role in the final victory against Germany: a role that he saw as his destiny.

Patton should have been basking in praise as the liberator of Sicily's capital Palermo and the joint victor, with the commander of the British Eighth Army, Bernard Montgomery, of the race to take Messina (Patton was always intensely competitive; he got there first). Instead, as a storm of adverse publicity began to erupt in the American press, his commanding general, Eisenhower, was struggling to decide whether not merely to strip Patton of command, but also to send him home in disgrace. Eisenhower needed Patton for a role in the coming conflict in northern Europe and knew that Patton was "a truly aggressive commander." Eisenhower's real and nagging doubt about Patton was whether his vanity, his desperate search for military glory, might lead him to make wrong and costly military decisions. As it was, Patton was forced to apologize personally to every division of the Seventh Army—though in some case his attempts to apologise were drowned by cheers of support. At one such gathering (of the 60th Regiment, 9th Division) the troops just shouted "Georgie! Georgie!" and threw their helmets in the air. He finally gave up the attempt to make his speech, and as his staff car drove off, he stood up in the car to take the salute of the regiment, helmets now firmly back on heads, chinstraps properly fastened in the approved Patton fashion. Tears streamed down his face.

Patton was no longer in the field of candidates for command of all US ground forces in Europe. Later, as the invasion of Europe drew closer, Patton didn't even get the army command that he so desperately wanted: the First Army—the army chosen to spearhead the cross-channel invasion. The job went to Omar Bradley. Patton was heartbroken.

With supreme irony, the German High Command thought that the whole affair was a ruse; Patton was the man they feared most. Wherever the main thrust against them came, they were convinced that Patton would be at its head. They could not believe that he would be relieved of his command over such an incident. This speculation helped immensely in the final (real) Allied plot to convince Germany that the attack on Europe would come, not via Normandy, but by way of Calais, spearheaded by Patton who, without any real active command to occupy him, was busy making speeches for the benefit of German spies about his intention to do exactly that, at the head of an entirely fictional invasion force.

In the end Patton got control of the Third Army, though it was unclear exactly what role was expected from the Third in the coming invasion, and the suspicion lingers that Patton's superiors hoped that they might not have to call on him. His speech to his staff officers at their headquarters in England was classic Patton:

"I can assure you that the Third United States Army will be the greatest army in American history. We shall be in Berlin ahead of everybody. To gain that end we must have perfect discipline [...] You are here to fight [...] ahead lies battle. That means just one thing [...] you can't afford to be a goddamned fool, because in battle, fools make dead men."[65]

Patton's way of working with his new Army demonstrates his true strengths. Patton wanted discipline, and he wanted efficiency. Everyone worked seven days a week. Everyone wore steel helmets, neckties, leggings, and side-arms. Briefings were punctual and short; once they were over, he had no interest in staff officers hanging around to "show willing." Every campaign was discussed in detail by senior commanders: everyone got to have their say. Once a plan was decided, the debate was over; it would be implemented (preferably "with violence"). Orders were clear and simple, often one page of paper. One of Patton's most enlightened maxims was, "Never tell people how to do things. Tell them what to do and they will surprise you with their ingenuity." Officers were given their tasks politely and left to get on with it in their own manner.

He insisted on strict discipline: "There is only one kind of discipline—perfect discipline." In one of his speeches to the troops he illustrated his point with one of his graphic (and almost certainly fictitious) illustrations. "There are 400 neatly marked graves somewhere in Sicily, all because one man went to sleep on his job. But they are German graves, for we caught the bastard asleep before they did."[66]

Patton's Third Army broke out of Brittany in a remarkable feat of military logistics—moving 200,000 men and 40,000 vehicles through the tiny roads of Avranches, at the base of the Cotentin peninsula. Patton famously jumped onto a police box in the center of town and personally directed the log-jammed convoy, which slowly but surely began to flow. The Third Army emerged onto the plains of southern Normandy with divisions intact and ready to advance at speed. Bradley was convinced that their first objective was to secure the deep-water port of Brest on the most westerly tip of Brittany. It was only when Allied Headquarters realized that Brittany was a false objective (in the event, Brest proved to be too far away usefully to supply a frontline moving rapidly to the east) that they finally tore up the paper strategy and responded to the opportunities that events on the ground had presented to them. The Third Army was finally released from the distraction of Brittany and sped eastward: bypassing fortified positions; defeating German positions by maneuver rather than assault.

Patton was in his element. He tore through France in a victorious charge, like one of his ancient heroes. Soon Patton was able to claim that they had "advanced farther and faster than any army in the history of war."[67] They overran German defences, side-stepped fortifications—leaving them to be mopped up later—and moved so fast that they prevented the German army from organizing successive defensive positions.

Eventually, this heroic dash ground to a halt as fuel began to run out. Eisenhower needed to keep the Allied advance moving on all fronts. He agreed to divert fuel to Montgomery's British 21st Army Group 'Market Garden' operation—the ultimately unsuccessful attempt to cross the Rhine, Germany's great natural western border, at Arnhem, using paratroopers carried by a fleet of gliders.

Patton had reached the Lorraine in eastern France; he had roared past Verdun—scene of bitter trench warfare in World War I—and was close to Metz, on the Moselle river. A little farther on lay Germany's western defences—the Siegfried line—which were then still sparsely defended. Beyond that lay the Rhine. "Dammit, Bradley," begged Patton, "just give me 400,000 gallons of gasoline and I'll put you inside Germany in two days."[68] It was not to be. The pause allowed Germany to regroup its defences and, since Patton was considered to be a greater threat than Montgomery, German defences gathered at the old Siegfried line facing Patton's attack.

Montgomery's attack on Arnhem failed. Germany gathered its forces for a desperate counter-offensive through the forest of the Ardennes. The Allies were taken by surprise; there was a real risk of the Germans achieving their goal of bursting out of the Ardennes and turning north to the coast at Antwerp, splitting the Allied forces in two and destroying all Allied armies north of the new line. Hitler believed that this would force the Allies to surrender. German troops poured through the small roads of the Ardennes forest as they had in 1940. Paratroopers of the American 101st Airborne Division reached the key road junction of Bastogne by truck and put up a stiff resistance, holding up the advance. Called on to surrender, the acting commander of 101st replied with the historic one-word answer: "Nuts!" A translator was summoned by the confused German commander to interpret the precise colloquial meaning of this enigmatic response.

On December 19th 1944, Patton and the other Allied generals were summoned to Verdun for an emergency meeting with Eisenhower. Patton was certain that the Third Army would be called to help the First Army, which was facing the brunt of the German attack. Patton had briefed his staff at 7.00 a.m. that day; within two hours they had devised a plan to take three divisions to relieve the First Army by one of three possible routes. They gave each route a codename: when Patton was given his brief at Verdun he would phone with the codeword for the chosen line of attack. The Third Army could begin to move almost immediately. Patton was at Verdun for the 11.00 meeting. When it came to Patton's turn to volunteer what the Third Army could contribute to the situation, he confirmed that he could attack with three divisions in 48 hours. There was genuine disbelief: Eisenhower at first assumed that Patton was being boastful as ever, and reprimanded him. It began to dawn on the meeting that Patton was deadly serious: "When can you start?" he was asked; "As soon as you're through with me here," he replied.[69]

Patton pulled off his momentous maneuver; the Third Army had to change direction by 90 degrees in freezing weather, often in the dark, and attack an entirely unexpected target. It was something that had never been done before in so short a time. Patton spent the next few days driving around the Third Army's positions. He visited seven divisions and briefed every one in detail, making adjustments to dispositions, chatting to GIs, making sure that everyone knew what was needed of them. As the Third Army moved, night and day, Patton was everywhere, driving in an open-top jeep in freezing temperatures—his face actually frozen on occasions—so that the troops could see that he was driving forward; sometimes he got out and helped shove vehicles back onto icy roads. Everywhere he went he was cheered by his troops, inspired by just a sight of 'old blood and guts'. Bastogne was relieved on December 26th.

The vicious Battle of the Bulge was still to come—a desperate battle in freezing conditions that cost up to 100,000 casualties on both sides. The German losses were more significant, because they were irreplaceable. The German reserves thrown into this last ditch offensive were now gone, and the Luftwaffe was fatally damaged.

Patton continued throughout the battle to demonstrate the intense level of personal, on-the-ground leadership that had enabled the Third Army to make its famous maneuver to relieve Bastogne. One historian has said that Patton's greatest achievement as a leader was his ability to make things happen—his outstanding ability as a mover and shaker. Patton's own verdict is certainly that of a great leader: "Yes, we broke all records moving up there. It was all done by the three of us [...] me, my chauffeur, and my chief of staff. All I did was tell my division commanders where they'd got to be tomorrow. Then I let the others do it."[70]

Patton got to cross the Rhine with his army in March 1945, with the German army in full retreat. Characteristically, Patton urinated flamboyantly in the Rhine: "I have been looking forward to this for a long time."[71] He died in a mundane car accident on his way to a pheasant shoot in Germany in December 1945, after the German surrender, one day before he was due to return home. But Patton had always dreaded the come-down after his historic action in Europe:

"Civil life will be mighty dull—no cheering crowds, no flowers, no private airplanes. I am convinced the best end for an officer is the last bullet of the war. *Quelle vie.*"[72]

ZHOU ENLAI
(1898–1976)

A dedicated and lifelong communist, Zhou Enlai's political instincts were moderate and progressive—unlike those of many of his fellow communists. Famous for his punishing work routine, despite increasingly fragile health, Zhou worked all his life to improve the lot of the Chinese people. He also worked to mitigate and even subvert the more destructive policies of Chairman Mao Zedong: Mao was Chairman of the Communist Party of China; Zhou was Premier of the People's Republic of China. Zhou was attempting to run the country while Mao, the most powerful man in the Party, was busy having revolutionary ideas.

Zhou can be criticised for not having taken a stance against disastrous policies with which he clearly disagreed, but it also could be argued that by surviving—when so many of Mao's opponents worked so hard to engineer his downfall (and at a time when downfall could be fatal)—Zhou was able to retain his influence and to continue to move China's development in a positive direction, away from the destructive chaos and the impractical, ideologically-driven programs advocated by Mao. The affection with which Zhou is remembered in China today, where he is often referred to as "beloved father of modern China," suggests that Zhou's compromises were correct, and arguably self-sacrificing. It is also likely that Zhou simply considered it his duty to continue to work for the People's Republic and for the Party, even when the Party had taken a direction that he considered to be wrong.

Zhou was a tireless and fearsomely efficient administrator. His goal was always to modernize China through increasing use of technology and modern skills, often in the face of massive ideological bias: Zhou constantly promoted the importance to China's development of knowledge-workers, even when all such "intellectuals" were being condemned and even purged as non-revolutionary. He used his subtle intellect to turn ideologues' arguments against them. One of Zhou's most defining characteristics was his commitment to talking to people—not arguing, but talking. When the hot-headed Red Guards of Mao's Cultural Revolution were running out of control, Zhou seemed at times to be the only voice of reason—in an entirely literal sense—facing armed groups fired-up on ideology and brute power; talking, cajoling; insisting that issues be resolved by dialog and not by force. Zhou was one of the twentieth century's great diplomats, both at the highest international levels and down on the shop floor. More than anything, Zhou was tireless in promoting his program, in making things happen, even in the face of potentially lethal opposition.

At the end of World War II, the Communist Party of China (CPC) took control of China, ousting Chiang Kai Shek's Nationalist Party. The Republic of China set up a government in exile on the island of Taiwan; the Communist People's Republic of China became the government of mainland China.

The People's Republic of China began life ominously. Mao instigated the mass execution of so-called counter-revolutionaries: the definition was wide-ranging and included members of the Nationalist Party (Kuomintang), former employees of Western businesses, members of the rural gentry, businessmen, and intellectuals. At least one million people died, probably considerably more. Another million or more were transported to "Reform through Labor" camps. It is impossible to imagine that Zhou can be exonerated from complicity in these bloody purges.

China embarked on a Russian-financed Five Year Plan to boost industrial output, reducing China's almost total dependence on agriculture. Land was redistributed from landlords and wealthier peasants to poorer peasants. Zhou set about the reconstruction, welcoming support from communist and non-communist alike: "All those who can contribute to the rebuilding of China must do so. We welcome them irrespective of politics." Nearly half of the ministers appointed by Zhou to the State Council were non-communists.[73] Working at a fearsome pace—he had a routine of working until five in the morning and rising again at ten—Zhou set about undoing the damage done by decades of warfare, and to begin the industrialization and modernization of China.

In January 1956 Zhou delivered a report to the CPC, entitled *On the Question of Intellectuals*, in which he argued implicitly against the demonization (and worse) of China's "intelligentsia" and explicitly for China's desperate need for scientists, teachers, and "knowledge-bearers" to transform China from an essentially medieval agricultural society into a modern state. "All our plans for development, our advance, depend on the proper use of the knowledge-bearers [...] Without scientists, without teachers, we shall not be able to lift ourselves out of backwardness." Zhou pre-empted the classic Marxist concern that the revolution belonged to the proletariat—the workers: "Mental labor and manual labor are both needed. Our intellectuals, by deploying mental labor, are part of the working class."[74] Mao, with his tendency towards radical involvement from the grass roots up, was not content with embracing this idea as a guiding principle: intellectuals must be encouraged to criticise; the party must be 'rectified' through critique. Over time the country's "intellectuals," many of whom had suffered beatings and abuse, became emboldened. They told the party what they really thought. Among the entirely sensible and reasonable demands for such essentials as a proper legal system and police regulation came criticism of the Communist Party and even of Mao himself (and, indeed, of Zhou). Some non-communist party leaders thought that some sort of power-sharing might be acceptable: perhaps different parties should be allowed to govern in turn. It had all got out of hand.

The Communist Party stepped in. There was such a backlash against intellectuals—now clearly shown to be of unsound and "rightist" opinions—that some historians believe that Mao had encouraged the movement in order to identify subversives so that he could move against them. The total number of deaths in these "anti-rightist" purges could well be in the millions.[75] Zhou attempted to protect the non-party members of his cabinet, but ultimately failed. In a sense, the non-party members were lucky: party members who had joined in the criticism were in general harshly (i.e. fatally) dealt with; many non-party members' lives were spared, but Zhou's plans to harness the skills of non-party intellectuals in his cabinet were at an end.

Mao's next Big Idea was the Great Leap Forward. There had already been a degree of collectivization of agriculture leading to "higher-cooperatives," which brought several hundred family units together into communal units. The process was now accelerated: private plots ceased to exist; thousand of family units were brought together to work on communal farms. Wages were replaced by "points." Mao also introduced a technologically illiterate drive to double steel production by encouraging local steel furnaces. Steel manufacture needs controlled, high-temperature furnaces that enable iron to combine with carbon to make steel. It is possible to make steel in small furnaces, but only if you know what you are doing— ironically, it was a skill well-known to the ancient Chinese. As unrealistic production targets were forced on local communities, manpower was recruited from agriculture, factories, schools, and hospitals. All kinds of metal utensils were requisitioned to meet the targets. Woods were cut down; furniture and doors were used to fuel the backyard furnaces. The end result was poor-quality pig iron of little value. Many dams, canals, and other engineering projects, built by peasant labor without supervision by engineers—forbidden by Mao on ideological grounds —also proved to be useless. Zhou had rashly commented about the haste of these ideas and was obliged to write a "self-criticism." "I have committed errors," said Zhou. "My thinking has not caught up with the thinking of Chairman Mao."[76]

As agricultural output fell, China was hit by bad weather, floods, and even plagues of locusts (Mao had also instigated a "Kill a Sparrow"campaign, because sparrows eat grain; unfortunately, they also eat a lot of insects, such as locusts.) Grain production fell by 15 percent in 1959, and a further ten percent in 1960. Local officials tried to pretend that the policy was working by inflating figures for harvests: when they were required to requisition grain to send to the cities or for export, they found themselves obliged to deliver a percentage of their own inflated figures. Peasants went hungry. Starvation set in. The total death toll of this man-made disaster is estimated to be in the tens of millions.[77]

The disaster was a political blow for Mao. He relinquished the role of President of the People's Republic to Liu Shaoqui, who denounced the Great Leap Forward at a Party Conference in Beijing. Liu and another moderate, Deng Xiaoping, the General Secretary of the Communist Party, began to plot to move Mao into a symbolic role and to take over control of economic policy. There was a period of general liberalization. Zhou, with his customary diplomacy, refrained from criticising Mao directly. In one of his trademark sleights of hand, he quoted Mao in apparent support of a line of thought that was diametrically opposed to Mao's current position:

> "There has been a bad tendency in the party for the past three years. There is not enough democracy. Our aim is to liberate thought, to abolish superstition, to dare to speak, to think, to act […] We must speak the truth, encourage democracy, strengthen it in the party. This is the thought of Mao Zedong for Party Building."[78]

Despite Zhou's clever words, democracy—in its usual form—was the last thing on Mao's mind. Mao was in danger of being sidelined. He launched his counter-attack: the Cultural Revolution.

Mao seemed to have a genuine belief in the role of disorder: as revolutionary movements accumulate bureaucracy and lose the cutting edge of their vision, so they must be purged in a brief spell of violent anarchy, driven by the people, the masses. Mao seems to have seen himself as the Chinese Monkey King—a rebellious spirit causing uproar. Even he was dismayed by the anarchy that he was about to let loose.

A new problem had arisen within the party, said Mao, the problem of "revisionism"—of capitalist tendencies appearing within the party, of elitism and bureaucracy that divorced the party from the people. Mao accused Zhou himself of being a threat to the Party's revolutionary spirit. But Mao's new revolution was to be much more than a debate amongst Party members: the masses would be set free to purge the country, bypassing the Party hierarchy. Students, peasants, workers, and soldiers were all called upon to abolish the "Four Olds": old customs, old culture, old habits, old ideas. It was a wide brief. The Red Guards—a term used for all young people embarking on Mao's new mission—were offered free travel to anywhere in the country. Exhilarated by their new powers and fired up with revolutionary fervor, they began to take China down the road of mere anarchy.

Tribunals were set up to try capitalist-roaders and anti-revolutionaries. People were beaten and humiliated. There were many suicides and many murders. Teachers, academics, writers, and journalists were attacked; museums, temples, and shrines were ransacked; ancient books and works of art were destroyed. The human cost was very high. One poignant personal note was recorded by the Chinese author Han Suyin, who records the words of her own niece: "In our school we were told to beat our teacher. We did, and he died."[79]

Mao's aim in launching the Cultural Revolution was quickly achieved: party members who could be accused as capitalist-roaders would find a mob of Red Guards camped outside their homes, screaming slogans night and day. Wall-posters and banners became a popular way of denouncing politicians. Zhou was to be attacked later by these means: "Which class does Zhou represent?"; "Ten questions to address to Zhou"; "Bury Zhou alive."[80]

Liu Shaoqui was sent to a detention camp, where he died. Den Xiapoing was sent for re-education on three different occasions, ending up as a worker in an engine factory. He was later rescued by Zhou and brought back into politics.

During these terrifying times, Zhou trod a difficult path, rescuing those whom he could, but never stepping so far out of line that he became an easy target for the Red Guards. His favorite ploy became the despatch of senior figures who were at risk to Hospital No. 301, which was reserved for high-ranking party members. The medical staff at the hospital were happy to diagnose illnesses that prevented their 'patients' from leaving the hospital grounds. Zhou smuggled many targeted party figures into Hospital No. 301, from which they emerged, years later, miraculously cured. He closed museums to protect their contents and drew up lists of temples and shrines that were to be preserved as national treasures—though this was often ignored at a local level. On occasions, Zhou would join the ranks of those denouncing "enemies of the people" so that he would be included in the panel of those who would pass verdict on them, whereupon Zhou would plead extenuating circumstances.

During the Cultural Revolution, Mao's last wife, Jiang Qing, had become a power in her own right at the head of the infamous Gang of Four. The relationship between the Gang and Mao himself is unclear, but the Gang were at the heart of the worst, later excesses of the Cultural Revolution. In 1967, the Gang of Four began the ultimate, logical extension of the anarchic madness of the Cultural Revolution: the Red Guards should now take over the army, the final symbol of hierarchical authority. The Red Guards stole weapons from the PLA (People's Liberation Army) and looted army barracks while helpless officers looked on. Rival gangs of Red Guards began to shoot each other with the liberated weapons.

Zhou continued to run China. By 1967, 40 million workers demanded to be allowed to travel to Beijing to parade before Mao Zedong, as millions of Red Guards had done. Zhou wisely limited delegates to one or a few per factory. Factory workers in Shanghai overthrew their local government, unassisted and therefore untainted by any army involvement. The Gang of Four were ecstatic: here was true workers' power, unmediated by any party, government or military involvement. Zhou presented the figures on the economy to Mao. Production was collapsing; the Chinese economy was facing ruin. Mao called in the Peoples Liberation Army to end the Cultural

Revolution. The Red Guards' power over the army came to an abrupt halt and army units moved into areas controlled by the Red Guard. Mao began the "Down to the Countryside Movement," which required all recent middle-school graduates (the bulk of the Red Guards) to move to the countryside and work on the land. The Red Guards were being sent off to earn their proletarian callouses on the land. They were allowed back to the cities a decade later.

Mao's Cultural Revolution had achieved its political aim—his opponents had all been purged—at the expense of bringing the entire country to the brink of anarchy. Zhou Enlai, the survivor, remained and began to reassert his program. Mao named his successor as Lin Biao, a man who seemed merely to parrot Mao's thoughts. Lin can not have been quite so subservient, however, as there are indications of a KGB plot to assassinate Mao involving Lin Biao. Soon afterwards, Lin died in a suspicious plane accident over Mongolia, apparently trying to flee China after the failure of a planned coup or assassination attempt.

The Gang of Four continued to attack Zhou, but by 1975 he was able to reassert his prime concerns: the Four Modernizations—of agriculture; of industry; of national defence; of science and technology. Zhou had already achieved perhaps the greatest diplomatic achievement of his policy of establishing normal relations between China and the outside world: the visit of United States President Richard Nixon to China in 1972.

In 1974, Zhou was diagnosed as having bladder cancer; he began to delegate work to Deng Xiaoping, now Executive Vice Premier—the man whom Zhou had rescued from a tractor factory and restored to office. Zhou died in 1976, eight months before his Party Chairman Mao Zedong. After Zhou's death, the Gang of Four hoped at last to seize power. Deng Xiaoping delivered Zhou's funeral oration; there was an outpouring of national grief. Later that year, on the traditional day of mourning, huge crowds gathered in Tiananmen Square in Beijing, to mourn the dead premier. The Gang of Four cleared the square, accused the mourners of being "counter-revolutionary", and put Deng Xiaoping under house arrest under suspicion of having organized the event. The public reaction against this action hastened the political end of the Gang of Four. Deng Xiaoping—heir to Zhou's modernizing and liberal agenda—became the de facto leader of China after Mao's death, repudiating the Cultural Revolution and ushering in the liberalizing Beijing Spring.

Zhou Enlai is widely regarded as one of the twentieth century's greatest negotiators: calm, reasonable and subtle; able to turn opponents' arguments on their heads; a master, in times of political turmoil, of making the politically correct statement that nevertheless expressed the view that he wished to promote. He negotiated with Soviet Russia and the USA in times of international crisis—he was Foreign Minister during the Korean War when Chinese troops directly entered the conflict against the USA, but it was also his initiative that saw ambassadorial talks between the two countries begin again in Warsaw. He was central to negotiating the peace settlement between France and Vietnam at the 1954 Geneva Conference, to end the French Indochina War. He was also instrumental in supplying Chinese aid to the Vietcong in the war against America—the Vietnam War—that followed the French Indochina War.

Zhou developed relations between China and Africa, and with neighboring Asian countries. His greatest diplomatic achievement is still seen—by both China and the West—to be his 'ping-pong' diplomacy with the United States, by means of which the two countries eased diplomatic hostilities by negotiating a series of sports exchanges, and which led eventually to President Nixon's symbolic visit to China early in 1972. The People's Republic of China had been admitted to the United Nations some months earlier, in late 1971. China, thanks largely to the tireless efforts of Zhou in maintaining dialog with all parties, both inside China and internationally, was once again a major player on the world stage.

7

TAKING THE
OFFENSIVE

We have to put up with the fact that a lot of management terminology borrows heavily from military concepts: we take on the opposition head-on or we try to outflank them; we discuss our strategies and our tactics; we worry about our logistics; we attack new markets and we defend our market position.

There is a good reason for this: for several millennia, the most common testing ground of our leadership skills has been warfare. Also, and perhaps equally significantly, it was the military affairs of nations that were recorded in detail. Complex leadership decisions within sophisticated political structures will have been taken by statesmen throughout the ages: sadly, we know very little about them. We can see glimpses of this civilian leadership through the documentation of advanced societies with surviving written records such as ancient China, Athens, and Rome; nevertheless, we still know a great deal more about Julius Caesar's conquest of Gaul than we do about his contemporaries' political actions in the senate, or about the leadership shown by Roman businessmen in developing the international trade in copper.

There is also something dreadfully compelling about leadership in times of war—it has always provided the most demanding testing ground of leadership skills. The stakes are so high: life and death; the survival of nation states; the creation of empires; the overthrow of oppressive governments. We should be conscious and wary of the tendency to link corporate affairs with military thinking, since modern corporate life is not actually warfare (no, really)—but nevertheless, there is still a great deal to be learned.

As a manager you will, at several key moments in your career, have to seize the initiative; you will have to take the offensive. A review of many managers' careers would show that they have, in fact, spent their time defending a position; they have "stopped things from getting any worse" or, less negatively, "have maintained our very high standards." It is a job that has to be done, but it does not represent great leadership. Great leaders counter-attack. They defend a position but then they shake the opposition with some unexpected move—now it is the turn of the opposition to try to hold on to what they have. This kind of action is not the preserve of major corporations. The head of a school can decide to manage the school successfully and to keep his or her various constituencies—pupils, parents, local authorities, government watchdogs—entirely happy. Or they can decide to take on ambitious new programs and challenging targets to try to take the school to a different level. A small business can make a living doing what it does very well, or it can decide that it could be a much bigger business. It can take the offensive.

The first two leaders from history in this section are, indeed, military men. Hannibal's name entered the hall of fame 2,000 years ago as the man who took the fight to the enemy. Carthage and Rome were the two great rivals for control of the Mediterranean. Carthage had recently been heavily defeated by Rome and was paying crippling annual indemnities to her conqueror. Hannibal's father conceived a strategy that his son executed: Hannibal conquered southern Spain to provide the Carthaginians with new resources, and then he attempted the impossible: he attacked Rome itself. Hannibal famously crossed the Alps with a large army and a number of war elephants, in the face of hostile tribes and apparently impossible physical obstacles. He surprised the Romans and defeated their first attempt to stop him in northern Italy. He then performed another impossible task, crossing the "impassable" marshes at the mouth of the River Arno on the northwest coast of Italy. His troops were unable to sleep for three nights as they waded through water; they snatched what sleep they could on abandoned wagons, supply packs, or on the carcasses of dead animals—such as those of Hannibal's last remaining elephants. Hannibal emerged behind the Roman army that was supposed to be preventing his attack on Rome. He destroyed it in a surprise attack and then met the Romans again in a major engagement at Cannae. His tactic of enveloping the Roman army within the pincer movement of the two wings of his army has been successfully copied by commanders ever since. Hannibal stayed in Italy, undefeated, for 15 years, but never received enough local support or reinforcements from Carthage to be able to take Rome itself.

Salāh ad-Dīn Yūsuf ibn Ayyūb (Saladin), by way of contrast, did lead his people to the victory of which he dreamed, although the final achievement of his grand vision was only fully realized a century after his death. Saladin's goal was to drive the Christian Crusaders out of the Middle East. The Crusaders had established the Kingdom of Jerusalem on the Levantine coast after their conquest of the holy city of Jerusalem in 1099. Their small but significant kingdom had become a potentially permanent feature of the region's local politics. The Middle East at the time was more like a collection of city states than of nations. Local rulers sometimes fought the Crusaders and sometimes they fought each other. Sometimes they formed alliances with the Crusaders against their local enemies. Very often, and understandably, they just tried to keep their heads down. To achieve his grand strategy, Saladin needed first to unify the region, and then to inspire it with the common objective of expelling the Crusaders. He achieved this unification with the occasional use of force but, more typically, through negotiation and diplomacy. Finally, he led the combined Islamic forces against Jerusalem, the symbolic capital of the Crusaders' empire, and re-conquered the city—showing great mercy to the inhabitants, in stark contrast to the Crusaders' own bloody sack of the city 88 years earlier. The capture of Jerusalem was to be Saladin's greatest achievement. The Crusaders were reduced to occupying a rump kingdom, based around the city of Acre on the Mediterranean coast. This Kingdom of Acre, as it became known, was finally swept away a little over 100 years after Saladin's re-conquest of Jerusalem. Saladin had united the factious groupings of the region's city states in a common cause against the invaders. He refused to accept the new status quo represented by the Crusaders' invasion of the region, but taking the offensive was, in his case, far from a simple act of bravado and aggression; Saladin's claim to fame as a great leader lies in his ability to use his diplomatic and political skills to create a coalition of forces with a common aim: to take the offensive.

There is another side to the idea of taking the offensive: the notion of attacking an apparently impregnable position; something that seems so well-defended that it is impossible to defeat. History shows us that this is never the case. A smaller force can defeat a larger one; the greatest citadel can be brought low. The technique remains the same in every case: to concentrate one's own forces; to strike an unexpected blow at a vital point of the opposing forces; to use speed, maneuverability, and surprise to catch the opposition unawares. All of these techniques translate directly into modern corporate affairs. So, who better to illustrate this militaristic theory than an apparently unassuming young Victorian lady from a middle-class family from Suffolk, England? Elizabeth Garrett Anderson wanted to be a doctor—a simple enough ambition that brought her into direct conflict with the all-male Victorian medical profession, who blocked her every attempt to advance, with defences as strong and daunting as any heavily-defended military position. Garret Anderson was the Hannibal of her day: she took the fight to the enemy; she constantly surprised them with her audacity; she out-maneuvered them all and, finally, she wore them down with her tenacity. She refused to give up—even when she could have achieved her goal simply by moving to America. Unlike Hannibal, Elizabeth Garrett Anderson laid siege to the capital of her enemies and succeeded in razing it to the ground.

HANNIBAL BARCA
(247–183 BCE)

Hannibal had the advantage that he was brought up to be a leader. His father, Hamilcar, had been commander of the Carthaginian forces against Rome in what is known as the First Punic War; his son was brought up, famously, to hate the Romans, and to expect to lead a Carthaginian army against them. Hannibal's brother-in-law, Hasdrubal, who took command of the army when Hamilcar died, appointed Hannibal as head of cavalry when he was just 21-years-old. It could be that Hannibal was simply an able soldier who, thanks to his family connections, was given early promotion, but there are clear indications that Hannibal was a natural leader. The Roman historian Livy (who never missed an opportunity to portray Hannibal, Rome's most feared enemy, in an unflattering light) wrote this:

> "No sooner had he arrived than Hannibal drew the whole army toward him. The old soldiers fancied they saw Hamilcar in his youth given back to them; the same bright look; the same fire in his eye; the same trick of countenance and features. But soon he proved that to be his father's son was not his highest recommendation. Never was one and the same spirit more skilful to meet opposition, to obey, or to command. It was hard to decide whether he was more dear to the chief (Hasdrubal) or the army. Neither did Hasdrubal more readily place anyone at the head when courage or activity was required, nor were the soldiers under any other leader so full of confidence and daring. He entered danger with the greatest mettle, he comported himself in danger with the greatest unconcern. By no means could his body be tired, his ardor damped. Heat and cold he suffered with equal endurance […] The time of waking and sleeping depended not on the distinction of day and night. What time was left from business he devoted to rest, and this

was not brought on by either a soft couch or by quiet. Many have often seen him covered by a short field-cloak lying on the ground betwixt the outposts and the sentinels of the soldiers [...] He was by long odds the best rider, the best marcher. He went into battle first, he came out of it the last [...] Hannibal served three years under Hasdrubal's supreme command, and left nothing unobserved which he who desires to become a great leader ought to see and to do."[81]

During the nearly 15 years that Hannibal was to spend in Italy, undefeated by the Romans despite being a short march away from Rome for all of this time, Hannibal was never significantly reinforced by Carthage: he recruited new troops from local tribes; as the years passed, the army with which he had marched from Spain to Italy had disappeared and been replaced by soldiers who had never known his father or his brother and who owed no allegiance to either Carthage or to Hannibal. Pay was scant or absent; food was short; for all of his last years in Italy it must have been clear that Hannibal could not defeat Rome. Yet he never faced a rebellion and his army never deserted him.

Hannibal was one of the great military strategists of all time. The Romans relied on discipline and manpower to win their battles: they marched up to the front and slugged it out with their opponents. Hannibal, like Alexander the Great, the young Greek military genius who had conquered most of the known world a century earlier, used maneuver, stratagems and the concentration of forces at decisive points to defeat much larger Roman forces. The Romans adopted a strategy of containment of Hannibal's army in the later years; it seemed that none of their generals would risk facing Hannibal in battle. When Hannibal was recalled to defend Carthage against direct attack by Rome, he was finally defeated by a Roman general who made good use of what were essentially Hannibal's own strategies—an inventive approach to the battlefield that would never have occurred to a Roman before Hannibal had demonstrated what was possible. Hannibal, without any cavalry, nearly won that last battle—but not quite.

Carthage, on the north coast of Africa, is located on a spit of land that juts out from the North African coast opposite Sicily. All ships passing between the eastern and western Mediterranean have to pass the relatively narrow channel between Carthage and Sicily: it was a key strategic location. Carthage became a major Mediterranean power. As such, the city-state came inevitably into conflict with Rome, as the Italian city-state began its rise to power. The final defeat of Carthage (nearly 40 years after the death of Hannibal) shifted the future center of western civilization from the coast of North Africa to Europe. Rome destroyed Carthage completely—its city walls and its harbor were dismantled and its people were killed or sold into slavery. Legend has it that the Romans then sowed the fields of Carthage with salt so that no crops could be grown there. This is extremely unlikely, as the rapidly expanding city of Rome soon came to rely heavily on grain imported from North Africa, and the legend may well stem from a twentieth-century source.

Carthage lost their first major war with Rome (the First Punic War) when Hannibal was a young boy. The Romans had destroyed the Carthaginian fleet. They took control of Sicily from Carthage and imposed a huge annual indemnity on Carthage for the next ten years, crippling the city's finances. A little later, Rome also conquered the Carthaginian islands of Sardinia and Corsica. Rome, not Carthage, was now the preeminent naval power in the area. They took to calling the sea around Sicily, Corsica, and Sardinia *Mare Nostrum* "our sea." As the Roman Empire expanded, the whole of the Mediterranean was to become *Mare Nostrum*.

Hannibal's father, Hamilcar, proposed a grand strategy to the impoverished and defeated Carthaginians: they should conquer Spain—a country rich in natural resources—to provide them with a new base of money and men with which to renew the attack on Rome.

If Hamilcar represented the war faction in Carthage, then his political enemy Hanno represented the peace faction. Hanno had been keen for Carthage to acquire more territories in Africa (which had financial benefits for Hanno) rather than to fight a war with Rome. He demobilized the Carthaginian fleet in 244 BCE, while the Romans were building the fleet that would be instrumental in the defeat of Carthage three years later. He then refused to pay the mercenaries who had fought for Carthage, provoking a revolt. His attempt to lead the army to defeat the mercenaries failed, and he handed over control to Hamilcar, who succeeded. It was in the interval caused by this distraction that Rome seized Corsica and Sardinia. When Hannibal was in Italy, it was Hanno who led the faction opposing the despatch of the reinforcements that would almost certainly have resulted in the defeat of Rome. Hanno, like two other Carthaginian Hanno's, was known as "the Great." In his case, it is very hard to see why.

Hamilcar, without a fleet, had to march his troops through North Africa and then ferry them across the Straits of Gibraltar. He succeeded in conquering much of southern Spain. When he was killed in battle, his son-in-law Hasdrubal took command, and negotiated a truce with Rome—which was invading Spain from the North—that made the Ebro River a border between Carthaginian and Roman territorial ambitions. Hasdrubal also began a tentative alliance with the Gauls of the Po River valley in northern Italy in order to threaten Rome, which quickly made a pre-emptive strike and annexed the Po valley. When Hasdrubal was assassinated, Hannibal took control of the army in Spain. Rome made an alliance with a Spanish city south of the Ebro, which Hannibal felt to be a breach of the treaty. He besieged and captured the city; Rome protested, but Hannibal's popularity in Carthage made the government stand firm: war between the two city states was declared once more.

Hannibal's father, Hamilcar, had already conceived of a plan to attack Italy from the west, across the Alps. Hannibal decided to put this plan into action. It was an astonishing undertaking. Hannibal's whole strategy for invading Italy was based on the idea that the Italian tribes and city states—like those in the Po valley—would join Carthage in a war against Rome. He crossed the Pyrenees, fighting the local tribes, and marched through Gaul managing, in general, to reach an agreement with local chiefs. A Roman force had been despatched to stop Hannibal from crossing the Rhone; he turned north. It has never been certain where Hannibal crossed the Rhone, but recent theories suggest it may have been at or near Montelimar, and that he marched into the Alps up the Drôme valley with some 40,000 infantry, 8,000 cavalry, and 37 war elephants. In the mountains the army faced appalling weather, hostile tribes, treacherous roads, and deadly precipices. Hannibal lost half of his force and most of the famous elephants crossing the Alps. However, he achieved his objective: the Romans were taken by surprise as an army suddenly appeared in the north of Italy, in the Po valley. The consul who had been sent to stop Hannibal from crossing the Rhone hurriedly shipped his army back to Italy by sea. The Gauls of the Po valley joined forces with Hannibal against Rome.

Hannibal moved down the Po valley and won an early minor victory thanks to his superior cavalry, encouraging more local tribes to support him. Another Roman consul was ordered to bring his army back from Sicily to join forces with the army shipped back from France. The first major engagement was at the river Trebia, a tributary of the Po. Hannibal's cavalry made an appearance near the Roman camp and allowed themselves to be driven off, retreating across the Trebia. The Romans, who were probably too keen to engage the enemy, sent their whole army across the river to meet the main Carthaginian force. The Carthaginian and Roman cavalry —Hannibal's cavalry included his terrifying elephants—were both positioned at each end of the lines of infantry to protect their vulnerable flanks.

Hannibal's cavalry began to push back the Roman cavalry; the flanks of the Roman line were exposed and attacked. At this point, a force of light infantry and cavalry that Hannibal had hidden in the steep banks of a nearby stream attacked the rear of the Roman forces. The Roman army broke; many were drowned trying to cross the River Trebia; others were trampled beneath the elephants; most were cut down.

The Romans withdrew to the south; to reach Rome Hannibal needed to cross the Apennine Mountains that run diagonally down the backbone of Italy from north to south. The main road across the mountain was guarded by a Roman army. The other route to Rome was impassable: it was blocked by the huge marshes around the mouth of the River Arno. It is not certain that Hannibal actually said: "We will either find a way, or make one." If Hannibal didn't actually utter the words, then he should have done, and somebody else must have written them into history for him. Hannibal led his troops through the marshes. They marched for four days and three nights, unable to sleep except on wagons, dead animals, or discarded packs because there was no dry land. There were many casualties—including Hannibal's last remaining elephants—but he emerged into southern Italy, cutting off the defending Roman army from Rome itself. He began to pillage the countryside that the Roman army was supposed to be protecting to draw them into battle. The Romans again rushed to meet Hannibal with their full force, and he met them on the northern shores of Lake Trasimene, where he had laid the perfect ambush. He concealed his troops in the heavily wooded hills above the lake; the road ran beneath them on the shores of the lake. His men lit campfires on distant hills to persuade the Romans that the Carthaginians were still ahead of them. As the Roman army entered the road along the lake's northern borders, Hannibal's troops sealed off the exit and attacked. The Romans were unable even to form a line of battle. About 15,000 Romans were killed or drowned in the lake; another 5,000 were captured. The vanguard of 6,000, which had been drawn away from the battle by Carthaginian skirmishers, were captured the next day and sold into slavery; perhaps 10,000 managed to return to Rome. The entire army was destroyed. Hannibal lost between 1,500 and 2,500 men.

In their panic, Rome appointed a dictator, Fabius Maximus. Fabius chose a strategy of avoiding battle with Hannibal (giving rise to the word Fabian—"a cautious strategy designed to wear out an enemy"). Fabius failed to pin down Hannibal, who extricated his whole army from the region around Naples, right from under the nose of Fabius, and moved to Puglia, on the Adriatic coast. Rome dismissed Fabius and resumed Consular elections, appointing two Consuls, Varro and Pallus. In the Roman Republic, Consuls, the highest elected officials of Rome, were also expected to do duty as army commanders. Success in battle, in Rome's highly militarized society, was a sure route to political success.

Hannibal had taken Cannae, on the fertile plains of Puglia, a vital source of food for Rome. The Consuls marched to meet Hannibal with an army of unprecedented size; nearly 90,000 men. The battle of Cannae is one of the masterpieces of ancient warfare. Its strategy of an encircling pincer movement has been copied by generals throughout the ages to modern times. The two Roman consuls, by republican tradition, took command on alternate days. Hannibal knew his opponents: Varro was the more impetuous and reckless; he had won a minor skirmish against Hannibal's troops earlier, and was eager for the kill. Hannibal tempted Varro into battle on an open plain where there was no cover for one of Hannibal's ambushes; Varro strengthened his center in order to smash through the Carthaginian center. The wings of the opposing armies, as ever, were covered by cavalry. Hannibal's was better, both in quality and in number. Hannibal also made use of the variable quality of his infantry: he placed his weakest, newly-recruited local troops at the center—facing the awesome might of the strengthened Roman center—and placed his veteran Carthaginian troops on the wings. As the battle progressed, Hannibal, at the center, in the thick of battle, organized on orderly fall-back of the center, which had started the battle in a crescent formation, bulging out towards the enemy, but which slowly allowed itself to be forced into a concave formation, drawing the enemy into the center. As more and more Roman troops were poured forward into the attack, their room for maneuver—even the room to wield their weapons—became limited. The Carthaginian cavalry to the left had defeated their Roman counterparts and now raced along the rear of the Roman army, attacking the Roman cavalry at the far side of the battle from behind and cutting them down. As the Romans pressed ever forward into the weakening Carthaginian center, certain of victory, the veteran troops on Hannibal's wings began to crowd in on their flanks: the Romans were being forced into a wedge-shaped trap that was closing around them. The attack of the successful Carthaginian cavalry from their rear sealed the trap.

The Roman army was, quite literally, slaughtered. Of some 87,000 Romans, only 14,000 escaped; 50,000 were killed and the rest were taken captive. Hannibal was only interested in prisoners who might genuinely defect to his side: allies of Rome, not citizens. Hannibal was urged to march on Rome, but he calculated that final victory could only be achieved if the Italian tribes and city states would side with him against Rome. If he attacked Rome and lost, it was all over—and he had no siege equipment or experience in siege warfare. If he stayed in Italy as a magnet for disaffected forces, he might find allies that would ensure the defeat of Rome.

The Romans showed their mettle in this crisis. Every man over 17 years of age was enlisted. Engineers strengthened the city's fortifications. Women were forbidden to cry in public. Rome would fight to the last man. A long stalemate ensued. Hannibal enlisted the support of Macedonia and Syracuse, and the Italian city of Capua came over to the Carthaginian side, but reinforcements from Carthage were blocked by the pusillanimous Hanno. Hannibal remained in southern Italy, holding his increasingly rag-tag army together and running circles around the Roman armies, who dared not face him in a set-piece battle.

Rome slowly began to wear Hannibal down. Capua fell to Rome after two sieges; the Romans conquered Syracuse and defeated a Carthaginian army in Sicily. Hannibal's last hope was his brother (another Hasdrubal) who retraced Hannibal's footsteps across Spain, France and across the Alps. His crossing of the Alps was far easier than Hannibal's, partly because many of the bridges and constructions that

Hannibal had made were still in place, and partly because the Gauls were now allies of the Carthaginians. Hasdrubal was defeated in northeastern Italy by four Roman legions and his army was wiped out. Hannibal's brother's head was cut off and thrown into Hannibal's camp to reinforce the point that reinforcements were not, after all, on the way.

In 203 BCE, Hannibal was recalled to Carthage and was finally defeated by a Roman army, largely because the Numidians—allies of Carthage and suppliers of the skilled cavalry contingents so essential to Hannibal's battle tactics—switched sides. The new Roman superiority in cavalry, and the strategic lessons that they had learned at Hannibal's hands, won the day. The Roman cavalry defeated the Carthaginian horse and swept onto the rear of the Carthaginian army.

Hannibal survived the battle and became a successful politician, reforming the corrupt Carthaginian oligarchy so successfully that it was able to make the payments of further swingeing reparations to Rome without increasing taxation. Rome was so alarmed by the economic resurgence of Carthage that they demanded that Hannibal be handed over; he went into voluntary exile. He helped Syria to land a force in southern Italy, but was denied his request to command troops; when it seemed that the Syrians would betray him to Rome he moved to Crete and then to Asia Minor. When his latest hosts were, in their turn, finally persuaded to hand him over to his lifelong enemy, Hannibal took the poison that he had kept always with him, hidden in a ring. He was 64 years old.

The military tactics of Hannibal's great battles are still studied as text-book examples. Germany's plan for enveloping the French armies at the outset of World War I—the Schlieffen Plan—was explicitly based on the battle of Cannae. The broader lessons from Hannibal's leadership are the gains to be made from taking the offensive: had Carthage had the sense to reinforce Hannibal, ascendancy in the Mediterranean region might have belonged to Carthage and not Rome. It was when Rome launched its own counter-attack and crossed the Mediterranean to invade Carthage that Hannibal was recalled to defend the capital. Rome, narrowly, won the ensuing battle.

A leader who can stay on the offensive keeps the initiative and forces the opposition onto the back foot (to mix a military with a sporting metaphor). The other great lesson to be drawn from Hannibal is that nothing is impossible, and that it is achieving the 'impossible' that gives a leader the advantage.

SALADIN
(1138–1193)

In 1187, the army of Saladin stood outside the walls of Jerusalem. The great city, sacred to Jews, Christians, and Muslims alike, had been occupied by Christian Crusaders since 1099. When the Crusaders first entered Jerusalem, they embarked on a terrible massacre of its inhabitants. The mayhem lasted for three full days and shocked the Islamic world, confirming their belief that the Crusaders—also known as Franks, because of the predominance of French troops and leadership—were mere barbarians.

Now, 88 years after the Christian occupation of Jerusalem and the creation of the Kingdom of Jerusalem, Saladin was poised to recapture the sacred city. He had won a significant victory only two weeks earlier by taking the port of Ascalon, north of Gaza. Jerusalem's defenders could no longer be supplied by sea from Europe; the nearest Christian army was at Tyre, 100 miles to the north. The beleaguered city found that it could muster only two knights to lead its defence. Christian knights were the generals and fighting machines of their day; it is not too fanciful to say that the knights, with their mighty horses and heavy armor, were not so much the cavalry as the tank corps of their day. Knights were born and bred to fight in the medieval (and ancient) tradition of lords whose main function in life was to offer protection to their subjects in return for the latter's rents and labor.

One of the knights about to defend Jerusalem was Balian of Ibelin. Balian, after the earlier defeat of the Crusaders by Saladin at the battle of Hattin, had retreated to the safe haven of Tyre, but his wife and family were in Jerusalem. He petitioned Saladin to be allowed to travel safely to Jerusalem in order to bring his family back to Tyre. Saladin agreed, on the condition that Balian would return to Tyre with his family after only one night at Jerusalem and that he would never take up arms against Saladin again. Once Balian was in Jerusalem, he came under impossible pressure to stay and help in the defence of the city.

The Christian Patriarch of Jerusalem quickly absolved Balian from the sin of breaking his oath, arguing that it would be a greater sin to keep the oath (to an infidel) and to abandon the Christians of Jerusalem. Balian, in a demonstration of the chivalric warrior code that overrode the supposedly clear lines of religious conflict, wrote to Saladin, saying that he had been forced to break his oath and begging protection for his family. Saladin sent 50 soldiers to escort the Lady Ibelin and their children to the safety of Tyre.[82]

Balian, freed (remarkably) from concerns about his own family's safety, set out to defend Jerusalem. Saladin attacked the walls of the city with siege engines, hurling stones and fire canisters. Sappers, protected by the shields of their comrades, began to undermine the walls: the foundations were propped up with timbers that were then set alight; the walls crumbled. The Crusaders prepared to die fighting, certain of a place in heaven for such a martyr's death. The ordinary inhabitants of Jerusalem knew, however, that if the city resisted further, then the attackers would sack the city—this being the long-established fate of besieged cities that refused terms of surrender. The awful sack of Jerusalem by Christian soldiers in 1099 was still recent history; the inhabitants could expect no mercy from the besieging Muslims.

Saladin was loath to see such bloody mayhem in the streets of the sacred city. He also wanted to preserve the city's sacred sites and artefacts: plundering soldiers make indiscriminate looters. On the other hand, his coalition of emirs and their troops had to be rewarded—the plunder of a rich city was the expected reward for services given. Also, when ambassadors from Jerusalem had refused to surrender the city after the fall of Ascalon, Saladin had sworn an oath to take Jerusalem "by the sword."

Balian led the negotiations for the defenders: if Saladin refused to offer terms then the Crusaders, with nothing left but the opportunity of a glorious death, would die fighting to the last man, having first destroyed the sacred Islamic sites of the city and killed the 5,000 Muslims who were held captive within the city. It was almost certainly a bluff—Balian was unlikely to be allowed enough time to carry out his threats—but it was a bluff that Saladin was happy to use as an excuse to avoid the sack of the city.

Saladin took counsel from his advisors. If the city was formally surrendered, then Saladin could be said to have fulfilled his oath. The occupants of the town could be ransomed, thus allowing the emirs to get their fair share of plunder though a reasonable 'take' on the official ransom which, of course, was destined for various treasuries. The administration of this surrender was not only as fair as Saladin could contrive (some emirs managed their own private ransom schemes and pocketed all of the proceeds) but was in some aspects extraordinarily generous and humane. The remnant of a treasure donated to the Knights Hospitallers in Jerusalem by King Henry II of England was accepted as a ransom for 7,000 people too poor to raise the sum through any other means. Saladin's brother asked for 1,000 slaves as his just reward for his services in battle, all of whom he promptly freed. Saladin responded by releasing many thousand old and infirm inhabitants in the same spirit. Great ladies, who had no problem in raising their ransom money, were nevertheless now dispossessed by Saladin of the lands that they had previously held and their husbands, if not dead, were imprisoned. Saladin promised to trace the lords and reunite them with their families. He made cash grants to the ladies, depending on their status, as compensation for their losses.[83]

The legend of Saladin is all here. A great general, able to unite the divided factions of the Islamic world and to drive the infidel out of Jerusalem (if not yet out of the country); a man of great chivalry in his treatment of the Christian warriors with whom he fought; a humane and magnanimous victor. But, in many ways, Saladin's claim to great leadership lies not so much in the headline achievement of having recovered Jerusalem for the Islamic word as in the remarkable achievement of having achieved control over the various factions of the twelfth-century Islamic world and in his ability to bring these factions together to face a common enemy. For many local potentates, the Crusader's presence in the region was a less pressing concern than their own local political issues. Saladin had a clear vision: the recovery of Jerusalem and the expulsion of the Christian infidels from the Middle East. Saladin's leadership set the directions that the Islamic communities of the northern Middle East would need to follow in order to achieve this vision. Having consolidated his control of Cairo, he gradually forced the whole of Syria to acknowledge his leadership. He unified the region under his control, primarily by means of negotiation and political pressure, and gradually created the platform from which to launch an attack on the Christians' most symbolic stronghold, Jerusalem.

Saladin was born to a Kurdish family. His father and his father's brother were both commanders for Nur ad-Din Zengi, the Turkish ruler of Aleppo. The key cities of the middle-eastern region at that time were Baghdad and Mosul, on the River Tigris in Mesopotamia, and Damascus and Aleppo in Syria. The caliphs of Baghdad were the nominal heads of the Sunni Islamic world, but the rulers of the various city-states were in a state of constant minor warfare amongst themselves. In Cairo, Shi'ite caliphs (considered as heretics by the Sunni caliphs of Baghdad) ruled Egypt.

Nur ad-Din conquered the great fortified Christian city of Edessa, the first major city that the first Crusaders had captured. Edessa was strategically important, as it constantly threatened the cities of both Aleppo and Mosul. In 1154 Nur ad-Din took over Damascus in a bloodless coup to become the undisputed ruler of Syria—his brother was the ruler of the other strategic city of Mosul. Nur ad-Din was the first Muslim leader to position himself as leading a long-term Holy War—a *jihad*—against the Christian enclave.

Nur ad-Din had taken Damascus with the help of Saladin's father and his uncle, Shirkuh—a formidable warrior (and a formidable trencherman) who was later to kill Raymond of Antioch in single combat. Saladin's father was left to govern Damascus, while Nur ad-Din and Shirkuh returned to Aleppo. Young Saladin grew up in

Damascus, the richest city in Syria, in a privileged position. He was educated in philosophy, science, religion, rhetoric, and poetry. Central to a young gentleman's education was the concept of *zarf*—elegance and refinement. Saladin entered the army at the age of 14 and later left Damascus to join his uncle Shirkuh at Aleppol, to complete his military training. He was a fine horseman, a hunter, and a famous polo player.

In 1167, Saladin joined Shirkuh on Nur ad-Din's military expedition against the Shi'ite Caliphs of Egypt. They were successful, and Shirkuh was installed as military governor of Egypt. Saladin took over the role on the death of Shirkuh (who finally ate and drank himself to death); he quietly dismissed officials loyal to the Egyptian Caliph (still alive, but now powerless) and installed his own. His father and brothers were installed in key roles. In 1170, Saladin launched an attack on a fortress at the southern edge of the Christian kingdom. The Templars held out until the Christian army arrived, and Saladin's Egyptian army slipped away to sack the city of Gaza. Saladin then transported a fleet of prefabricated ships by camel from Cairo to the Gulf of Suez and sailed them round the Sinai Peninsula to the Gulf of Aqaba, launching a simultaneous land and sea attack on Christian-held Aqaba—a major port and a key staging-post on the pilgrimage to Mecca. Saladin's Egyptian army was now a fighting force to be reckoned with; the re-taking of Aqaba was a major victory for Islam. Saladin was becoming a force in the land; Nur ad-Din was not happy.

Saladin used Egypt's agricultural riches to build up his treasury. He pursued a policy of non-confrontation with Nur ad-Din, sending regular tributes in cash and goods. Nur ad-Din considered a military expedition against Saladin. When Nur ad-Din died in 1174, leaving his 11-year-old son as boy-king, Saladin took on the title of Sultan of Egypt and began his campaign to take control of Syria.

He rode with only 700 troops to Damascus at the invitation of the city and began to argue his case to be recognized as the ruler who could unite the Islamic world against the Franks. To consolidate his power, in the time-honoured way, he married Nur ad-Din's widow. He petitioned

Baghdad—religious capital of the Muslim world—for a diploma recognizing his conquests. Saladin had brought Egypt back to the Sunni fold; he had expanded his Egyptian territories into the Yemen, on the southeastern coast of the Red Sea, south of Mecca; he had gained territory in North Africa; his claim to Syria was necessary to enable him to re-conquer Jerusalem; all of his future conquests would be in the name of the caliph of Baghdad. Nur ad-Din Zengi had never offered so much recognition to Baghdad; the prestige of the Caliph of Baghdad was greatly enhanced. Saladin got his diploma, and was proclaimed as King of Syria. The Zengid Turkish sultanate had been effectively by-passed.

In 1177, Saladin marched out of Cairo as champion of the Holy War, intent on capturing Jerusalem. He marched up the coast of Palestine; the Crusaders were just able to reinforce the port of Ascalon with 500 knights under King Baldwin, who smuggled a message through the besieging Muslims to the Knights Templar at Gaza. Saladin had turned inland to attack Jerusalem. As the Templars arrived, Baldwin was able to break out of Ascalon; the combined forces surprised Saladin's army in the ravines near Montgisard and slaughtered them. Only one tenth of the army is said to have returned to Egypt.

Baldwin was not strong enough to move on to Damascus, but he built a new fortification on the upper Jordan at Jacob's Ford, an important crossing of the River Jordan on the main road from Damascus to Acre. Baldwin hoped that the fortress would block attacks on Jerusalem and put pressure on Damascus. Saladin was unable to prevent the building of the great tower because he was busy putting down rebellions by various of his Muslim subjects. He tried to bribe Baldwin to stop the work, but Baldwin refused. In 1179 Saladin was able to attack the new tower; he had only a few days to overwhelm its defences before Baldwin would arrive with reinforcements from Tiberias, on the lake of Galilee. Saladin succeeded, his sappers undermining the walls as they were later to do at Jerusalem. The Christian garrison were killed. Saladin and Baldwin signed a truce the following year.

Christian attacks continued, despite the truce. A Christian hot-head, Raynald of Chatillon, raided rich caravans in the south from his fortress of al-Karak: a stronghold that constantly threatened both the caravan and pilgrim trails between the port of Aqaba on the Red Sea and Jerusalem and Damascus to the north.

In early 1187 Saladin summoned all provinces to the holy war. The Christians were comprehensively defeated at the battle of Hattim, where they had gone into battle carrying what was believed to be the True Cross (the actual cross on which Jesus had been crucified), and had lost this mighty talisman to the Muslims. The defeated King Guy of Jerusalem was led before Saladin with the hated Raynald, whom Saladin had sworn to kill. Water was brought for the exhausted King Guy, who then passed it on to Raynald. Saladin immediately insisted that Guy tell Raynald that the water was given to Raynald without Saladin's permission: if Saladin had offered food or water to Raynald then the latter would be able to claim the protection of his 'host'. Later that evening Raynald was killed; Saladin may have struck the first blow himself. The King and even the Grand Master of the Templars were spared and later released, but 100 Templar and Hospitaller Knights were executed: these committed and fanatical shock troops of the Crusades were too dangerous to spare. The chivalrous Saladin was humane, but he was not above occasional ruthlessness.

The fall of the port of Ascalon brought Saladin to the walls of Jerusalem; after the fall of Jerusalem, the Third Crusade was launched to recapture it; bringing Saladin into battle against Richard I ("The Lionheart") of England. The two never met, but seemed to develop a genuine admiration for each other. Saladin sent fruit, chilled with snow, to Richard when he was ill and offered the services of his personal physician; when Richard's horse was killed in battle, Saladin sent a gift of two horses. Richard proposed a dynastic marriage between his sister and Saladin's brother to create a united Palestine with the two of them as joint rulers. The wedding never came about, and it is unlikely that Saladin would have countenanced a marriage to an infidel.

The Third Crusade never did regain Jerusalem. In 1192 a treaty was signed that left Jerusalem in Muslim hands but granted rights of Christian pilgrimage. The Kingdom of Jerusalem was reduced to a few cities around Acre, the new capital. Saladin died of a fever in the spring of the following year.

Saladin, above all, was a great unifier. He emerges as a humane and generous man, and these civilized instincts allowed him to rise above the politics of revenge: Saladin's habit of treating a defeated enemy with kindness and even with generosity won him many friends, while his firm control from the center prevented this from being exploited as weakness. It had practical benefits: cities were relatively happy to surrender to Saladin, in expectation of decent treatment, while they would have held out against an attacker likely to wreak destruction on a vanquished city. In his struggle to assert his leadership over the Zengid dynasty, Saladin managed on every occasion to strike a deal, to negotiate a treaty, to use politics to gain the upper hand rather than to engage in outright civil war. He set a clear direction: a program of unification in order to drive out the Christian invaders. After his death, his realm disintegrated.

ELIZABETH GARRETT ANDERSON
(1836–1917)

Elizabeth Garrett (Anderson was her married name) had no intention of being a leader, but she did have to take the offensive. She wanted a career, and she chose medicine, although even her dauntless spirit might have faltered if she had known just how many obstacles, over how long a period of time, would be strewn in her path by the male medical establishment.

Garrett became the first woman to have her name entered on the medical register and the first woman doctor to open a practice; the first European woman to gain a doctorate in medicine (from Paris); the first woman to become a member of the British Medical Association; the first woman member of the London School Board; the first female Dean of a medical school—and, later in life, almost as an afterthought, Britain's first woman mayor (of Aldeburgh, Suffolk). Along the way, she founded the New Hospital for Women and Children.

What is concealed within this marvellous list of achievements is the reality of how astonishingly difficult it was for her to achieve any of these things. Women simply did not become doctors. All of the medical schools and examining bodies had been founded in the clear expectation that mediciine was, and would always be, a male preserve. Sometimes their charters and constitutions spelled this out; sometimes they didn't. Sometimes they were vague. When Elizabeth presented herself, to the astonishment of the various hospitals, schools, universities, and licensing bodies, there was often a scramble for ancient documents. If it was not possible to prove that the founding charter or constitution prevented the admission of women, another good reason would be found, or a vote would be taken, with the inevitable result.

Garrett stands out as the leader that she never intended to be by virtue of the sheer difficulty of the pioneering trail that she blazed. No sooner would she manage to find one loophole in the system than it would be closed behind her to prevent other women from following suit. She faced unremitting hostility from a formidable establishment —though in person, of course, they found her impressive and persuasive.

It is worth trying to get some flavor of the depth of prejudice that existed at the time against women entering the medical profession. It had many facets, and was always accompanied by that air of amused superiority that is the hallmark of the true bigot. In 1873 (by which time Elizabeth Garrett was the only woman to have managed to get her name onto the Medical Register), an editorial from *The Lancet*, the magazine of the medical profession, had this to say:

> "It is asserted by the advocates for female doctors that there is a field for the usefulness of women in the medical treatment of diseases of women and children, and that women themselves would rather be attended in their labours and various ailments by members of their own sex than by men. We must demur to this, for from an extended experience we are convinced that the mothers of England prefer to be attended in their labors by medical men, and that, in fact, the idea of female medical attendants is positively repulsive to the more thoughtful women of this country. Judging from the mental, moral, and emotional characteristics of the female organisation [by this the leader-writer means the female mind and body] we should say that women are not well fitted to regard calmly and philosophically the pains and agonies of their sisters, nor are they constituted to battle seriously and determinedly with many of the dangerous and alarming accidents of parturition, which always require prompt and vigorous action."[84]

There was a deeply held belief that men and women were different not only physically but mentally. The leader writer from *The Lancet* went on to say (with a nod towards evolutionary Darwinism), "It cannot be doubted that it is possible to make women more man-like, but it is not possible to produce in them the characteristics of man without destroying many of their feminine attractions and possibly also their feminine functions."[85] Too much "unnatural" effort by a woman (too much intellectual strain, for example) would affect not only her health, but her fertility. The affect on her attractiveness was, of course, unavoidable.

The medical profession shared (and promulgated) the notion that women's God-given nature was simply not up to a wide variety of stern or demanding tasks; not only were women likely to have a fainting fit at the sight of another woman in labor or pain (an interesting notion, since women had been midwives and healers for many millennia before the arrival of the Victorian male doctor), but they were also incapable of the "prompt and vigorous action" that a medical emergency might require.

Sexual politics played a largely unacknowledged role. Five years later, the same editor of *The Lancet*, James G. Wakeley (son of the founding editor, Thomas Wakely) had this to say:

"In the economy of nature [...] the ministry of women is one of help and sympathy. The essential principle, the key-note of her work in the world, is aid; to sustain, succour, revive and even sometimes shelter man in the struggle and duty of life, is her peculiar function. The moment she affects the first or leading role in any vocation she is out of place and the secondary, but essential, part of helpmate cannot be filled."[86]

Furthermore (and this was a problem that Elizabeth could not possibly have foreseen), her fellow male students—hard-drinking, rat-baiting, horse-betting, cadaver-slicing young medical students—began to fret about the effect on their sensitivities of observing dissections in the presence of a woman. They raised a petition against her presence: "Young females as passive spectators in the operating theatre is an outrage on our natural instincts and feelings and calculated to destroy those sentiments of respect and admiration with which the opposite sex is regarded by all right-minded men." Even worse, their lecturers were apparently likely, "to feel some restraint through the presence of females in giving that explicit and forcible enunciation of some facts which is necessary for their comprehension by the student."[87]

Finally, apart from women losing their "femininity", not being up to the task, subverting their proper role as helpmate, and offending the sensibilities of male medical students, there was the altogether more delicate problem of bodily functions and, in surgery, of blood and guts. The notion that a nice young lady would willingly choose a career that would involve her on a daily basis with these unmentionables was unthinkable, and a woman who did so choose was, in many subtle ways, questionable.

Elizabeth, the second of ten children, was born into a well-to-do Victorian family; her father, Newson Garrett, was a self-made man. He had started out as a pawnbroker in London's East End before moving his family to Aldeburgh in Suffolk, and setting himself up in the brewing industry. The family was a perfect example of successful, self-made, affluent, middle-class Victorian Britain. The expectations for Elizabeth, as a young woman, were depressingly limited. While her brothers went to public school, to university, and out into a world full of excitement and potential, she was expected to become that most recent of inventions: the middle-class lady of leisure. For the young ladies of the late-nineteenth century, everything seemed possible, yet nothing was expected of them.

On a visit to family friends in Gateshead, Elizabeth met Emily Davies, six years older than herself, the wife of the Rector of Gateshead. Emily Davies was to become a leading feminist and an early suffragist. She helped to collect the names for the 1866 petition that John Stuart Mill presented to Parliament—the first ever petition for women's right to vote. She was to edit the feminist *Englishwoman's Journal* and to campaign for the right of women to be admitted to London, Oxford, and Cambridge Universities. With Barbara Bodichon (soon to be another acquaintance of Elizabeth), Emily later founded Girton College, Cambridge, the first residential college for women. Emily, as might be expected, made a profound impression on the young Elizabeth, which grew over time as they kept up their friendship.

In 1859, visiting her sister in London, Elizabeth Garrett met Dr Elizabeth Blackwell, thanks to an introduction via a business connection of her father's. Although English, Dr Blackwell grew up in the United States and was the first woman to graduate from medical school with an MD (Doctor of Medicine). She later returned to England and established the Women's Medical College. Blackwell assumed that Elizabeth must have decided to follow in her footsteps and spoke encouragingly to her. Elizabeth was rather daunted by the notion, but her new friend, Emily Davies, was a firm believer in the need for women physicians: Elizabeth must become a pioneer and lead the way for other women. With considerable doubts as to her abilities, Elizabeth warmed to the idea. Had she known of the obstacles that the British male establishment would put in her way, Elizabeth might have dropped the idea. Elizabeth's father was won over to the idea of her chosen career in time, but her mother struggled with the idea of her daughter leaving home to go into any kind of profession, let alone medicine. She shut herself in her room and cried. Elizabeth Garrett, with her father's support, set out to become a doctor in 1860. Darwin's *Origin of the Species* had recently been published, as had Dickens' *Tale of Two Cities*; Abraham Lincoln had just been selected as presidential candidate for the new American Republican party.

With no prospect of entering a medical school, Elizabeth took a job as a nurse at the Middlesex Hospital in London. Hygiene at the hospital was not so much rudimentary as non-existent. It was still believed that illnesses were spread by miasma or 'bad air', which led to an obsession with fresh air—explaining why hospitals of the time were built with such high ceilings and tall windows. They were not, sadly, obsessed (or even interested) in cleanliness. Surgeons wore the same blood-spattered frock coats from one operation to the next, carrying their unwashed surgical implements with them. Doctors also went straight from dissecting cadavers to inspect pregnant mothers, without washing their hands. Gangrene was endemic in amputees; puerperal fever was endemic in maternity wards.

Elizabeth found that she had a strong stomach and a cool head. Surgeons noted that she was calm and efficient when minor surgery was performed on the wards; they began to invite her to follow them on their rounds. She attended her first operation with other (male) students. She began to be treated as a real medical student. Concerned that this might be seen as unfair, she offered to pay her student's fees. The hospital would not accept a fee, since that would recognize that she was a student, but she was allowed to make a donation and to continue to help the surgeons on their rounds as an 'amateur'. Her studies intensified; she asked to be allowed into the dissecting rooms; the Dean and the lecturers became increasingly impressed, but her fellow male students became increasingly concerned. Eventually, a group of students raised a petition. Faced with a potential revolt of fee-paying students, the hospital refused Elizabeth admission as a full-time medical student. With a letter of regret that praised her conduct at the hospital from the lecturers, she was forced to leave the Middlesex.

She was already becoming the subject of controversy and debate. *The Lancet* ran several supposedly humorous editorials with introductions such as, "How Should the Fair Intruder be Received?", but concluded that the whole issue was irrelevant since no examining body would issue the necessary diploma.[88] There was the rub: several other London schools voted not to allow Miss Garrett to study; since no examining body would accept her in order for the qualifications essential to be able to practice medicine, they would be educating somebody who could only be able to practice illegally.

Elizabeth wrote to the examining bodies—Oxford, Cambridge, Glasgow, Edinburgh—but was rejected. There was, however, one last examining body that could offer the minimum qualification needed to have one's name entered on the Medical Register and to be able to practice as a doctor: the Society of Apothecaries, whose charter referred to "all persons" desirous of practicing medicine, without reference to their sex. Elizabeth's father took legal advice. It was agreed that "persons" did include "women." The Apothecaries agreed to accept Elizabeth to their examinations if she could find herself an apprenticeship and attend a list of statutory courses—which, in the normal course of things, would mean spending three years at medical school, all of whom, to date, had refused to accept her. The apothecary at Middlesex Hospital, with whom she had worked during her time there, willingly agreed to take her on as his apprentice.

To continue her studies, Elizabeth tried the University of London. The charter of the University said that it had been founded to provide education "for all classes and denominations." The Garretts again took legal advice, but it was decided that women were neither a "class" nor a "denomination", so the university was not obliged to accept them. The University was about to receive a new charter, so Newson Garrett submitted a proposal to Senate that, under this new charter, the University should open its examinations to women on the reasonable grounds that, "it appears very desirable to raise the standard of female education, especially in the more solid branches of learning." Elizabeth and her friend Emily Davis distributed 1,500 leaflets to various notables. There was support from William Gladstone, the Chancellor of the Exchequer. The Senate of the University was split down the middle; the Chancellor cast his deciding vote…against.

A well-disposed Professor of Medicine at St Andrews University, Professor Simpson, invited Elizabeth to attend his lectures. There was another moment of hope: the Professor suggested that Elizabeth try for matriculation to the University; there was no examination, only payment of a fee of one pound. If allowed to matriculate, Elizabeth would have been accepted into the University and would be eligible to sit their examinations for a Doctorate of Medicine, whereas her qualification from the Society of Apothecaries would only be sufficient to get her on to the Medical Register and allow her to set up as a General Practitioner. Elizabeth wanted the coveted letters

"MD"after her name and feared she would get few patients without it. Elizabeth approached the genial Secretary of the University, told him that she was attending the professor's lectures, and asked to matriculate. She paid her one pound and was accepted. The next day a crestfallen Secretary was forced to return Elizabeth's pound: Senate had decided that she could not be accepted. Elizabeth refused the returned pound and took legal advice. Was the acceptance of the money a form of contract? No, the University could not be bound by the actions of its Secretary unless they had specifically authorized him to take such action. Was there a case to be made in court? For damages, possibly, but Senate could not be forced to do what their Charter did not permit them to do.

Elizabeth's friendly professor at St Andrews made light of her distress: the supposedly magical letters "MD" meant little, he assured her; a practitioner was judged more by his (or her) character than by the letters after their name.

There was a minor, but essential, piece of good news. The Society of Apothecaries confirmed that Elizabeth was able to cover the necessary course-work for her qualification by private tuition from recognized lecturers of acknowledged schools of medicine. Her certificates from Middlesex Hospital and her other studies could also all count towards her qualification. Professor Simpson referred her to an eminent lecturer in Midwifery at Edinburgh. She studied and worked for a year at the Edinburgh Maternity Hospital, gaining essential clinical experience, but she still needed a course in practical anatomy. Finally, a bright young orthopaedic surgeon agreed to take her on.

Bit by bit, Elizabeth gained the necessary experience and qualifications. She got clinical practice at the London Dispensary, which served the poor of London's Spitalfields area. She attended the London Hospital for more nursing experience and, now a minor celebrity, put up with a great deal of hostility. She entered the fifth and final year of her studies. She used her good relations with the Middlesex to be allowed onto certain wards by permission of individual physicians and surgeons.

The Society of Apothecaries suddenly realized that this young woman really did intend to take their examinations, and that they would be blamed throughout the medical profession for allowing a woman to qualify as a medical practitioner. The Court of Examiners wrote to say that, regretfully, they could not examine her after all. Elizabeth's doughty father threatened to sue. The Society took Counsel's opinion and was told, once more, that their charter did not disbar women. They backed down, but immediately set about changing their regulations so that no other woman might embarrass them in this way. From now on a female applicant would be required to graduate from an accredited medical school. Since none of the medical schools would enrol women, this was an effective Catch-22. It was another 12 years before another woman would get her name onto the Medical Register.

Elizabeth passed the examinations. She set up in practice off London's Edgware Road and built up her list of patients. After six months she set up an outpatient dispensary for poor women. An outbreak of cholera meant that St Mary's Dispensary for Women and Children was embraced by the establishment more warmly than it might normally have been, as it provided treatment in impecunious Marylebone. By the end of the outbreak, the idea of an all-women dispensary was established. After six years, the Dispensary became the New Hospital for Women and Children.

In 1870, Elizabeth Garrett finally received her MD, from Paris University. She had commuted from London to Paris during her studies, faced a public *viva* examination (in front of a packed theatre of male students and lecturers and conducted, of course, in French), and submitted a thesis on migraine, which was well received.

As free education for working-class children in Britain became a reality with the passing of the Elementary Education Act in 1870, Garrett was urged by her local community to stand for the new London School Board, which not only allowed women to stand as potential candidates, but even to cast their own votes. Elizabeth spoke at public meetings of up to 1,000 people—at a time when it was virtually unheard of for a woman to speak in public. She won by a proverbial landslide.

A year later, Elizabeth married James Anderson. They were to have three children (one of whom was to die in infancy of meningitis) and, flying yet again in the face of accepted behavior, Elizabeth continued with her career. In 1874 Elizabeth helped to found the London Medical College for Women, where she taught for 23 years, including 20 years as Dean. In 1876 an MP steered a bill through Parliament that would oblige all medical corporations to allow women to enter for their examinations, regardless of their charters. In 1877 the London Medical School for Women was affiliated to the Royal Free Hospital in Hampstead, which could then issue the degrees to female graduates of the School, allowing them to enrol on the Medical Register.

There was one final clash with the medial profession. In 1874, her brother-in-law proposed Elizabeth for membership to the Metropolitan branch of the British Medical Association. The secretary found that the only condition for membership was that candidates should be registered medical practitioners—there was no mention of gender. He signed the application. It took some years before the Association woke up to the fact that a female member had been elected. In 1878 a conference listened politely while Dr Garrett Anderson pointed out that there were now eight women on the Medical Register, that there would soon be more, and that they should be eligible to become members of the BMA. She was listened to with politeness—they even laughed at her witticisms—then they voted to ban all future women members; though, in honour of Elizabeth, not retrospectively. For 19 years she was the only female member of the BMA. In 1902 the Andersons retired to Aldeburgh, and in 1908 she was elected Mayor of the town—the first female mayor in Britain.

8

CREATING
OPPORTUNITIES

Creating opportunities is a bit like the elusive skill of making your own luck. No manager can achieve everything by themselves. Creating opportunities is a different skill from that of successful delegation or of genuinely empowering team members. Once the team is empowered, they need chances that they can take, opportunities that they can exploit. A really good manager helps to create these opportunities—and a really well-run team eventually begin to create their own opportunities, which is when the whole thing really begins to take off.

We all recognize this in sport. When a team is playing at its best, with every player making the best use of their individual skills and playing at the top of their game, then opportunities start, as if by magic, to appear. The individual skills of one player create the opportunity for the next player. The cumulative effect of a number of small opportunities suddenly becomes one big opportunity. A coach can set out the general strategy for a team like this, and encourage them to play a certain sort of game, but even the best coach cannot plan for the precise opportunity that will win the game.

Opportunities can be created in many ways. Building the right team is essential: highly talented individuals will bring opportunities to a manager's doorstep. Developing a really outstanding marketing idea can do the same thing: suddenly a particular image or a slogan incorporates the organization's goals so well that other things start to fall into place; apparently unrelated bits of activity suddenly make more sense from this new perspective; different departments suddenly come up with new ideas that fit neatly into the new perspective. Entering a new market, or entering a market at a particularly well-judged time can do the same thing: suddenly opportunities are falling at a team's feet. Some apparently mundane structural changes can be highly effective—something as simple as the way in which information is presented and handled, or the way in which individuals report to their team managers. If information begins to flow more smoothly through the organization, then people will more easily be able to pick up on the bits that matter to them. Suddenly, people start to have ideas.

The leaders from history in this chapter illustrate very different ways of creating opportunities. Firstly, the surprising ways in which ideas can begin to flow around an organization that brings together unexpected partners, and facilitates the exchange of information without heavy-handed control from the top (illustrated, surprisingly and strikingly, by Genghis Khan); the opportunities that can arise from sheer persistence—from simply hanging in there and keeping options alive (Chiang Kai Shek); the dramatic breakthroughs that can be achieved by getting out into the world, talking to people, keeping your eyes open, and bringing back an intelligent report (Marco Polo).

Genghis Khan is an entirely counter-intuitive choice with which to illustrate the concept of creating opportunities. In the West, we still tend to see Genghis as one of the most destructive forces in history. The Mongol hordes swept out of the Eurasian steppe in the thirteenth century, overrunning the stable and sophisticated Islamic empires of Central Asia and reaching as far as the Black Sea. The descendants of Genghis would reach the Mediterranean and threaten Vienna in the north. The terrifying Mongolian cavalry overwhelmed all opposition, and utterly destroyed those who opposed them, razing entire cities to the ground. It seemed that a new dark age would spread across Asia and Europe. In fact, although they were ruthless in conquest, the Mongols were surprisingly benign in peace. They had no interest in imposing any particular ideology on the new empire; different regions of their increasingly vast territories were allowed to develop in their own way. The very existence of the empire—stretching eventually from China to the Mediterranean—created a *Pax Mongolica* that has been compared with the *Pax Romana* created by the Roman Empire at its height, more than 1,000 years earlier. Goods, cultures, religions, and ideas began to flow around the globe. Genghis Khan does not, in himself, make a good role model for managers (though you may have dealings with managers who exhibit some of his characteristics), but he was an exceptional leader—completely reorganizing Mongol society from a set of feuding tribes into a unified force—and his legacy shows how a large but focussed organization, governed with a very light touch from the center, can create huge opportunities.

Chiang Kai Shek can take much of the credit for making the emergence of modern China possible. After the final collapse of China's last imperial dynasty, represented by the poignant figure of Puyi, "The Last Emperor," there was an attempt to create a new, democratic republic in China. The Nationalist Party—the Kuomintang—was the new republic's main political party. The republic turned for its new President to an ex-imperial general with the necessary military clout to ensure the stability of the new government, but he attempted to turn himself into a new emperor; the Provinces rebelled once more and the world's oldest civilization descended into a series of feudal states governed by modern-day barons—"the warlords." As leader of the Nationalist Party and of its new army, Chiang Kai Shek defeated the most significant warlords and created a national government once more, though he was plagued by continued wars against the remaining warlords, and a full civil war later broke out between the Kuomintang and the Chinese Communist Party. Chiang was persuaded to join forces with the Communists to fight the threat of invasion from Japan (Chiang was kidnapped by one of his generals and given no option; he had been determined to destroy the Communist Party before taking on Japan). He then performed another of his miracles on behalf of China: his Nationalist forces, aided by Communist guerrilla actions, managed to slow down the Japanese invasion long enough to prevent a rapid conquest of China, buying sufficient time to see America enter the war after Japan's bombing of the American Fleet at Pearl Harbor. The Sino-Japanese war became part of the wider conflict of World War II and Chiang became Supreme Commander of Allied Forces in the region. After the war, Chiang lost his battle against the Communist Party; his Republic of China became a government in exile on the island of Taiwan, while mainland China emerged as the People's

Republic of China. On Taiwan, Chiang helped to engineer Taiwan's economic revolution, turning the country into one of the 'tiger economies' of the Far East and changing the economic status of the region for ever. Chiang, often remembered as "the man who lost China," will go down in history as the man who did the most to keep the Chinese nation intact in one of its darkest periods.

Marco Polo is famous as a traveller and a merchant, but he ought to be famous as a merchant of ideas. With his father and his uncle, he traveled from the Mediterranean to China, an almost unimaginable journey made possible, perversely, by the success of the terrifying Mongol invaders. The Mongol Empire's control of vast regions made travel across huge distances possible and—relatively speaking—safe. The Polo family traveled to see the grandson of Genghis Khan: Kublai Khan, ruler of Mongolia and the northern and western regions of modern China. Marco Polo's true skills lay both in his ability to get on with people from very different cultural backgrounds, and in his abilities as a reporter. Kublai Khan, like any great leader, was hungry for information. Marco Polo became the Khan's trusted ambassador: he traveled around the Khan's Empire and he brought back well-told tales of the wonders of the Khan's lands and of his people. These tales, and Marco's notebooks, formed the basis of Marco's great book, *Il Milione*—now known as *The Travels of Marco Polo*. This book not only brought the discoveries of the advanced Chinese civilization to the rest of the world—paper currencies; the use of coal; town-planning; postal systems—it also opened up entirely new horizons. Roughly 200 years after Marco Polo, Columbus sailed west from Europe with a heavily annotated copy of the *Travels*, hoping to find a new route to the fabled riches of the East, described so enticingly by Marco. Marco's dissemination of ideas changed the development of Europe (and the New World) by presenting new ideas and opportunities to the world—by bringing different cultures together.

GENGHIS KHAN
(*c.*1162–1227)

The Mongols were nomadic steppe-dwellers from northeast Asia, similar to (and possibly related to) the Native Americans and closely related to the Huns or Xiongnu who had plagued China some 1,400 years before. They worshipped the Eternal Blue Sky and a pantheon of lesser gods, and were entirely tolerant of, and even embraced, other religions alongside their essentially shamanistic beliefs. They left no architecture or manufactured goods; they painted no pictures and carved no statues. At first glance, Genghis Khan's armies seem to us to have brought only death and destruction, and to have left nothing behind.

There were occasions when the Mongol hordes would not simply capture and sack a city, but would reportedly slaughter every living creature inside, tear down the city walls, and remove all traces of the city's existence. Genghis Khan razed cities partly to deter future resistance, and partly as a strategic move to destroy population centers in relatively inaccessible areas of his expanding empire, in order to funnel the movement of people and trade through the more accessible routes, which he could then monitor and control. There can be no doubt about the utter devastation visited on some regions by the Mongol army, nor of the horrors experienced by many civilians—such as being herded in front of the advancing Mongol army as living shields, or being thrown into defensive ditches as living ballast.

Paradoxically, the impact of Genghis Khan and the Mongol hordes on the history of civilization is perhaps greater than that of any other world empire. The one thing that the Mongols did build—both physically and metaphorically—was bridges. The conquests of Genghis linked China with Central Asia, the Middle East, and Europe for the first time in history; forging commercial and diplomatic links between nations who were previously barely aware of each other's existence (Genghis invented the concept of diplomatic immunity for ambassadors and envoys between nations). The Mongols facilitated the flow of goods around the emerging new world, and with the goods traveled technologies, ideas, and cultures. Mining and noodles, carrots and carpets, science and tea, Christianity and gunpowder, paper currencies and Buddhism began to move around the world in an unprecedented way.[89]

The Mongol clans of the twelfth century lived in a small part of what we now call Mongolia; north of the Gobi desert and south of the mountain ranges that separate Mongolia from eastern Siberia. Arctic winds release what little moisture they carry onto the northern mountains. When the spring thaw comes, frozen lakes and snowdrifts feed the streams and rivers that water the vast grasslands. In a good summer, the steppe turns green and feeds the great herds of horses, cows, sheep, and goats that sustain the people who live there. There are far more animals than people; life is a battle for survival.

The Mongol tribes were surrounded by many others, including the Tatar, Kerait, and Merkit. Tribes fought each other in a constant round of raids and retaliations; within the tribes, family clans bickered and feuded. In the winter, hunting parties searched for game in the forests in the mountains. In hard times, hunting parties would raid groups of humans instead. Women were kidnapped as wives; young boys as labor. At the approach of a raiding party, adult males were the first to escape on horseback—if the community was to survive the raid, then the young men were the most valuable members and also the ones most likely to be killed as rivals; this was not a land for heroics. Genghis Khan's own mother had been captured while returning with her new husband to his home territory. The bride persuaded her husband to flee, to save his life; she never saw him again. She became the second wife of her captor, a Mongol chieftain, and bore him a child called Temujin—the man who would become known as Genghis Khan.

When Temujin was a young man, his father was killed by Tatars. His family, without a man to hunt food for the two widows and seven children, were abandoned and expected to die of starvation: there were too many of them to support, and the rival families did not want Temujin to succeed to his father's eminent position. The family survived by scavenging what food they could: roots; fruit; fish; small game. They were at the very bottom of the social system of the steppes, little better than animals. The experience forged what became Temujin's core beliefs: the need to break down the caste system and to forge new alliances that went beyond family and tribe.

When still a young man, Temujin was captured and enslaved by another tribe, but eventually escaped with help from a local family, who risked everything by helping him. His fame began to grow. Temujin had been betrothed to a young girl before the death of his father; he now sought out her family, who agreed to the long-delayed marriage. Soon afterwards, Merkit raiders attacked Temujin's camp. With the bitter but pragmatic logic of the steppes, he fled with his companions, leaving his new wife behind. Temujin could choose the traditional course of action—to find, or kidnap, a new wife—or he could fight back. He chose to fight. He approached the leader of the Kerait tribe, Ong Khan, whom his father had served, and offered his wife's dowry (a coat of black sable) as a gift. Ong Khan was happy for the excuse to raid his local Merkit rivals with Temujin as his captain.

Temujin won back his wife in a raid and began to become a successful warrior. The traditional approach on raiding a rival tribe was to plunder its goods, killing or driving away the young men and capturing young women and boys. Over time, as Temujin conquered more minor tribes, the leaders were killed but the remainder of the tribe was absorbed, not as slaves but on an equal footing, along with all their goods and animals. Temujin's mother adopted children from conquered tribes, making them Temujin's 'brothers'. Temujin also began to systematize looting. Warriors had been more concerned about plundering goods than they had been in chasing down the enemy: under Temujin, the enemy was hunted down and totally defeated; only then could the looting begin. The proceeds were distributed evenly, one share being set aside for the widows and orphans of any soldiers killed in the raid. This broke with the old aristocratic system where chieftains would distribute the plunder as they saw fit, reinforcing their power and status. Temujin's reforms began to break down not only inter-tribal rivalries but also the structure of society. After 20 years of inter-tribal warfare, including the defeat of his previous mentor, Ong Khan, who had turned against him, Temujin had united the various tribes under his rule and was acknowledged as "Khan" (leader). He was given the name "Chinggis" Khan, which later became more familiar in its Persian spelling of "Genghis".

The new leader now did away with all previous aristocratic titles and privileges. All offices belonged to the state—to the Great Mongol Nation that he had created from the warring tribes.

In a final, radical move, he organized the army into a system of decimal units. The basic unit was the unit of ten: regardless of tribal differences or social status, these men were now brothers; no unit could leave behind a wounded member. The eldest member was the leader, but the team could choose a different leader. Ten units of ten formed a company, whose leader was elected. Ten companies formed a battalion; ten battalions made an army of ten thousand, with a leader chosen by Genghis. Old loyalties and ties were effectively destroyed: ultimate loyalty was now to the Khan. The reorganization was remarkably similar to the changes introduced to Athenian society by Cleisthenes, nearly 2,000 years earlier, which were also designed to break up old aristocratic and feuding clans—though Genghis at the time would not have heard of the Mediterranean Sea, let alone an ancient Athenian civilization. The unification and democratization of both societies was similarly successful. Genghis Khan was more than 40 years old before he finally succeeded in uniting the tribes and reorganizing Mongolian society; it would take him the remaining 20 years of his life to conquer the world.

To prepare for war, Genghis Kahn called a council. The issue was known beforehand, not turning up at the council was an effective vote of no confidence. Genghis Kahn got his quorum. The main purpose of the council was to ensure that everyone, down to the lowliest warrior, understood the purpose of the war and agreed with its principles—such as to avenge past wrongs and to acquire wealth from the cities of China. On the battlefield, soldiers had to obey orders unquestioningly. Before the Mongols rode off to war, however, there was debate and involvement.

Genghis Khan's first attack on China showed his grasp of strategy and of politics; his territory was bordered to the west by the Tangut and to the east and south by the far more powerful Jurchens, a tribe from Manchuria who had founded the Jin dynasty in northern China, and who demanded tribute and obeisance from the Mongolians. He decided that, if he attacked the Tangut, the Jin would not come to their aid. He was right. In order to capture Tangut cities, the Mongols learned to cut them off from their surrounding food supplies. They tried to divert the Yellow River to flood the Tangut capital, but flooded their own camp instead. They defeated the city anyway and learned from their mistakes. The Tangut were subdued; it was time to move on the Jin—in an unprecedented move, the Mongols crossed the huge and forbidding Gobi desert.

Every soldier carried everything that he needed, including dried milk and meat. They could go many days without the need for fresh supplies; their high-protein diet made them able to go hungry for longer than people living on high-carbohydrate diets, like most of their agricultural opponents. Scouts went ahead of the army to check the terrain, water supplies, and resting places. As they emerged from the desert through a pass they destroyed the waiting Jin army.

The Mongols knew only steppe warfare, on horseback. The whole army consisted of cavalry; the bow was the key weapon. Since every Mongolian made a living by herding animals and hunting, these skills were second nature—the whole nation could be mobilized. The Mongols did not seek out a battlefield on which to conduct a set-piece battle, they attacked across a huge front, many miles wide. They treated the people in their path much as they treated the vast herds that they were used to managing on the steppe: it was a Mongol tactic to stampede animals towards their enemies; now they also started to herd huge numbers of refugees in front of them, clogging roads, overwhelming cities, consuming supplies. At times they would use this mass of humanity as living shields, or even as living ballast to fill moats or other obstacles.[90] They were indifferent to loss of human life if it preserved Mongol life. The Mongols laid siege to the Jin capital, Yanjing (modern Beijing) and sacked it; the Jin Emperor was forced to move south.

Captured riches flooded into Mongolia; unheard of luxuries became necessities and Genghis Khan was driven to conquer further territories. His conquests took the Mongol horde into modern-day Kyrgyzstan and Kazakhstan. He conquered the city of Kashgar in the modern Chinese province of Xinjiang, having been asked for support by the local Muslim population against a repressive king. The Mongols liberated the city without damage and proclaimed freedom of worship to every community. The Mongols single-mindedly pursued a simple and effective policy: those who welcomed or supported them were rewarded; those who opposed them died.

Genghis began to make great use of military intelligence, using a network of scouts and a sophisticated system of communication via way-stations situated one day's ride apart. This system also supported his armies' chain of supplies: a system to rival that of Alexander the Great and one that Genghis, without access to the relevant written histories, had to reinvent. The Mongol army had no concern for individual honor: if a battle was lost, no soldier could claim that he had won some special honor from it. The means to victory were also unimportant; the Mongols were delighted to win by trickery, as when a Mongol soldier dressed himself in the clothes of a captured envoy and entered a besieged city. As he did so, the Mongols withdrew, and the pretend envoy persuaded the city that they were victorious. He organized the dismantling of the cities defences, and the horde returned.

With the entire Silk Road from China to the eastern borders of the Middle East under his control, Genghis Khan now wanted to trade with the rich and technologically advanced territories of the Islamic world, stretching beyond the mountains of Afghanistan to the Black Sea. Genghis Khan sent an envoy to the ruling Turkish Sultan of the Khwarezmid Empire, saying that he had no need of conquering any further territories and had a sincere interest in fostering trade between their two empires. The Sultan expressed cautious interest, but the first caravan of goods sent from the east was captured; its merchants and drivers were killed. Genghis Kahn sent a mission asking for the arrest and punishment of the local governors who had captured the caravan.

The envoys were killed or returned to Mongolia with their heads and faces shaved. The consequence of this violent and short-sighted episode was about to change the world. The Mongols crossed more than 2,000 miles of desert, steppe, and mountain to attack Bukhara; with the help of local nomadic tribes, they crossed the feared Red Desert, the Kyzyl Kum, to appear deep behind enemy lines. The city surrendered, but the Turkish soldiers barricaded themselves in the inner citadel, confident that no marauding band of steppe warriors could defeat its massive defences, and with water and enough food to sit out a protracted siege. But by now the Mongol army had learned much. Engineers constructed siege engines that they had copied from the Chinese; devices entirely unknown to them a few decades before. The astonished defendants of the inner fortress of Bukhara found themselves attacked by catapults, mangonels, and trebuchets, hurling not only stones and great arrows but also exploding devices and incendiaries. Great towers allowed the attackers to rain arrows and missiles on the defenders of the battlements; sappers undermined the foundations. Prisoners were herded into the moats to form living bridges for the great siege machines to cross. The defenders were wiped out.[91]

Such was the shock of the defeat of Bukhara that the capital of the Sultan's empire, Samarkand, surrendered. The Mongols moved on: south across the mountains of Afghanistan to the Indus River (in the footsteps of Alexander the Great) and west to the plains of Russia and to the shores of the Mediterranean. Baghdad fell in 1258. The descendants of Genghis Khan were to rule in Bukhara for 700 years, until the city was overrun by the Soviet Empire of the twentieth century.

Genghis Khan conquered the largest contiguous land empire in history, stretching from China, through central Asia, into the Caucasus, and the Russian Principalities. Once the empire was conquered, however, the Mongols were surprisingly benign rulers. They had no interest in cities, or in accumulating great wealth. They liked manufactured goods, and encouraged trade. The huge Mongol Empire became a vast free-trade zone. Taxation was relatively light, with exemptions for doctors and teachers. Wars died out as the overwhelming force of the Mongols overrode all other power struggles—just as the overwhelming might of the Roman Empire of Augustus had begun a long period of peace one thousand years earlier. Trade between East and West became far safer and far easier. Ideas and goods began to flow around the world. What Genghis Khan's empire had created was opportunity.

CHIANG KAI SHEK
(1887–1975)

Chiang Kai Shek is often described as "the man who lost China." It is also true to say that, without Chiang, there would not have been a China to lose. After the collapse of China's last Imperial Dynasty, a brief period of republican government was hijacked by its new President—a previous commander of the Imperial army. He declared himself to be the new Emperor. Chinese provinces rebelled once more, but with the collapse of any form of central government, the country fragmented into a collection of territories governed by various strongmen who had sufficient troops and resources to control a territory. The age of the warlords had arrived; China, the birthplace of civilization, had been knocked back into a kind of feudalism.

The Republic of China, which seemed to have been strangled at birth, had envisaged the emergence of a democratic, representational government. A new national party, the Kuomintang—also known as the Chinese Nationalist Party—was formed to embody these aims. Chiang Kai Shek became the leader of this party and the supreme commander of Nationalist forces. He succeeded in defeating the most significant warlords in China's northern and central territories, and reunified China.

It was Chiang's misfortune that events, both internal and external, never allowed him to consolidate this success. Continued wars with remaining warlords sapped resources, while the Communist Party of China—which Chiang became increasingly determined to destroy—proved to be a resilient force. Chiang's greatest misfortune was the invasion of China by Japan: his attempts to build up the armed forces in order to repel the expected invasion were constantly distracted by his efforts against the warlords and the Communists. In the end he was persuaded—literally at gunpoint—to join forces with the Communist Party in a united front against the Japanese. This may have been in the interests of the country's defence (though this can be debated), but it was certainly in the interest of the Communist Party, who used the years of war to rebuild their army and to increase their power base in the countryside, fighting a guerrilla war while the Nationalist Armies bore the brunt of the conventional warfare, suffering heavy losses.

Chiang's greatest success, after the reunification of China, was to prevent its rapid conquest by Japan, something that Japan itself considered to be entirely feasible. By holding off the Japanese invasion—trading space for time—Chiang was able to keep the country intact for long enough to see America enter the war and for the Sino-Japanese war to be subsumed into World War II. After the war, the Communist Party defeated the Nationalist forces and Chiang's Republic of China withdrew to the island of Taiwan, while the People's Republic of China was established on the Chinese mainland.

Chiang, as a leader, managed to create a number of opportunities that have changed the world: by recreating a nation from an incoherent collection of warlord territories, he allowed China to re-emerge; by holding out against a Japanese invasion for long enough to gain international support, he kept the reborn nation alive; and after his defeat and exile in Taiwan, he helped to create the conditions from which one of Asia's earliest 'tiger economies' could emerge, helping to transform the economic conditions of the Far East.

The Qing dynasty—the last imperial dynasty of China—ended in 1912 when the Empress Dowager abdicated on behalf of the six-year-old Emperor Puyi, "The Last Emperor." A series of mutinies and uprisings against the succeeding weak central government led to a number of southern provinces declaring themselves to be independent. They formed a National Assembly and elected a provisional President of the Republic of China: Sun Yat-sen, a quiet and moderate revolutionary who had been trying for many years to replace the ailing imperial government with a democratically-based republic. The new National Assembly represented only the breakaway southern provinces, while the Imperial Qing government retained control of the north. The new republic also had no significant military power: the man in control of the Imperial army, Yuan Shikai, was now wooed by both the new Republican government and the old regime. In return for the Presidency of the new republic, Yuan sided with the revolutionaries.

Sun Yat-sen and others formed a new political party that was to become the Kuomintang (KMT), or Chinese Nationalist Party. Sun was elected as leader, and the new party campaigned for the first elections to the National Assembly on a platform promoting constitutional, parliamentary-style democracy. The Kuomintang won a majority in the new Assembly. Unsurprisingly, the new President, ex-Army Commander Yuan Shikei, began to behave in an increasingly autocratic manner and to ignore the National Assembly. The parliamentary leader of the KMT spoke out against Yuan and was assassinated at Shanghai railway station. Sun Yat-sen led a badly-organized and unsuccessful revolt against Yuan and fled once more into exile in Japan. Yuan, true to type, proclaimed himself Emperor in December 1915, but several provinces immediately rebelled and foreign powers, especially Japan, withdrew their support. Yuan delayed his coronation ceremony, but failed to appease his growing number of opponents. He died in June 1916, leaving a power vacuum that was filled by local warlords who were able to retain control of elements of the fragmenting army. Their main powerbase was in the north. Yuan is remembered, not fondly, as the "Father of the Warlords" who were to plague China for the next two decades.

In 1920, Sun Yat-sen and the Kuomintang managed to form a government of sorts—in effect a limited military government—in Guanzhou (Canton), on the coast of southern China. Sun proclaimed his intention to govern under the Three Principles of the People: a personal vision of a representational government, with proper separations of power between the legislative and administrative branches of government, and a program of social welfare. Sun founded the Whampoa Military Academy near Guanzhou to develop an army in order to take on the warlords in the north, and accepted Soviet aid. The developing Communist Party of China (CPC) was instructed by Soviet advisors to collaborate with the Kuomintang, forming the First National Front—in this case, against the warlords, and in an attempt to establish a national Republic of China. The Academy was to have a profound influence on the development of China. Communist and nationalist cadets trained side-by-side: the Director of the Academy was Chiang Kai-Shek, the future leader of the Republic of China; the Director of the political department was Zhou Enlai, the man who would become Premier of the People's Republic of China under Chairman Mao Zedong. At Whampoa, Chiang Kai Shek trained a generation of future army offices who would remain loyal to him and to the Kuomintang, but he found it difficult to work alongside Communist party officers (including Zhou Enlai) as part of the United Front. Before taking up his appointment at Whampoa, Chiang had been sent to Russia for three months to study the new revolutionary government's political and military models. He had decided that the Russian revolutionary model was not for China.

In 1925, Sun Yat-sen died. He was replaced as Chairman of the National Government by Wang Jingwei, a left-wing politician who supported continued collaboration with the Communist Party. In 1926, Chiang exploited an incident in which it was alleged that the Communist Party and Wang Jingwei had attempted to have him kidnapped. Chiang used the opportunity to rid the Kuomintang of communist members and Russian supporters, jailing many, and forcing communists out of some senior party positions—the acting head of the propaganda department, Mao Zedong, lost his job.

As supreme commander of the Kuomintang's army, Chiang launched the Northern Expeditionary Force to win northern and northeastern China back from the warlords and, within a year, had brought much of China under Nationalist control, defeating the less well-trained warlord armies and finding popular support in the regions under the warlords' control. At this point the Kuomintang forces still contained both nationalist and communist troops. Chiang's left-wing opponent, Wang Jingwei, had led KMT forces to take Wuhan, in eastern-central China; Wang, with support from the Communist Party, now declared that Wuhan was the center of the National Government. Zhou Enlai had organized a worker's rebellion and general strike in Shanghai, putting the communists in effective control of the city. Chiang decided to move against the communists and Wang. His forces attacked Shanghai and began a brutal suppression of communists that soon spread through the provinces, starting a civil war between the nationalists and the communists.

Chiang declared a national government at Nanjing, near China's east coast, further down the Yangtze River from Wang's power-base in Wuhan; two months later he was able to overthrow the rival government. The Nationalist army went on to take Beijing from its warlord ruler and, finally, the huge area of Manchuria in northeastern China also pledged allegiance to Chiang's Kuomintang.

China had been reunified—a remarkable achievement—and it had a national government. Chiang married a younger sister of the widow of the revered Sun Yat-sen and established himself as the rightful heir to the founding principles of the Kuomintang party. For the next decade, Chiang Kai Shek and the Nationalist Party began to move towards the modern, progressive China envisaged by Sun Yat-sen. The legal and financial systems were modernized, foreign concessions were abolished, a program of road and railway construction improved communications within the country, an early aviation service began. There was progress in health care provision and in promoting industrial and agricultural production, but the government was beset by both internal and external problems. In 1930, Chiang fought a civil war against remaining warlords in China's central territories that involved some 300,000 casualties, and nearly bankrupted the Nationalist government.

In 1931 Japan invaded Manchuria. The Nationalists were forced to sign a humiliating Accord acknowledging Japan's presence on Chinese territory. Chiang resigned as Chairman of the National government, but soon returned to power. His slogan became: "First internal pacification, then external resistance." He needed time to build up China's armed forces and its defences, and he wanted to defeat the Communist Party in China before he faced Japan. Chiang faced increasing levels of Japanese "incidents"—serious attacks on Chinese territory that managed, nevertheless, to fall short of all-out war. In 1932, the Japanese bombed Shanghai on the pretext of defending their "concession" against anti-Japanese protests (several foreign powers owned territories or "concessions" in Shanghai, which were technically foreign soil).

The war against the Communists continued. In 1934, the Nationalists succeeded in encircling Communist forces in Jiangxi province in southeastern China, having painstakingly built up a ring of fortified blockades around Communist-held territory; parts of the Communist army and its civilian and administrative support systems broke out and began what was to become the epic Long March to a safe haven in the central northern province of Shaanxi. In the course of the Long March, Mao Zedong emerged as the leader of the Communist Party.

Chiang expected the warlords to destroy the retreating Communist army as they retreated through their territories; he can be forgiven for believing that the Communist Party had been destroyed as a fighting force. In fact, the survival of the Communist army—despite the fact that only some 8,000 out of the 100,000 who originally broke out of the encirclement in Jiangxi were to complete the march—enabled the communists to regroup and to create a new political base. The fact that an opposing army must be completely destroyed is a recurring lesson from history. This is not to say that they must be killed to the last man (this is a very rare occurrence—Hannibal's slaughter of the Roman army at Cannae being a notable exception), but that they must cease to exist as an organized fighting unit. George Washington's greatest military achievement was to keep the American revolutionary army (also numbered in tens of thousands) intact and viable. It went on to defeat the British Army. Napoleon was, unwisely, allowed to keep some of his elite Imperial Guard in exile on the island of Elba. Despite their tiny numbers, they formed the seed of a new army once he had escaped from Elba and landed on the coast of Provence.

Chiang continued to work to build up an army that could hope to defend the country against a full Japanese invasion. He hired a veteran of the US Army Air Corps—an early advocate of air power—and struck a deal with Germany for $100m of weapons in exchange for supply of minerals. He also continued his attempts to destroy the tenacious Communist Party. Many felt that Chiang was more obsessed with the destruction of the Communists than he was with driving the Japanese out of China. He argued that, "The Japanese are a disease of the skin; communism is a disease of the heart."

In late 1936, Chiang flew to the city of Xi'an, capital of the Shaanxi Province where the Communist Party had made its new base. Zhang Xueliang, the son of the previous warlord of the Manchurian region, had joined forces with Chiang—an event that had helped to precipitate the Japanese invasion of Manchuria: the Japanese had assassinated Zhang's father by blowing up the train that he was on, hoping that the son would prove to be an amenable ally. Zhang's decision to form an alliance with the Kuomintang caused the Japanese to invade.

Chiang Kai Shek was now using Zhang to attack Communist positions, but did little to support his efforts: Zhang had good reason to fear that, as inheritor of his father's warlord forces, Chiang Kai Shek would not lose too much sleep if Zhang's troops were weakened or destroyed in the attack on the Communists. Zhang negotiated a ceasefire with the Communists and may even have swapped camps. Zhang himself says that he applied for membership of the Chinese Communist Party but was refused ex-warlords not being welcome, in general, as new members of the Communist Party. There are suggestions that he did in fact become a CPC member but that this was concealed from everyone except a select few, such as Zhou Enlai. Zhang, in any case, was about to play a momentous part in Chinese history.

Zhang and his colleagues tried to persuade Chiang to join forces with the Communists in order to resist the Japanese invasion; when he refused, Chiang was taken hostage. It was generally assumed that Zhang had staged a coup; in fact he invited a communist delegation, led by Zhou Enlai, to join them. The CPC pledged to support the war effort against Japan under a Second United Front, in return for an end to Chiang's suppressions. Chiang would gain valuable military support and manpower, he would emerge as the leader who had unified the nation in a time of great crisis, and he wouldn't be taken out and shot. Chiang accepted.

Chiang did indeed return to Nanking as a national hero. He later took his revenge on Zhang, who was court-martialled and spent most of the rest of his life in custody. Zhang has been seen as a patriot who did what he felt was in the best interests of the country by bringing Nationalists and Communists together. If, on the other hand, it is discovered that Zhang had indeed joined the CPC before the "Xi'an Incident," as it is generally known, then the event could be seen as a sophisticated CPC plot to prevent Chiang's continued suppression of the movement and to allow the communists to regroup during the ensuing war. Whatever the motivation of the various players involved, there can be no doubt that the eventual winners were the Communist Party.

War between China and Japan was finally declared in 1937. To defend Shanghai, 600,000 of Chiang's best-trained troops were mobilized: one third of them were killed—most of Chiang's political base, his Whampoa Military Academy graduates. Nevertheless, the dogged Chinese resistance proved that Japan could not quickly overrun the country. The Japanese had claimed that they would defeat Shanghai in three days and China within three months; it took them three months to subdue Shanghai. Chiang began to play a clever game of trading space for time: fighting rearguard actions that eventually ceded territory to the Japanese, but at the expense of drawing in Japanese troops that were needed in the other Asian and Pacific theatres of war. Most importantly, it allowed Chiang to show the Western powers that the new Chinese government was deserving of foreign aid. When Japan invaded the United States of America by bombing the American naval base of Pearl Harbor in Hawaii, the war between China and Japan was subsumed into World War II, and China became one of the Allied powers. Chiang Kai Shek became Supreme Commander of Allied forces in the China theater, which included India and Southeast Asia.

During the war, Chiang's Nationalist forces took the brunt of the conventional set-piece battles, while the Communists fought guerrilla actions in the countryside: the Japanese were only ever effectively able to control cities and railroads. Though the Communists' guerrilla efforts were significant, their forces suffered far lower casualties than the Nationalist front-line troops. The Communists also began a policy of recruiting all-Chinese guerrilla forces to the CPC, regardless of their political allegiance, sometimes by force. The Kuomintang lost perhaps three million troops during the war, while the CPC, who started the war with negligible forces, increased their forces to around 1.7 million.

On August 6th 1945, America dropped the first atomic bomb on the Japanese city of Hiroshima; three days later, Russia invaded Japanese-held Manchuria as part of its pledge to the Allies at the end of the war in Europe, and destroyed the depleted Japanese army there. On the same day as the Russian invasion of Manchuria, the second atomic bomb was dropped on Nagasaki. On August 15th, Japan surrendered.

Toward the end of the war, Chiang's Nationalist government had lost much of its support. Inflation had turned into hyperinflation; a wartime measure confiscating precious metals and foreign exchange, in return for government scripts that became worthless within a year, left many Chinese convinced that the Nationalist government was inept at best and corrupt at worst. In the meantime, the Communists had consolidated their political base in a countryside devastated by the effects of war, exacerbated by the scorched earth measures that had been used to frustrate Japanese advances into China's heartland, including the deliberate flooding of huge areas.

Full-scale civil war broke out again between the CPC and the Nationalists. The Communists' popular support was increasing; they received financial support from Russia and had been allowed to enter Manchuria, after Russia's victory against the Japanese, to acquire the weapons left behind by the Japanese army. (The Soviets also dismantled and removed huge amounts of industrial equipment from Manchuria, further weakening the Nationalist government's already-devastated economy.)

In 1947 the Kuomintang declared a new constitution as part of the move towards representational democracy; a new National Assembly elected Chiang Kai Shek as President. But, in the meantime, Communist forces were winning the Civil War.

Chiang finally left mainland China for the island of Taiwan and carried on his duties as President of the Republic of China, continuing to claim sovereignty over China as a whole. He was re-elected by the National Assembly on four occasions, dying in office in 1975. Chiang himself laid the blame for the defeat of the Nationalists more on internal corruption and foreign intrigue than on the successes of the Communists. In Taiwan, Chiang maintained a state of martial law on the basis of the ongoing state of war between the KMT and the People's Republic of China. Many Chinese intellectuals and businessmen had fled to Taiwan with the KMT; Chiang's government, though authoritarian, encouraged the economic developments that would turn Taiwan into one of the Asian 'tiger economies'.

Chiang's career was plagued by circumstances that prevented him from making the most of the opportunities that he had created—and some of his disasters were of his own making. His Northern Expedition against the warlords was a hugely significant campaign that enabled the reestablishment of a national government. His failure to destroy the Communist army before the Long March may or may not have been a critical failure: a new Communist force may have been able to re-emerge even after the total destruction of the army of Mao Zedong, Zhou Enlai and others, since there were other Communist forces at large. The kidnapping that forced him to fight alongside the Communists in the war against Japan was a golden opportunity for the Chinese Communist Party but not for Chiang. The Communists fought bravely in the countryside, winning hearts and minds, while suffering relatively light losses. The Nationalist army bore the brunt of the Japanese onslaught. Finally, while Chiang's Nationalist Party was in government during the war—in admittedly disastrous financial conditions—Chiang nevertheless failed to deliver an impressive party performance: the Nationalists became tainted with perceptions of poor and even corrupt government. But the reunification of China and the defence of China against the Japanese created the opportunity for the re-emergence of China as potentially the greatest nation on earth—a destiny that the People's Republic of China seems about to fulfil—while Taiwan, which did not wholeheartedly welcome or enjoy the arrival of Chiang's Republic of China on its doorstep, has emerged as one of the world's leading economies. Without Chiang Kai Shek, none of these opportunities might have existed.

MARCO POLO
(1254–1324)

In the middle of the thirteenth century, Europe was still reeling under the terrifying attacks of the Mongol hordes that had appeared so suddenly from the East. The Mongol cavalry crossed the mountains and deserts that had always been the natural barriers between east and West, destroying mighty cities in Central Asia previously thought to be invulnerable to mere tribesmen. They smashed down city walls with siege engines they had adopted following their conquest of northern China, massacred the occupants, and devastated the surrounding countryside, sweeping all before them. Led at first by the mighty Genghis Khan and then by his descendants, the Mongols destroyed a Persian dynasty that had ruled Greater Iran and much of Central Asia for the previous century. Within seven years of their first emergence from the east, the Mongols had reached the Caspian Sea. They invaded Poland and Hungary, defeating the mighty Teutonic, Templar, and Hospitaller knights of medieval Europe, and pushed into Syria, Iraq, Palestine, and parts of Turkey. Baghdad—at that time the center of the Islamic world—fell in 1258. Vienna was threatened. The barbarians were at the gates.

Strangely, however, a perverse benefit was beginning to emerge from the terror. The Mongols—at a huge cost in human life—had established an empire that stretched from the Sea of Japan to the Mediterranean and, despite their ferocity and destructiveness in war, the effects of the Mongol peace were surprisingly positive. Historians now talk of the *Pax Mongolica*, a thirteenth-century equivalent of the *Pax Romana*. The Mongolian Empire, rather like the Roman Empire, had joined previously warring or hostile nations together and imposed central control by means of overpowering physical force; it was suddenly possible to travel around the huge new empire in relative safety. Trade routes became more active; goods and ideas were exchanged at greatly accelerated rates. The ancient Silk Road between

East and West (though it was only given this name in the nineteenth century, and silk was only one of the many goods traded along the route) became far safer to travel—though still arduous and dangerous.

Niccolò Polo and his brother Maffeo were established and successful merchants from Venice. The great city had been a center for international commerce for centuries; as a result, it had the most advanced banking system in Western Europe, and operated relatively sophisticated forms of commercial contracts, business loans, and even insurance.[92] For the Polo family, trade was second nature and the whole world was an opportunity. At a time when the West was terrified at the prospect of further Mongolian incursions into Europe and the Middle East, the Polos calmly traveled into the heart of the beast, doing business at every opportunity.

They were to meet Kublai Khan, to return to the west, and then to return once more to the courts of the Mongolian Emperor, this time with Niccolò's son, Marco, who was to become the Great Kahn's most trusted ambassador. Marco Polo's great skills as an observer and as a writer proved that the most valuable commodities—the things that can most transform and enhance human societies—are not goods, but ideas.

Niccolò and Maffeo left their native Venice in 1252 for Constantinople (modern-day Istanbul). Constantinople had been sacked in 1204 by the Christians of the Fourth Crusade. The Christian Church had previously split between the Church in Rome and the Eastern or "Greek" Church in Constantinople. The Crusaders aimed to make the Eastern Church subservient to Rome. Venice had helped the Crusaders in the sack of Constantinople, and benefited greatly from the plunder of the city's wealth: the four bronze horses that grace the roof of the Basilica di San Marco on St Mark's Square in Venice were looted from Constantinople.

As Venetians, Niccolò and Maffeo would have received special status and tax reliefs in the newly conquered, and now Roman Catholic, city.

By 1259, the two merchants sensed that the political wind was changing. They were right. In 1261 a descendant of the old Greek emperors retook Constantinople and burned the Venetian quarter in revenge. The two brothers moved on to the Crimea, in the Black Sea, by then a part of the Mongolian Empire, but an area long-connected with Venetian trade. They moved on further east to Sarai, on the lower Volga, now the capital of the Golden Horde, which was ruled by a grandson of Genghis Kahn. The Golden Horde was the Western region of the Mongolian Empire, covering what we now know as Eastern Europe. (The name derives from the Mongolian "Altan Orda" or "Golden Camp," gold being the imperial color; the Mongolian/Turkish word "orda" providing the root for the Polish "horda" and the English "horde".)

Local Mongolian wars made it unsafe for the brothers to return to the west; they traveled on to Bukhara, in modern-day Uzbekistan, where they stayed for three years, happily doing business. They became fluent in the Mongolian language and even in some dialects. At this point they were invited to join an embassy to the Great Khan (King of all the Khans): Kublai Khan. Their safety in the passage to the Far East was ensured by the presence of the Mongolian ambassador, but it was an astounding journey to undertake; a journey to the edge of the world to meet the most hated man in Christendom. But, then again—there was good business to be done.

The Polo brothers met the great Kublai Khan. Kublai was a clever man. The Mongols were few, the Empire was vast: he needed outsiders to help administer the Empire and he needed commerce and new technologies to make it prosper. In particular, he wanted knowledge. He asked the brothers about the rulers of the West, about their relative importance, about their systems of justice. He was especially interested in Christianity: the Mongolians were essentially shamanists—they believed in one great deity, the Eternal Blue Sky, and a pantheon of lesser gods who governed the affairs of mankind. They had no problem with the worship of other gods or prophets and allowed complete freedom of religious worship throughout the Mongolian

Empire: some Mongolians were Nestorian Christians; others were Buddhist or Islamic. Kublai engaged the brothers on a mission: they were to return to Europe with a message for the pope, asking him to send 100 Christian scholars to educate Kublai's court in Christian beliefs; if they were persuaded, Kublai and his court would convert to Christianity (though almost certainly on a non-exclusive basis). It was an intriguing offer from a leader that the pope considered to be the devil incarnate. Kublai also wanted some oil from the lamp of the Holy Sepulchre: the fame of the miraculous healing powers that the oil was believed to possess had obviously spread. This, the Polo brothers knew, they could deliver; like almost everything else in Christendom, it was available—at a price.

The Polos returned to the Mediterranean, carrying a remarkable symbol of the power of the Great Khan: a tablet or rod of gold, called a *paiza*, which confirmed that the travellers were emissaries of the Great Khan himself, and that other rulers throughout the Empire must provide them with food, lodging, and horses, "on pain of their disgrace" if they should fail to do so. They retraced their steps across Central Asia, reaching the Mediterranean and setting sail for Acre, capital of the Kingdom of Jerusalem, where they told their story to the papal legate. Pope Clement IV had recently died and a new pope was yet to be elected. There would be an exceptional delay of almost three years before the election of a new pope—the longest papal election in the history of the Roman Catholic Church. The legate expressed wonder at the Great Khan's request, and advised them to go home to Venice while the election dragged on. They had been away from home for 16 years; Niccolò found that his wife had died. He also found, to his surprise, that she had left him a 15-year-old son, Marco.

As chance would have it, the papal legate who had shown interest in their mission from the Great Khan was elected as Pope Gregory X. The Polo brothers, with Marco, presented themselves to the new pope, who greeted them warmly and welcomed the opportunity to spread Christianity throughout China and perhaps throughout the whole Mongolian Empire. He gave them the services, not of the requested

100 wise men (the Great Khan obviously over-estimated the worldly powers of the Pope) but of two learned friars, who were also given extraordinary ecclesiastical powers to appoint bishops and priests on behalf of the pope himself.

The Polos now equipped themselves for a major expedition. They were no longer mere traders stumbling into the east, but ambassadors both of the Great Khan (under whose protection they still traveled, thanks to their golden *paiza*), and of the pope himself. Because of the impossibility of carrying large amounts of currency, the family carried precious stones and pearls, often sewn into the lining of their clothes for safe-keeping. This was their big opportunity; they expected to return as rich men.

The Polo entourage were only in Armenia, still at the very start of their great journey, when the two friars refused to continue. There was some local difficulty with a Sultan, whom the Polo's almost certainly bribed, but the preceding unpleasantness and the threat of imprisonment was enough for the friars. The Polo family, undaunted by the distinct lack of even two of the one hundred wise men they had promised to bring to Kublai Khan, pressed on to Mosul on the Tigris, and then to Tabriz, in northern Iran, an important pearl market supplied from the Persian Gulf. They traveled through the Persian mountains, where they were troubled by bandits. They fled to Hormuz, on the Persian Gulf, thinking to take a ship to India, but were so horrified by the apparent un-seaworthiness of the ships, made without nails and tied together with coconut fiber, that they returned to Kerman, an important trading depot surrounded by mountains, on the edge of the Lut Desert. Here they took to the Silk Road, and crossed the desert by camel into Afghanistan, to the city of Balkh (ancient Bactria). They had been traveling for two years, and the worst obstacles were yet to come.

They crossed the Pamir Mountains, the traditional border between east and west. Radiating out from the Pamir are the mountain ranges of the Hindu Kush to the northwest, the Celestial Mountains to the northeast, and the Karakorum and the Himalayas to the southeast.

This is the roof of the world. After the mountains was the oasis town of Khotan, on the edge of the dreaded Taklamakan desert. Travellers could go round the northern or southern rims of the desert stopping at the life-saving oasis towns. Trying to cross the desert was certain death. At the easternmost tip of Taklamakan is the city of Lop, at the edge of yet another desert, the Desert of Lop. At the end of this desert was the marshy sea, Lop Nur (now dried up). The travelers emerged into regions that owed allegiance to Kublai Khan, and traveled ever eastward until they came to the Great Khan's summer residence: Shangdu—the fabled "Xanadu".

Marco described the huge marble palace, its walls marvelously gilded and painted, and the incredible 'summer palace'—an elaborate structure with bamboo pillars and a bamboo-tiled roof, that could be dismantled in its entirety and moved from place to place ("In Xanadu did Kublai Khan / a stately pleasure dome decree"[93]). After a great feast, the summer palace was indeed dismantled and the court retired to the winter palace of Khanbaliq ("the Khan's city") on the site of modern-day Beijing. The family were at last presented to the Great Khan and prostrated themselves on the floor before him. After a presumably tense moment, the Khan raised them up and greeted them warmly. The two brothers talked of their exploits and trials on the journey with great eloquence and, quickly glossing over the absence of the Christian scholars, they presented the papal documents that they had been given and, of course, the healing oil from the Holy Sepulchre, which was received with great excitement. (The oil had not been so very difficult to obtain, as it was sold from a side window of the Church of the Holy Sepulchre for pilgrims to use in lighting lamps around the Sepulchre)[94]. Finally, Niccolò presented his son, Marco, saying that Marco was now the servant of the Great Khan. The Khan was pleased.

Marco's fluency in Mongolian—and, soon, in several other languages and scripts—was a great asset. But as his relationship with the all-powerful Khan developed into a real bond, he began to demonstrate his true talent. Despatched as an emissary on important imperial business, he returned and delivered, not just an account of the business for which he had been despatched, but details of his journey, and the people and many interesting things that he had seen along the way. He brought back what the Khan wanted most of all: knowledge of his empire. Marco became the Khan's indispensable diplomat and tax collector, but also his eyes and ears. The notes that Marco took on his travels through Kublai's empire formed the basis for his *Travels*. The wonders that Marco saw were at first dismissed by Europeans as inventions of his imagination. As the ideas and technologies described by Marco began to reach the West in concrete form, they helped to drive the European Renaissance and bring an end to the Medieval period.

It was the city of Khanbaliq itself that first caught Marco's attention and his awe. Unlike the narrow, twisting streets of Europe's medieval cities, Khanbaliq was laid out on a grid structure, with broad, straight avenues. A system of gates could isolate any section of the city in case of trouble; guards patrolled at night. Inside the walls of the huge city were lawns, gardens, orchards, meadows, and great lakes full of fish. City roads were raised so that rainwater ran off them; there was a sophisticated drainage system that collected rainwater for irrigation. The great city was free of the mud and filth of European cities: clean, healthy, secure, and more or less crime-free.

The countryside was dotted with staging posts, both on the main roads to the provinces and on lesser highways, each stabling some 400 fresh horses; the Khan's messengers would change to a fresh horse every 25 miles as they brought news from the outlying provinces. Foot-runners, covering stages of three miles each, delivered messages over shorter distances and brought the couriers' messages to their final destination. The postal system had arrived.

Marco saw "stones that burn like logs"—coal had been used in China for a thousand years, but was little-used in Europe; it heated the water that allowed people to bathe, "at least three times a week, and in the winter every day if they can do so." Marco mentions printed books and pamphlets, but the potential significance of printing with movable type seems to have escaped him. He comments on the government practice of buying forward stocks of corn and releasing them at low prices in times of famine, and of donations of corn and bread to destitute families. He was especially astounded by the paper currency. The Chinese had used a form of paper currency for some 400 years, but Kublai replaced all currency with Mongol notes and confiscated all forms of coinage. The Mongol currency was backed by reserves of silk and silver; it worked. Marco could hardly believe it—though he was very impressed by how light it was to carry. He noted that the Khan "made so great a quantity of them (banknotes) that he could pay for all the treasure in the world, though it costs him nothing."[95] Well, not quite. Overprinting of money soon led to inflation, and by 1272 a new currency had to be issued at a ratio of five to one. By 1309—some 50 years after Kublai introduced the Mongolian paper currency in 1260—the currency had depreciated by 1000 percent.[96]

The Polo family were to spend 17 years with Kublai in China; Marco was finally released from his service. The Polos sailed from southern China via Sri Lanka and southern India to Hormuz on the Persian Gulf—but in far better ships than the local ships that they had dared not charter from Hormuz itself nearly 20 years before. The Polos arrived back in Venice in 1295, and had to make an ostentatious display of their wealth to prove to the cynical Venetians that there was substance to their exotic tales. The Polos had by now become accustomed to their Mongolian clothes; the wife of Maffeo disliked them so much that she gave her husband's clothes to a beggar. Unfortunately, Maffeo had sewn the jewels that represented most of the accumulated wealth of 20 years of traveling and trading into the lining of his clothes. He took to sitting in St Mark's Square, working a spinning wheel without any wool. Venice being a small place, even the beggar eventually came to see the madman in St Mark's Square, and Maffeo retrieved his coat and his jewels.[97]

The older Marco Polo was to dictate the story of his travels when in prison in Genoa after his capture during a war between the city-states of Venice and Genoa. His amanuensis was a writer from Pisa, who had himself been captured in another little war between Genoa and his own home town. The book became known as *The Travels of Marco Polo*. It became an instant international best seller, translated into many languages, some 200 years before the printing press was to make an appearance in Europe—every copy was transcribed by hand. Christopher Columbus made copious notes in his copy as he set off hoping to find a westward passage to this land of riches. Unfortunately, Marco's writings led him to believe that this land could not be far from the Caribbean, since nobody knew that a continent called America and an ocean called the Pacific lay between Portugal and China, traveling westward.

The *Travels* began, literally, to open up a new world. The exploration of this world would be driven by trade—as much for Columbus (dreaming of Marco's descriptions of great plantations of pepper, cinnamon, and cloves) as it was for the Polo family.

NOTES

1 Nigel Hamilton, *Monty: The Making of a General* (1981), p627.

2 Ibid. pp622–625.

3 Ibid. pp628–629.

4 Ibid. p655.

5 Ibid. p668.

6 <http://www.anc.org/ancdocs/history/mandela/1960s/ rivonia.html>.

7 Anthony Sampson, *Mandela* (1999) p72.

8 <http://www.anc.org.za/ancdocs/history/mandela/1960s/rivonia.html>.

9 Sampson, pp521–523.

10 Winston Churchill, first speech as Prime Minister, House of Commons, 13 May 1940.

11 Winston Churchill, speech in House of Commons, 18 June 1940.

12 Abraham Lincoln, address at Baltimore, 18 April 1864.

13 Abraham Lincoln, speech at Peoria, 16 October 1854.

14 Abraham Lincoln, second inaugural address, 4 March 1865.

15 'Thucydides, Pericles Funeral Oration' <http://www.fordham.edu/halsall/ancient/pericles-funeralspeech.html>.

16 Stephen J. Lee, *Aspects of British Political History* 1914–1995 (1996) p91.

17 Winston Churchill, *Great Contemporaries* (1937) p225.

18 Winston Churchill, House of Commons, 13 May 1940.

19 Winston Churchill, House of Commons, 18 June 1940.

20 Claude Manceron, *Austerlitz* (1966) pp76–78.

21 David G. Chandler, *The Campaigns of Napoleon* (1966) ppxxxv–xxxvi.

22 Ibid. p386.

23 Ibid. p410.

24 Ibid. p412.

25 Ibid. p422.

26 T.J.S. George, *Lee Kwan Yew's Singapore* (1973) p22.

27 Ibid. p50.

28 'List of countries by GDP (nominal) per capita', Wikipedia, <http://en.wikipedia.org/wiki/List_of_countries_by_ GDP_(nominal)_per_capita>.

29 <http://www.africa.upenn.edu/Articles_Gen/Letter_Birmingham.html>.

30 Andrew Lambert, *Nelson: Brittania's God of War* (2004) pxxx.

31 Robert Southey, *The Life of Nelson* (2005) p127.

[32] Terry Coleman, *Nelson: The Man and the Legend* (2001) p259.

[33] Patrick Kinross, *Ataturk: The Rebirth of a Nation* (2003) p189.

[34] Ibid. p78.

[35] Ibid. p93.

[36] Ibid. p154.

[37] Ibid. p175.

[38] Ibid. p204.

[39] Ibid. p278.

[40] Mike Marqusee, *Redemption Song: Muhammad Ali and the Spirit of the Sixties* (2005) p44.

[41] Ibid. p20.

[42] Ibid. p43.

[43] Ibid. p44.

[44] Ibid. p8.

[45] Ibid. pp82–83.

[46] E.L. Woodward, *War and Peace in Europe 1815–1870* (1960) p274.

[47] Ibid. p199.

[48] Claude Manceron, *Austerlitz* (1966) p92.

[49] Duff Cooper, *Talleyrand* (1932) p352.

[50] 'Charles Maurice de Talleyrand-Périgord', *Wikipedia*,
<http://en.wikipedia.org/wiki/Talleyrand>.

[51] 'The Papers of George Washington', <http://gwpapers.virginia.edu/
documents/revolution/letters/bfairfax2.html>.

[52] Joseph J. Ellis, *His Excellency George Washington* (2005) p100.

[53] Ibid. p143.

[54] Antonia Fraser, *Cromwell, Our Chief of Men* (1977) p24.

[55] Ibid. pp97–98.

[56] Ibid. p158.

[57] Ibid. p142.

[58] Ibid. p268.

[59] Ibid. pp419–420.

[60] 'The Famous Patton Speech',
<http://www.pattonhq.com/speech.html>.

[61] Ibid.

[62] Carlo D'Este, *A Genius for War: a Life of General George S. Patton* (1995) p464.

[63] 'Patton in North Africa',
<http://worldwar2history.info/north Africa/Patton.html>.

[64] Ibid. p634.

[65] Ibid. p573.

[66] Ibid. p602.

[67] Ibid. p635.

[68] Ibid. p660.

[69] Ibid. p680.

[70] Ibid. p689.

[71] Ibid. p712.

[72] Ibid. p639.

[73] Han Suyin, *Eldest Son* (1993) p214.

[74] Ibid. pp250–251.

[75] 'Mao Zedong', *Wikipedia*, <http://en.wikipedia.org/wiki/Mao>.

[76] Suyin, p268.

[77] 'Famine', *Wikipedia*, <http://en.wikipedia.org/wiki/Famine>.

[78] Suyin, p313.

[79] Ibid. p323.

[80] Ibid. p344.

[81] Theodore A Dodge, *The Great Captains* (2002) pp39–40.

[82] Geoffrey Hindley, *Saladin* (1976) p4.

[83] Ibid. pp6–9.

[84] Deborah Brunton, ed., *Health, Disease and Society in Europe 1800–1930* (2004) pp124–125.

[85] Ibid. p126.

[86] Ibid. p117.

[87] Ibid. p351.

[88] Jo Manton, *Elizabeth Garrett Anderson* (1995) p114.

[89] Jack Weatherford, *Genghis Khan and the Making of the Modern World* (2004) pxxii.

[90] Ibid. p93.

[91] Ibid. pp6–9.

[92] Laurence Bergreen, *Marco Polo: from Venice to Xanadu* (2007) pp15–16.

[93] Coleridge's poem 'Kubla Khan' was inspired by Marco Polo's *Travels*.

[94] Bergreen, p39.

[95] Ibid. p128.

[96] 'Paper Money', <http://www.silk-road.com/artl/papermoney.shtml>.

[97] Bergreen, p318.

SELECTED BIBLIOGRAPHY
AND FURTHER READING

Bergreen, Laurence, *Marco Polo: From Venice to Xanadu* (London, 2008)

Bowra, C.M., *Periclean Athens* (London, 1971)

Branch, Taylor, *Parting the Waters: Martin Luther King and the Civil Rights Movement* (London, 1988)

Chandler, David G., *The Campaigns of Napoleon* (New York, 1966)

Coleman, Terry, *Nelson: The Man and the Legend* (London, 2001)

D'Este, Carlo, *Genius for War: A Life of General George S. Patton* (London, 1995)

Dodge, Theodore A., *The Great Captains* (Stevenage, 2002) [Hannibal Barca]

Ellis, Joseph J., *His Excellency George Washington* (London, 2005)

Fenby, Jonathan, *Generalissimo Chiang Kai Shek and the China He Lost* (London, 2005)

Fraser, Antonia, *Cromwell, Our Chief of Men* (London, 1977)

George, T.J.S., *Lee Kwan Yew's Singapore* (London, 1973)

Hamilton, Nigel, *Monty: The Making of a General* (London, 1981)

Harris, Robin, *Talleyrand, Betrayer and Saviour of France* (London, 2008)

Harris, Tim, *Revolution: The Crisis of the British Monarchy 1685–1720* (London, 2006) [John Churchill]

Hindley, Geoffrey, *Saladin* (London, 1976)

Keegan, John, *Churchill* (London, 2003)

Kinross, Patrick, *Atatürk: The Rebirth of a Nation* (London, 1995) [Mustafa Kemal]

Lambert, Andrew D., *Nelson: Britannia's God of War* (London, 2004)

Lawday, David, *Napoleon's Master: A Life of Prince Talleyrand* (London, 2006)

McPherson, James M., *Abraham Lincoln and the Second American Revolution* (New York, 1992)

Manceron, Claude, *Austerlitz* (London, 1966) [Napoleon Bonaparte]

Manton, Jo, *Elizabeth Garrett Anderson* (London, 1965)

Marqusee, Mike, *Redemption Song: Muhammad Ali and the Spirit of the Sixties* (London, 2005)

Oates, Stephen B., *With Malice Toward None* (London, 1978) [Abraham Lincoln]

Sampson, Anthony, *Mandela* (London, 1999)

Suyin, Han, *Zhou Enlai and the Making of Modern China 1898-1976* (London, 1993)

Weatherford, Jack, *Genghis Khan and the Making of the Modern World* (New York, 2004)

Weir, Alison, *Elizabeth the Queen* (London, 1998)